D0435733

THE LAST DAY
OF THE OLD WORLD

ADRIAN BALL

THE LAST DAY
OF THE OLD WORLD

Doubleday & Company, Inc.
Garden City, New York
1963

For Eve and the quintet

AUTHOR'S NOTE

The author would like to acknowledge with gratitude, his debt to the translators and research workers who assisted him in the writing of this book.

Special thanks are due to a trio who translated numerous passages from European published sources and conducted personal interviews. Mr. Virgil Berger, in Bonn, handled the translation of German material and correspondence, while Mr. Christopher Powell covered books, official files and newspaper reports available in Paris. Mr. K. Zdziechowski, of the Polish Library, proved another valuable translator and adviser.

The author was also greatly assisted by Mr. Ian Ball in New York and by Messrs. Alfred Perles and Warwick Barraclough in London. The indexing and checking of Mr. Michael Cunningham and the careful preparation of the manuscript by Miss Jaleh Adl were further valuable contributions.

CONTENTS

ILLUSTRATIONS

PART ONE

Midnight to 6 a.m.

I

The men of war were talking anxiously but evasively of peace. The men of peace were preparing reluctantly for war. Their roles on the world stage had become strangely reversed for a few brief hours as mankind moved towards the greatest upheaval in its history.

Talk of peace was on the lips of both dictators at each end of the Rome-Berlin axis as the minutes ticked by towards midnight on that Saturday night of 2nd September, 1939. The German invasion of Poland had been in full swing since dawn the previous day, Hitler's Panzers were cutting long, cruel swathes through the lightly armed Polish forces and only the most chauvinistic Pole could have forecast that the resistance would continue for more than a few weeks. But Adolf Hitler was in a far from confident mood despite the successes of his armies in Poland. He was beginning to feel that his bluff was likely to be called—and his fascist partner, Benito Mussolini, was frankly terrified at the turn events were taking.

Both dictators were proferring olive branches to the British and French leaders—for different reasons and with very different motives— as the fateful Sunday approached. Hitler's last and most unusual peace proposal was being made in a queer, rushed way through a comparatively junior diplomat in London. Mussolini was anxiously awaiting the fate of a personal bid to secure an armistice in Poland and then negotiate a settlement favourable to Germany at another 'Munich'. Together, the dictators were providing, by their bizarre manœuvres, an ironic epilogue to a decade of violence and shattered diplomacy, and a prelude to five and a half years of world-wide conflict.

Midnight in Downing Street. The blackout, almost total though Britain was still at peace, made the little street off Whitehall look asleep and deserted. But inside the government buildings there was suppressed tension and excitement. Mr. Neville Chamberlain's Cabinet was in urgent session at 10 Downing Street, official working residence of the Prime Minister. In Number 11, an emissary from Hitler was begging Britain's top civil servant to place a new message from the Nazi leader before Chamberlain and his fellow ministers. The two men talked quietly, but quickly, and listened to one another courteously. They were Sir Horace Wilson, Permanent Secretary to the British Treasury and Head of the Civil Service, and Dr. Fritz Hesse, from the German Embassy, a few hundred yards away across St. James's Park.

Dr. Hesse was Press Attaché at the Embassy and also the London representative of the German News Agency, DNB. But in his interview with Sir Horace he was acting as Hitler's special emissary empowered to submit the Führer's proposal to the British Cabinet and to start negotiations immediately.

Sir Horace let Hesse talk without interrupting him, but his keen eyes never wandered from the German's face. He gave no sign of being impressed by Hitler's belated readiness to 'move out of Poland and to offer reparations for the damage done', on condition that he received Danzig and the road through the Corridor and that Britain acted as mediator in the German-Polish conflict.

These were the terms which Joachim von Ribbentrop, 46-year-old ex-champagne salesman and now Foreign Minister of the Reich had used over the telephone earlier in the day when giving Dr. Hesse his instructions. And he had added, 'So that there may be no misunderstanding, stress the fact that you are acting on the express instructions of Hitler and that this is no private step of mine.'

Ribbentrop's deep, booming voice still rang in Hesse's ears as he sat opposite Sir Horace studying the British diplomat's inscrutable face. He felt slightly unnerved by the prolonged silence that followed his exposition of Hitler's proposal.

At last Sir Horace spoke. And what he said made Dr. Hesse realize with a shock how utterly the attitude of the British Cabinet had changed since Germany's assault on Poland. It would be difficult, Sir Horace said, for him to approach the Cabinet with Hitler's proposal in the present situation. President Roosevelt had assured Chamberlain of his support in case Britain decided on a declaration of war, and Russia would not fight on Germany's side.

'How do you imagine that Chamberlain can go back in such a situation?' Sir Horace asked.

Dr. Hesse had no illusion of Hitler's suggestion being acceptable to the British Government but nevertheless begged Sir Horace to submit it to the Cabinet. It was the only chance of averting war, he pleaded, and perhaps a sign that Hitler realized he had made a mistake.

Sir Horace immediately seized upon the innuendo in the last sentence. Was he to understand that Hitler had changed his mind and was prepared to make a public apology? He went on to tell Hesse, according to the latter's later testimony, that if Hitler were to make a speech expressing regret for his actions and apologizing for acts of violence committed, there might 'still be a chance'.

Dr. Hesse hesitated. He knew full well that Hitler would never submit to the humiliation of a public apology. He clearly realized that even to suggest such a thing would make the dictator abandon any idea of a peaceful settlement. Being a diplomat, Dr. Hesse did not put it so crudely to Sir Horace, but suggested that it would be a 'psychological error' to ask Hitler for an apology, all the more as the responsibility of events could not be laid at Germany's door alone. There was some definite provocation on the Polish side, he declared. In any case, the German stressed, he was not authorized to make promises.

Sir Horace retorted bluntly that the situation had reached its danger-point through Hitler's fault and Hitler's fault alone. How could Hesse speak of 'psychological errors'? Hitler had deeply humiliated Chamberlain at Godesberg and Munich; had, in fact, treated him like dirt. He had overstepped all bounds and time and again had broken his word. He was no longer to be trusted. Nothing short of a public apology on the part of Adolf Hitler could now alter the situation.

Dr. Hesse fired his last broadside: Hitler had given Britain a chance of avoiding the war, he exclaimed. If Chamberlain stubbornly insisted on an apology before so much as examining Hitler's offer, the world would know who was responsible for the war.

At Sir Horace's request, Dr. Hesse repeated Hitler's proposal. Sir Horace got up from his desk and began pacing up and down the office. Presently the door was opened and a silent secretary handed Sir

Horace a piece of paper. He read it carefully as if memorizing it, then held it up to a candle and burnt it. There was a different tone in his voice as, turning to Dr. Hesse, he declared that he was no longer in a position to submit the proposal to the Cabinet, for it no longer had a chance of being accepted.

Sir Horace then explained curtly that Britain expected France to enter the war on her side within twenty-four hours. Mussolini had confirmed his Foreign Minister's statement that Italy would take no part in the war with Poland. M. Edouard Daladier, the French Prime Minister, had so far not committed himself to a definite time but had made it clear that the French declaration of war would follow Britain's within a matter of hours.

Britain had no other choice, he told Dr. Hesse. She would not only imperil her very existence but the basis upon which Empire and her prestige in the world were founded if she allowed Germany to wield a hegemony over the European Continent. He thanked Dr. Hesse for his effort but said he was sorry he could not give another answer. 'No Englishman could,' he added as the interview came to an end.

Dr. Hesse returned to the German Embassy in Carlton House Terrace. He was tired and haggard. At his desk in the sumptuous ambassadorial office, Herr Theodor Kordt, the *Chargé d'Affaires*, was waiting for him. He, too, seemed weary and exhausted, and one look at Hesse told him his colleague had failed. He had known all along that there was not a chance in the world and had even warned Hesse that he would only 'burn his fingers'. But it did not matter now.

For a while, the two tired men just sat there staring at each other in silence. Out of a framed picture from the wall above the desk, Hitler stared down at both of them. There was nothing to do except dispatch a coded telegram to Berlin, signed by them both: for the Führer and the Foreign Minister.

The text was quite short. No mention of any talk about an 'apology' on Hitler's part. The two diplomats merely reported that Sir Horace Wilson received the proposal in a 'friendly but negative manner'. The British Government would not enter into negotiations so long as the German aggression in Poland continued.

'It followed, therefore,' the telegram went on, 'that conversations of any kind were impossible for him, Wilson. The *status quo* must first of all be fully restored by the withdrawal of German troops from

Polish territory. After this, the British Government would be prepared to let bygones be bygones and to start negotiations immediately on the basis of the state of the conversations before the German aggression commenced.

'But for Mussolini's intervention, Henderson (the British Ambassador in Berlin) would this evening have presented in Berlin the British declaration of war, which the Cabinet had drafted this morning.'

The message to Hitler and von Ribbentrop then quoted Wilson as saying that Chamberlain's statement in the House of Commons earlier in the day on the reasons for Britain's delay in taking action had excited 'most violent indignation' in Parliament and the Cabinet. The latter had threatened to resign in a body that evening unless Chamberlain, during Sunday, gave Germany a declaration with a brief time limit. Chamberlain had just telephoned to Daladier in order to obtain the French leader's final assent. Thereafter, a Cabinet meeting was deciding that very night the final statement to be made in the Commons on noon, Sunday.

The gloomy report to Berlin concluded with these words: 'In view of these facts, it appeared to him (Wilson) impossible to agree to the suggestion. Nevertheless, he was at my disposal at any time should I have a further communication to make.

'I got the impression,' Hesse said, 'that Daladier was putting the brake on heavily, whereas public opinion here, owing to the German victories in Poland, was getting more and more excited at the inaction of the British Government.' Hitler could not have been presented with a more accurate summary of the state of British official and public opinion as 3rd September, 1939, dawned. It was to make bitter breakfast table reading for him a few hours later . . .

II

Midnight in Rome. There was no blackout and the lights blazed brightly in the windows of the Duce's Palazzo Venezia. Benito Mussolini, the 56-year-old dictator of Italy, who had seized power in his march on Rome as far back as 1922, was in a gravely perturbed state. Although he still clung desperately to his hope that a great power conference could be arranged to avert a major European war, all the signs were that the western democracies were not going to be bluffed again into a settlement favourable to Hitler. Mussolini had been released by Hitler, on 1st September, from the military obligations of their alliance, so he did not have to worry about providing troops for Poland. But he realized that he would have a mammoth struggle to avoid becoming involved ultimately in a European war.

Mussolini had faced few crises of the same magnitude. His mind was in a turmoil, but amid his anxiety and bouts of fury that night, he realized that it was imperative for him to think very clearly. There could be no question of Italy becoming involved in a major war. Not that he had any quarrels with his axis partner over the aims and principles of war; it was simply that he was not ready for a showdown. The timing of the conflict just begun by Germany was gravely wrong from Italy's point of view. The country was virtually exhausted from the Abyssinian campaign and the military help it had given to General Franco in the Spanish Civil War.

That night Mussolini must have gone over again and again the events that had led to the present impasse. His own conscience was clear. He had done everything in his power not to let the situation come to a head. His counsel had always been for a peaceful solution of the German-Polish conflict. It was from him, Mussolini, that the mediation attempts of the last few days had emanated.

On 31st August, he had urged Count Galeazzo Ciano, his 36-year-old son-in-law and Italian Foreign Minister, to clear the stage for a new conference on 5th September between the powers concerned. Under Mussolini's aegis, Britain and France were invited to discuss with Germany those clauses of the Treaty of Versailles which were the 'cause of the present trouble'. He saw no reason why Poland should not likewise take part in the conference.

But then on the next day, 1st September, had come the news of the German invasion of Poland. It hit Rome like a bombshell and Mussolini fumed with rage. He had not been consulted by his axis partner. Hitler's action was not only an affront to his Italian ally but had also endangered the success of the proposed conference.

Yet, on that same morning only a few hours after the German armoured divisions had begun moving into Poland, M. Georges Bonnet, the French Foreign Minister, had informed Ciano through M. François-Poncet, his Ambassador in Rome, that France was 'favourably disposed'. But France felt that all the interested and affected powers should be represented, and the conference should deal with the 'entire complex' of general problems which were at the root of all conflicts, and should lead to a general appeasement which would permit the 're-establishment and general organization of world peace on a solid basis'. Later that day, however, Britain and France sent notes to the Wilhelmstrasse warning the German Government of their treaty obligations to Poland.

The allied notes gave plain warning that Britain and France felt compelled to go to war unless German troops were withdrawn from Poland. But Mussolini, clutching at every possible straw, had made one further bid for peace during Saturday. He penned a personal note to Hitler which he instructed his Ambassador in Berlin, Attolico, to deliver at the German Foreign Office. In it, Mussolini declined to take the Anglo-French notes at their face value and expressed his conviction that there was still hope. A conference with Britain, France and Poland still had a chance of being called on the basis of an armistice which would leave the German forces in Poland where they stood. The new conference should be convened within two or three days, Mussolini suggested, and a settlement of the German-Polish dispute could be anticipated to be favourable to Germany in view of the situation.

In his fear of a major European war, Mussolini had tried to trick both the Nazi leader and the western allies into a resumption of negotiations on terms which clearly had no basis in reality. In that last desperate attempt to arrange a conference, Mussolini had even gone so far as to suggest that the idea which originally emanated from himself now had the strongest support in France. Ciano was later to claim that Mussolini's note was sent to Berlin as the result of 'French pressure', but there is nothing to indicate that such pressure was ever exercised.

The Duce's note, unanswered by Hitler for many hours, went as follows: 'Italy sends the information, leaving, of course, every decision to the Führer, that he still has a chance to call a conference with France, Britain and Poland on the following basis:

(1) An armistice which would leave the Army Corps where they stand at present;

(2) Calling the conference within two to three days;

(3) Solution of the Polish-German controversy which would be certainly favourable for Germany as matters stand today.

'The idea which originated from the Duce has its foremost exponent in France. Danzig is already German, and Germany is already holding securities which guarantee most of her demands. Besides Germany has already had her "moral satisfaction". If she were to accept the plan for a conference, it would achieve all her aims and at the same time prevent a war which already today has the aspect of being universal and of extremely long duration. The Duce does not insist on it, but he particularly emphasizes that the above be brought to the immediate attention of von Ribbentrop and of the Führer.'

Von Ribbentrop's reaction to Mussolini's letter on Saturday afternoon had been that the new peace proposal could not be reconciled with the Anglo-French notes of the previous evening, which he described as having the character of an ultimatum. That comment had provoked a day-long burst of Italian diplomatic activity, in both Berlin and Rome.

In the German capital, Attolico had been assured by the British Ambassador, Sir Neville Henderson, that it was 'not an ultimatum, but a warning'. In Rome, in mid-afternoon, Ciano had summoned both the British and French Ambassadors to the Palazzo Chigi and in their presence had telephoned to both M. Bonnet and Lord Halifax, the British Foreign Secretary.

Ciano told Bonnet—who thanked the Italian warmly for his peace efforts—that Hitler was not opposed to considering the projected conference. But he objected to the tenor of the British and French notes. If Hitler considered those notes had the character of an ultimatum his answer would be a categorical 'no'.

Ciano had then asked whether the French note was to be so regarded, adding that Sir Percy Loraine, British Ambassador in Rome, had assured him the British did not view theirs that way. Bonnet thereupon told Ciano by telephone that the French note also bore in no way the character of an ultimatum. Bonnet had appeared to be still hoping for a peace formula and Ciano told him Poland would be invited to any conference.

Halifax had spoken more sternly, denying in the hair-splitting way of diplomats of the day that an ultimatum had been delivered to Hitler but stating firmly that in his view Mussolini's proposal was unacceptable to Britain unless the German forces withdrew from Polish territory.

Halifax had stressed that it was his personal view and he would telephone Ciano later to give the decision of the British Cabinet. That came just after 7 p.m. and was identical with what Halifax had anticipated. Ciano was then obliged to tell the British and French envoys that he felt he could not address such a demand to Germany and that Mussolini shared that view. He had therefore advised his Ambassador in Berlin that Mussolini believed he could not follow up his suggestion and the Italian plan had to be abandoned. By 9 p.m. the allied attitude had hardened with a telephone call from Bonnet to Ciano saying that France associated itself with Halifax's stipulation. Once again, Ciano had said he did not think this condition would be accepted by the Reich Government.

By midnight, therefore, Mussolini's scheme for a 'second Munich' was dead to all practical purposes. Ciano, the realist, accepted that his efforts had got nowhere and retired to write up his diary and go to bed. He had scarcely got to sleep when the telephone rang. His Ministry reported that Bonnet had asked Raffaello Guariglia, the Italian Ambassador in Paris, if Italy could not at least obtain a 'symbolic' withdrawal of German forces from Poland.

The Count's diary noted his reactions in the middle of that fateful night: 'Nothing can be done. I throw the proposal in the waste-paper basket without informing the Duce. But this shows that France is moving towards the great test without enthusiasm and full of uncertainty. A people like the French, heroic in self-defence, do not care for foreign lands and for nations too far away . . .'

But if Ciano was resigned to the inevitable course of events and even had the tranquillity of mind to snatch a few hours' sleep, his father-in-law, nearly twenty years his senior, was of a temperament that allowed him no sleep. Donna Rachele, his patient wife, waited in vain for the Duce's return to their Villa Torlonia. 'Poor Benito,' she confided to friends visiting her. 'He works so hard and is so worried. If he would only eat and sleep properly . . .'

Mussolini had to avert the danger of an immediate major war at all costs. He knew that such a war would not only be disastrous to Italy but also his own undoing. He had presided over the destinies of his country for seventeen years and while he was regarded in European politics as the *bête noire*—a role in which Hitler subsequently supplanted him—he had always managed to steer clear of any major conflict.

How could Italy go to war anyhow? The country needed two or three more years to prepare for a major conflict. The national economy had still to recover from the adventures in Abyssinia and Spain. Raw materials were low and war factories needed to be moved to the south. The Army's artillery badly required to be modernized. The coast was unprotected. How could two Italian battleships stand up against the dozen the British and French could throw into the Mediterranean? Abroad, Italy's colonies, such as Libya, were exposed to attack, and the French were strong in Tunisia. Britain could be expected to cause trouble in Abyssinia. Albania, though potentially of great value, was now weak and undeveloped and could not be made a worthwhile base for years to come. Italy was also in grave need of boosting her overseas trade to bolster up the economy. Plans were well advanced for the 1942 Rome Exhibition which Mussolini hoped would give the nation's international prestige a tremendous fillip. At the other end of the globe, Japan, the as yet unproved ally, could not be expected to reach her peak strength before 1941 or 1942. Hitler might think he could localize the war in Poland, but the attitude of the British and French now was very different from the way they had behaved at Munich the previous year . . .

Many of these considerations must have passed through the burly dictator's anxious mind as he tried to think of a way to avert the crisis looming ahead for Italy. The hands of the clock moved past midnight but the lights still blazed in the Duce's rooms in the Palazzo Venezia. He was, however, wasting his time. The last fascist attempt to bluff through an act of appeasement by the democracies had failed— and Mussolini might as well have emulated his son-in-law and retired to bed early . . .

III

Neville Chamberlain's Cabinet had been half an hour in session when Big Ben chimed midnight. Downing Street was as inky as the rest of London and as black as the future as the Prime Minister and his colleagues wrestled with the question and the timing of a declaration of war.

The ministers gathered tensely around the table in the Prime Minister's room knew that the existence of their Government, perhaps the future of the Conservative Party, depended on the decision they would reach within the first few hours of Sunday morning. The mood of the country and of Parliament was for war. Angry conversations with back-benchers in the lobbies of the Commons, urgent chats over dinner at their clubs in St. James's, telephone calls from Press magnates and leaders of commerce and industry that night, had convinced every man present of that inescapable fact.

Chamberlain's Cabinet was meeting in the certain belief that many Conservatives, perhaps a majority, were in a mood to vote the Government out of office if no firm ultimatum were given to Germany when the Commons met again. Winston Churchill, leader of Chamberlain's critics within the party, would in all probability be pushed into Downing Street within twenty-four hours with the support of his growing army of followers and of the Liberal and Labour parties. Even as the ministers were beginning their deliberations, Churchill's aides were rallying support in every quarter. His son-in-law, Mr. Duncan Sandys, telephoned Count Edward Raczynski, the Polish Ambassador, as the Cabinet session began and said the Churchill group would 'not give way'. They had the moral support of the Labour Party and a wide circle of Conservatives. Sandys declared they were 'all agreed on no capitulation. If Chamberlain yields once more, we will oust him.'

The revolt against the administration had been gathering momentum since 6 p.m. that evening, the time the Prime Minister had been expected to announce the issue of an ultimatum to Hitler. Instead, he had to defer the statement for two hours while the discussions continued with the French over the Italian peace proposals and over the timing of the allied ultimata. While Chamberlain had clung to every slight hope of a peaceful settlement during those hours, the impatience and suspicion of the nation and its legislators had mounted. Few Parliamentarians would have stood for another Munich-type settlement—but that was just the prospect that Chamberlain had appeared to hold out in his statement to the House at 8 p.m. that night.

The packed house, already made impatient and restive by the delay, had heard Chamberlain say, 'His Majesty's Government will be bound to take action unless the German forces are withdrawn from Polish territory. They are in communication with the French Government as to the time limit within which it would be necessary for the British and French Governments to know whether the German Government are prepared to effect such a withdrawal.'

In the mood the House was in, the words had sounded stilted, unconvincing, almost beside the point. Chamberlain had nothing to add. He faced dark, sombre faces from the benches both on the Tory and Labour side. Tempers rose and for a moment it seemed that pandemonium would break loose.

Many of the most bitter listeners to Chamberlain that night had been on the Conservative side of the house. Men like L. S. Amery and Duff Cooper were red-faced and obviously speechless with fury. The House generally received the Prime Minister's temporizing statement as an indication that the days of appeasement had returned and the Poles were to be sacrificed. As the Labour leader, Mr. Arthur Greenwood, rose to speak there was a great cry from Amery of 'Speak for England', followed by Labour shouts of 'Speak for Britain' and 'Speak for the workers'.

Greenwood's firm but statesmanlike speech and its reception had been the gravest warning of all to the Prime Minister of the state of the nation's feeling. Greenwood said, 'I am gravely disturbed. An act of aggression took place thirty-eight hours ago. The moment that act of aggression took place one of the most important treaties of modern times automatically came into operation . . . I wonder how long we are prepared to vacillate at a time when Britain and all that Britain stands for, and human civilization, are in peril.'

Greenwood's fighting speech brought loud applause from both the Conservative and opposition benches. His words had echoed the widely held belief in the country, the lobbies and Press circles that Britain was weakening on her undertaking to Poland and that the French were 'ratting'. Had Greenwood turned on the Government then, 'he would have had Tory support and it might have meant the fall of the Government,' the War Secretary, Mr. Leslie Hore-Belisha, asserted later.

Chamberlain, aware that a revolt was brewing in his own ranks, and even among his ministers, had arranged the midnight Cabinet meeting immediately. He wanted to explain to his colleagues the reason for the deviation in his statement from a decision taken at an earlier Cabinet that afternoon that there should be an ultimatum expiring at midnight on 2nd September, whatever the French did.

Before receiving his ministerial colleagues, Chamberlain had dined with his Foreign Secretary, the Earl of Halifax, and had unburdened his heart to that sympathetic listener. The tall, gaunt Halifax had never known the Prime Minister so perturbed. Chamberlain told him bluntly that the statement to the House had not gone down well, members having misinterpreted the inability to give a time limit as the 'result of half-heartedness and hesitation on our part'.

While they dined, Chamberlain had confessed to his Foreign Secretary that he did not believe, unless they could clear the position, that the Government would be able to maintain itself in the morning. The two Government leaders, joined by Sir Alexander Cadogan, Permanent Under-Secretary at the Foreign Office and M. Corbin, the French Ambassador, had then spent an hour of what Halifax later called 'frantic telephoning' to Paris. Daladier, Bonnet and the British Ambassador (Sir Eric Phipps) had all been called to the telephone with the object of giving the Germans as short a time limit as possible.

Now it was after midnight and Chamberlain was having to explain wearily to his ministerial colleagues the difficulty in getting the French to synchronize the timing of a joint ultimatum. Mobilization was their great concern and French military leaders were still clamouring for a further postponement. Britain's Admiralty, War Office and Air Staff chiefs were as equally strenuously opposed to further delay.

Hore-Belisha, who had pressed for a midnight, 2nd September, deadline, now wanted an ultimatum to expire at 6 a.m. Chamberlain retorted that if the British ultimatum were to expire at noon, the French would deliver theirs at noon to expire at 9 p.m. on Sunday night. Apart from the mobilization problems, Chamberlain explained, Bonnet still felt under an obligation to consider the Italian proposal for a conference. By 1.30 a.m. everyone, according to Halifax, had 'frayed nerves' but agreement had been reached: A British ultimatum to Germany would expire at 11 a.m. that day. As the ministers dispersed in the street, there came the flashes and rumbles of a thunderstorm. The die had been cast. . . .

Chamberlain retired tired and harrowed after one of the most gruelling periods ever experienced by a British Premier. But his strength and nerve had held out through all the trials of the day. At 70, he was still a man of astounding elasticity, a mixture of being thickskinned and sensitive. Physically, he was still in excellent condition, due no doubt to the ordered course of his life. He still ate with relish and walked long distances through the London parks every day. His wife said of him at that period, 'It is so fortunate for us that Neville sleeps so well and has such a good digestion. I never have any trouble with him.'

Chamberlain did not express publicly his feelings in the early hours of Sunday as Whitehall began going through the official motions which would set Britain and Germany at war later that morning. But he did summarize much of what he felt at 1.30 a.m. on the morning of 3rd September, 1939, in a letter he wrote a few days later to his younger sister Ida from Chequers, his official country residence in Buckinghamshire.

The Prime Minister said: 'The final long-drawn-out agonies that preceded the actual declaration of war were as nearly unendurable as could be. We were anxious to bring things to a head but there were three complications—the secret communications that were going on with Goering and Hitler through a neutral intermediary, the conference proposals of Mussolini, and the French anxiety to postpone the actual declaration as long as possible until they could evacuate their women and children and mobilize their armies.

'There was very little of this that we could say in public, and meantime the House of Commons was out of hand, torn with suspicions,

and ready (some of them, particularly Amery, who was the most in-
sulting of all) to believe the Government guilty of any cowardice
and treachery.

'To crown it all, a certain number of my colleagues in the Government, who always behave badly when there is any trouble about, took
this opportunity to declare that they were being flouted and neglected
and tried to get up a sort of mutiny. Even Edward Halifax found
their behaviour unbearable and declared that I had the temper of an
archangel!

'The communications with Hitler and Goering looked rather promising at one time but came to nothing in the end as Hitler apparently
got carried away by the prospect of a short war in Poland and then a
settlement. It began with the advances of Goering through the neutral
and took the form of strong expressions of desire for an understanding,
if not an alliance, with us coupled with some doubt as to whether
we really wanted it.

'We made our position clear. We were equally anxious for an understanding but it must be based on confidence that the policy of
force was given up. The correspondence which has since been published in the White Paper was accompanied by verbal comments from
the neutral D. who flew backwards and forwards and alternately con-
versed with Goering and Hitler and Halifax and me.

'The comments didn't really go much beyond friendly expressions
and accounts of how the letters were received on the other side. But
they gave the impression, probably with intention, that it was possible to persuade Hitler to accept a peaceful and reasonable solution of
the Polish question in order to get an Anglo-German agreement which
he continually declared to be his greatest ambition.

'What happened to destroy this chance? Was Hitler merely talking
through his hat and deliberately deceiving us while he matured his
schemes? I don't think so. There is good evidence that orders for the
invasion on the 25th August were actually given and then cancelled
at the last moment because H. wavered. With such an extraordinary
creature one can only speculate.

'But I believe he did seriously contemplate an agreement with us
and that he worked seriously at proposals (subsequently broadcast)
which to his one-track mind seemed almost fabulously generous. But
at the last moment some brainstorm took possession of him—maybe

Ribbentrop stirred it up and once he had set his machine in motion he couldn't stop it. That, as I have always recognized, is the frightful danger of such terrific weapons being in the hands of a paranoiac.

'Mussolini's proposals were, I think, a perfectly genuine attempt to stop war, not for any altruistic reasons, but because Italy was not in a state to go to war and was exceedingly likely to get into trouble if other people did. But it was doomed to failure because Hitler by that time was not prepared to hold his hand unless he could get what he wanted without war. And we were not prepared to give it to him.

'As for the French, we had a bad time wrestling with them. We wanted our ultimatum to expire at midnight on Saturday; they required another forty-eight hours. You saw what happened in the end . . .'

Whitehall's most senior Civil Servants were at their desks at 2 a.m. that morning to translate the Government's decisions into deeds. One group of men, destined to occupy lofty positions in Britain's post-war period, watched the comings and goings in the darkened Downing Street from the window of a room in the Foreign Office. They included Mr. (now Lord) Gladwyn Jebb, private secretary to Sir Alexander Cadogan, Sir William (later Lord) Strang, Mr. (later Sir) Ivone Kirkpatrick, and Mr. Hugh Dalton, the Labour Party's foreign affairs expert of the day. For two hours while the Cabinet was in session they discussed the imminence of war and debated the events which had led up to the crisis.

Then, at 1.30 a.m., the Labour leader who was to become Chancellor of the Exchequer after the war, took another peek out of Jebb's window and noticed that the Cabinet meeting across the road had just come to an end. He took a hasty leave from the company as he intended to buttonhole Halifax in the street. As he left the room, Kirkpatrick said to him, 'If we rat on the Poles now, we are absolutely sunk, whatever the French do. We shall have no chance against Hitler. But if we go ahead now, we shall have two chances:

'First, we may shame the French into coming in, even though they would not have moved unless we had; second, even if the French stay out, we shall have the opinion of the world behind us, and we at least have the Poles on our side with the chance that the United States and others will come in before we are beaten.'

Descending the wide central staircase of the Foreign Office, Dalton bumped into Sir William Malkin, the Foreign Office legal adviser, running up in a great hurry. He had just come from No. 10. Dalton asked him, 'How are things going?' and he answered, 'I have got the declaration in the bag now. It's settled now.'

In Downing Street, the Labour politician accosted Halifax. 'I hope you have brought the French into line now,' he said. 'I warn you that if the House of Commons meets again without our pledge to Poland having been fulfilled, there will be such an explosion as you in the House of Lords may not be able to imagine. It may well blow up the Government altogether.'

According to Dalton, Lord Halifax said in reply, 'I quite understand. It has been very difficult. But it will be all right tomorrow (meaning later that day).' To Dalton's question, 'Who has really been the trouble?' Halifax replied: 'It is Gamelin and his mobilization time-table, but I have been speaking to Daladier myself tonight. We may have to go in a few hours before the French, but they will follow all right now.'

Lord Halifax recalled a different conversation later. He remembered Dalton saying to him, 'Can't you give me any good news?' Halifax replied, 'I didn't know what you will call good news—but we shall be at war in ten hours.' Dalton replied, 'I do call that good news, thank God.' But the Foreign Secretary parted from the Labour man feeling their meeting had been the 'last straw' and that the suspicions aroused by the delay in the Government's ultimatum had been 'wholly unjustifiable'.

As soon as the Cabinet meeting was over, Halifax went back to work at the Foreign Office. There was still much to do. Final instructions to Berlin had to be drafted and Paris had to be notified of the decision. Now there was no going back, but the tension had been momentarily broken. Even Halifax felt relieved as he called for beer. 'It was brought down by a sleepy resident clerk in pyjamas,' Kirkpatrick recalled later. 'We laughed and joked, and when I told Lord Halifax that news had just come in that Goebbels had prohibited listening to foreign broadcasts, he retorted, "He ought to pay me to listen to his."'

From 2 a.m. onwards, there was one telephone number that everyone in or near the Government wished to ring: the Polish Embassy. One after another, politicians telephoned Raczynski to tell him the news and to wish Poland well in its bleakest hour. The indefatigable

Dalton was one of the first callers, Churchill's associate Brendan Bracken another. Dalton told the Polish diplomat, 'Today both we and France shall be at your side. I hope this news will help you to get a little sleep tonight.'

Count Raczynski replied, 'Yes, it's true, it makes me just feel a little less unhappy.' He told Dalton of the speeches made in the Polish Diet during the day: 'They were all brave speeches, but one thing was missing. None of the speakers felt able to make any reference to our friends.'

Raczynski, however, had not been embittered by the delays in the presentation of the ultimatum. He wrote of his feelings that morning that Chamberlain's last attempt to buy peace at the risk of more concessions were 'in the end advantageous in that they showed without any doubt our goodwill to the rest of the world'.

As the early hours of 3rd September passed into history, Whitehall slipped into its war routine. In anticipation of hostilities, the Foreign Office released a joint Anglo-French declaration which had been agreed in advance. The war which was to result in 30 million deaths began with the most solemn and genuine of statements, which paid proper heed to the niceties of the conventions and protocols negotiated during the nineteen-twenties and nineteen-thirties.

It read: 'The Governments of the United Kingdom and France solemnly and publicly affirm their intention, should a war be forced upon them, to conduct hostilities with a firm desire to spare the civilian population and to preserve in every way possible those monuments of human achievement which are treasured in all civilized countries.

'In this spirit they have welcomed with deep satisfaction President Roosevelt's appeal on the subject of bombing from the air. Fully sympathizing with the humanitarian sentiments by which that appeal was inspired, they have replied to it in similar terms.

'They had indeed some time ago sent explicit instructions to the commanders of their armed forces prohibiting the bombardment whether from the air or from the sea or by artillery on land of any except strictly military objectives in the narrowest sense of the word. Bombardment by artillery on land will exclude objectives which have no strictly defined military importance, in particular large urban areas situated outside the battle zone. They will furthermore make every effort to avoid the destruction of localities or buildings which are of value to civilization.

'As regards the use of naval forces, including submarines, the two Governments will abide strictly by the rules laid down in the Submarine Protocol of 1936, which have been accepted by nearly all civilized nations. Further, they will only employ their aircraft against merchant shipping at sea in conformity with the recognized rules applicable to the exercise of maritime belligerent rights by warships.

'Finally, the two Allied Governments reaffirm their intention to abide by the terms of the Geneva Protocol of 1925 prohibiting the use in war of asphyxiating or poisonous or other gases and of bacteriological methods of warfare.

'An inquiry will be addressed to the German Government as to whether they are prepared to give an assurance to the same effect. It will, of course, be understood that in the event of the enemy not observing any of the restrictions which the Governments of the United Kingdom and France have thus imposed on the operations of their armed forces, these Governments reserve the right to take all such action as they may consider appropriate.'

By 4 a.m., Henderson, the British Ambassador in Berlin, had been alerted to arrange an early interview with von Ribbentrop. An hour later, he received the following telegram from Halifax: 'Please seek interview with Minister for Foreign Affairs for 9 a.m. today, Sunday or, if he cannot see you then, arrange to convey at that time to a representative of the German Government the following communication . . .'

Then followed the British ultimatum, couched in the polite, restrained tones of nineteenth-century diplomacy which sounded strange to many at the time but which make even more curious reading a generation later.

The ultimatum said: 'In the communication which I had the honour to make to you on 1st September, I informed you, on the instructions of His Majesty's Principal Secretary of State for Foreign Affairs, that unless the German Government were prepared to give His Majesty's Government in the United Kingdom satisfactory assurances that the German Government had suspended all aggressive action against Poland and were prepared promptly to withdraw their forces from Polish territory, His Majesty's Government in the United Kingdom would, without hesitation, fulfil their obligations to Poland.

'Although this communication was made more than twenty-four hours ago, no reply has been received, but German attacks upon Poland have been continued and intensified. I have accordingly the honour to inform you that unless not later than 11 a.m., British Summer Time today, 3rd September, satisfactory assurances to the above effect have been given by the German Government and have reached His Majesty's Government in London, a state of war will exist between the two countries as from that hour.'

Halifax added a postscript to his message to Henderson to provide for the unlikely eventuality of a Nazi retreat. He said: 'If the assurance referred to in the above communication is received, you should inform me by any means at your disposal before 11 a.m. today, 3rd September. If no such assurance is received here by 11 a.m., we shall inform the German representative that a state of war exists from that hour.'

IV

The telephone rang in the Polish Embassy in London. Mr. Winston Churchill asked to speak to the Ambassador, Count Edward Raczynski. The Count, accustomed for days to receiving a constant succession of calls from British politicians and journalists, answered the call himself. Churchill wanted to hear the latest news from the battle front. It could only be bad news from Poland and Churchill could not, late on that Saturday night, provide the Ambassador with any firm information about Britain's attitude to her ally's plight. But Churchill did his best to give the envoy some hope and encouragement.

Raczynski was tired and depressed, utterly despondent. He could only give Churchill depressing news from Poland. Time was running out, he declared, and the decision to be taken by Britain and France still hung in the balance. What was going to happen?

Churchill did not know. He muttered some words which Raczynski could not pick up, then added, 'I hope, I hope . . . that Britain will keep its . . .' The sentence was never completed. Churchill's voice quivered and broke, and the Ambassador distinctly heard him sobbing. 'He sounded bitterly humiliated and concerned,' Raczynski later reported in his diary.

The telephone was picked up by the then Mr. Anthony Eden who finished the conversation for his friend and leader. But there was nothing much he could tell Raczynski, either, beyond saying that he and his friends could not wait for action.

Churchill, tough, tempestuous opponent of appeasement within the ruling Conservative party, was surrounded by his friends and supporters that midnight at a meeting in his Westminster, London, flat. Duncan Sandys, Brendan Bracken and Robert Boothby were there in what a late arrival, Duff Cooper, described as a state of 'bewildered rage'.

They were a band of bitter, humiliated men, convinced that Chamberlain's indecisive statement in the Commons a few hours earlier was against the whole feeling in the country.

At 64, six years younger than the Prime Minister, Churchill was being urged by some of his political associates to go into the Commons on the Sunday morning, break Chamberlain, and take his place. Boothby felt that in no circumstance should Churchill agree to serve under Chamberlain. But by joining the Government, Churchill could save Chamberlain. Should he split the country or bolster up his party leader in time of crisis? Churchill pondered that and many other personal problems as his intimates talked on into the early hours of 3rd September, to the accompaniment of a tremendous thunderstorm. His shame and sadness at the thought that his country might fail to meet her obligations to an ally were exacerbated by anger at his personal treatment that day by Chamberlain.

Churchill, in fact, had already agreed to join the Chamberlain Government. On the Friday, a few hours after the beginning of the German onslaught on Poland, Chamberlain had summoned him to 10 Downing Street and invited him to serve in a projected War Cabinet. Churchill had agreed without comment, but the next day he had written to Chamberlain asserting that the average age of the suggested ministers was too high and urging the addition of Sir Archibald Sinclair, from the Liberals, and Anthony Eden. Churchill concluded that letter by saying he hoped Chamberlain would be able to announce the joint declaration of war when Parliament met that afternoon. But no such announcement was made, although the short, bitter debate which took place showed that the temper of the Commons was for war.

Churchill, considering himself almost a member of the Government, had not spoken in the debate. It had been a great strain to impose restraint at such a time. But he had done so, although Chamberlain had sent him no further word during the Saturday and was clearly hesitating to confirm Churchill's appointment until war had been finally thrust upon him. So, in the early hours of the morning while his closest political aides talked around him, Churchill drafted another letter to the Prime Minister recalling Chamberlain's undertaking to announce his ministerial appointment speedily.

Churchill said in his letter that he felt entitled to ask Chamberlain to let him know 'how we stand, both publicly and privately, before the debate opens at noon'. He went on to suggest a further review of the composition and scope of the War Cabinet and to say, 'There was a feeling tonight in the House that injury had been done to the spirit of national unity by the apparent weakening of our resolve. I do not underrate the difficulties you have with the French; but I trust that we shall now take our decisions independently and thus give our French friends any lead that may be necessary. In order to do this we shall need the strongest and most integral combination that can be formed. I therefore ask that there shall be no announcement of the composition of the War Cabinet until we have had a further talk.'

His letter concluded: 'As I wrote to you yesterday morning, I hold myself entirely at your disposal, with every desire to aid you in your task.'

Around 2 a.m., however, came a telephone call which caused almost all the anger in Churchill's flat to abate. The caller gave the news of the pending British ultimatum, with the near certainty that when the Commons met at noon the country would be at war. That altered the whole situation and the Conservative rebels prepared to leave the flat to wander home through the darkened streets. But before they went, Churchill told them he would send his letter to Chamberlain none the less. The thunderstorms were ending as the meeting which might have unseated a Prime Minister broke up, and night workers were sniffing the air and predicting a fine morning . . .

V

Franco-Polish relations were at their lowest ebb that midnight. One of the oldest friendships in Europe had been strained to breaking-point by the vacillation of the French in timing their ultimatum. To some Poles, it seemed at that hour as though even the question of France entering the war was in doubt. In every great capital of the world, during the night of 2nd–3rd September, French envoys were being harried by their Polish colleagues. But nowhere was the bitterness more intense than in Paris itself.

M. Lukasiewicz, the Polish Ambassador in the French capital, had walked out of the Quai d'Orsay that evening after a blazing row with M. Bonnet in which he had forgotten all the conventional etiquette of diplomacy. Bonnet had begun by assuring him that talks with London were still in progress, so no final information about an allied ultimatum was available. The Polish envoy had retorted, 'Talks, talks, talks! What's the use of talking? Poland needs action and very swift action.' He then stressed once more his country's firm view that the French engagement to support Poland with military force was automatic and could not be subject to delay.

Bonnet had shrugged his shoulders at the outburst and said nothing. He knew that no words of his could placate the Poles in the situation at that hour. The French General Staff were insisting that it needed until the Monday to complete the dispositioning of the Army and to evacuate large numbers of women and children. Bonnet puffed nervously at one cigarette after another as the Pole continued to make his representations. The room became full of the odour of his *gauloises bleues*.

Finally, Lukasiewicz had been able to stand it no longer and had jumped to his feet to explode in a violent tirade against French officialdom. 'It isn't right,' he shouted. 'You know it isn't right! A treaty is a treaty and must be respected! You have no justification whatever in delaying action! Or am I to assume that a French engagement is worthless? Am I to assume that your words are nothing but hollow sound?

'Do you realize that every hour that you delay the attack on Germany means further unimpeded attacks of the German air force on Polish civilian populations and death to thousands of Polish men, women and children?'

Bonnet had been taken completely aback. Outraged by the tone of the Polish diplomat, he had retorted angrily, 'Do you then want the women and children of Paris to be massacred?'

The Polish diplomat had returned to his Embassy bitter and dejected. He, like Raczynski in London, had become genuinely fearful that France and Britain were pinning their hopes on an Italian proposal halting the German advance into Poland. Both envoys believed the practical consequence of such a policy would be that Poland would be left to fight on alone. The American Ambassador in Paris, Mr. William Bullitt, warned Mr. Cordell Hull, his Secretary of State, of this fear of betrayal in an analysis of the situation which reached Washington at exactly midnight, European time. Bullitt, close to all the leading members of the Diplomatic Corps in Paris, considered the distrust felt by Lukasiewicz that night was an 'exaggerated and rather hysterical view of the present situation'. It was natural, the neutral envoy said, for the French and British leaders to be reluctant to plunge their countries into war if another Italian proposal might avert the catastrophe; but he felt that public opinion in either country would not permit negotiations with Germany prior to withdrawal of troops from Poland.

M. Edouard Daladier, the stocky French Prime Minister, was well aware of this public feeling. He was a man of the people, a baker's son, an ex-soldier whose common sense, businesslike attitude to national problems had earned him a greater measure of trust than France had accorded most of her politicians between the wars.

He had been aware all day and evening of the conflicting feelings in French minds over the threat of another world war. On one hand, France knew better than any other European nation what another conflict might mean. The horrors and the sufferings of the 1914–18 war were still fresh in the minds of everyone over middle age and a few even recalled the ravages of the Prussian invasion of their country in 1870. On the other hand, a majority of Frenchmen were clearly determined that Hitler must be stopped at all costs before Germany grew to a strength which could not be contained by any allied combination on land.

Daladier had no intention of backing out of France's commitments to Poland and had expressed himself forcibly on that point earlier in the afternoon to Lukasiewicz. He had told the envoy that he (Daladier) was going to 'take the direction of foreign affairs into his own hands'. There would be an 'end to delays and slippery conversations' and action would be taken immediately. Daladier, like most intelligent Frenchmen at that hour was resigned, fatalistically, to war, although he shared the strong desire for peace held by most of his compatriots and had been willing to go a very long way in probing Mussolini's peace proposals.

He had obtained from the Chamber of Deputies on the Saturday afternoon a vote of the necessary credits for opening hostilities, so on the night of 2nd September he had a free hand. The Deputies' vote had been unequivocal and sanctioned a declaration of war according to the procedure laid down by the French Constitution. No further parliamentary debate would therefore be necessary.

France's parliamentarians had given Daladier a standing ovation at the close of his speech in which he said simply and plainly, 'Poland is our ally'. Then he added that French pledges to Poland had been given and confirmed—'at the price of our honour we could only buy a precarious peace, which would be revocable, and when we had to fight tomorrow after having lost through it the esteem of our allies and other nations, we would only be a wretched nation, sold to defeat and to slavery'.

But, from the peak of patriotic acclaim in the Chamber, Daladier had been plunged into a valley of military indecision and over-caution. The French General Staff, led by 67-year-old General Maurice Gamelin, had stepped up their demands for more time to complete a complicated mobilization timetable. Frontier troops had been at war stations since 23rd August, and reservists had been obeying orders to join their units since the day after that. But more time was needed and the roads of France were crowded that night with military traffic which the military theorists in Paris felt would be assailed immediately in war by the German Luftwaffe. At the time, the tortuous French approach to war seemed to make sense and only a clairvoyant could have told the politicians and generals that Hitler had not the slightest intention of attacking the allies in the west while he was fully occupied in Poland. France would be in no direct danger for many months and could have synchronized her ultimatum with that of the British in complete security and tranquillity.

But the warnings of Gamelin and others made sense to Daladier, Bonnet and other French political leaders at the time. He had tried to explain all this in a personal telephone conversation with Chamberlain at 10 p.m. on Saturday night. Chamberlain had told him that if the French were to continue to insist on a 48-hour ultimatum to run from midday on Sunday, then the British Government would be unable to hold the situation. The British Prime Minister had then suggested an ultimatum at 8 a.m. on Sunday, to expire at noon. Daladier's cautious answer had been that unless British bombers were ready to act at once it would be better for France to delay attacks on German troops for some hours. Half an hour later, Bonnet had told Halifax in another telephone conversation that British insistence on an ultimatum expiring at noon on Sunday would create a 'deplorable impression'.

Around midnight, France took the first cautious step towards war with Germany. Daladier and Bonnet agreed to alert their Ambassador in Berlin, M. Robert Coulondre, that he would have to present a new *démarche* in the morning to the Wilhelmstrasse. In the early hours of Sunday a message from Bonnet to that effect was on its way to the French Embassy in Berlin. But it gave Coulondre no specific information about the contents of the pending ultimatum. That had still to be decided. So the Quai d'Orsay prepared for another all-night session while the nation, unaware of all the military and diplomatic mechanics involved, went to bed wondering what all the mystery was about . . .

At 2 a.m. M. Charles Corbin, the French Ambassador in London, called the Quai d'Orsay to report on the decisions of the British Cabinet. He told Bonnet that the British had finally abandoned the idea of an ultimatum expiring at 6 a.m. and would be presenting a two-hour ultimatum at 8 a.m. It would, however, still be most desirable if the French move could be made to coincide with the British. The Commons would be meeting within a few hours and it was vital that the ultimatum should be sent before, otherwise the Government risked being defeated.

'Could not the Commons sitting be put off until later?' Bonnet wanted to know. 'Impossible,' M. Corbin replied. 'But is there no way, on our side, to shorten the delay?' Bonnet gave a sigh and asked the Ambassador to hold the line.

Picking up another telephone, the Foreign Minister got into touch with the Ministry of War where the brass-hats were still deliberating. A long, verbal duel ensued, the voices rising in excitement. M. Corbin in London could hear every word that was spoken. At last, Bonnet asked the Ambassador to find out if the British bombing force could be put at the disposal of France. If so, the French General Staff could accept a shorter delay.

Daladier had already made the same request to London and drawn a blank. M. Corbin, nevertheless, conveyed Bonnet's suggestion to the Foreign Office, but soon had to report back to the Quai d'Orsay that the British General Staff could not immediately agree to this. The reason for the hold-up clearly was insufficient resources.

There was nothing that could be done. Bonnet told the Ambassador that he had already advised the French envoy in Berlin of the move planned for the morning. There was no reason why Chamberlain should not tell the Commons that France would send an ultimatum to Hitler at noon. Meanwhile he, Bonnet, would do his utmost to obtain an appreciable reduction in the delay insisted upon by the General Staff.

Corbin's anxiety had been heightened by the fact that, both before and after midnight, the French Embassy in London was—in his own words—under siege from British parliamentarians and journalists. The envoy later reported to his Government that he was forced as the hours wore on to adopt a peremptory tone with some questioners, asking them to compare the British effort, which was revealed above all in the factories, 'with the great national upheaval that is going to call six million Frenchmen to arms'.

Churchill was one of the callers who demanded angrily to know what France was ultimately going to do. His barks, Corbin recalled later, made the telephone 'vibrate'. Churchill, according to Corbin, said he had always striven for a Franco-British alliance and that this was perhaps the last occasion when France and Britain would be called upon to join forces. If they divided in such grave circumstances, Britain would isolate herself within her island and defend herself bitterly, but she would no longer want anything to do with European affairs. Churchill, however, gave another version of their midnight conversation seven years later. He told M. Paul Reynaud that his view at the time had been that Britain should have gone to war—even alone —by the side of Poland.

At 5 a.m. a telephone call from M. François-Poncet in Rome confirmed the collapse of the Italian intervention. Bonnet sighed; he was not surprised. The minutes were ticking towards the denouement. Six o'clock came. Bonnet yawned. He had smoked too much, he had talked too much, he was deadly tired, but rest was out of the question. Later, in his memoirs, he was to evoke those final hours: 'It was the fourth night we had been up, my colleagues and I. I read the latest telegrams which arrived on my desk. From my window I saw the Quai gardens lit up by the first rays of sun from a cloudless sky. I thought sadly that it would, alas, be a day of war. Memories of 2nd August, 1914, came to my mind: the mobilization drums, the departure for the front of trains covered with slogans, carrying away brothers and friends. And now, as twenty-five years before, it was war.'

VI

A 44-year-old Swede who enjoyed the confidence of both the British and German leaders, and believed that he was in a position to influence a peace settlement, arrived at the British Embassy in Berlin just before midnight on Saturday night. The Counsellor to the Embassy, Sir George Ogilvie-Forbes, received him at once and took him to a secluded office where they could talk at length in complete secrecy. The two men were together until the early hours of Sunday morning, discussing the latest moves of the remarkable Swede, who, within a period of just three months had built up personal contacts and a status without precedent in diplomatic history.

The man was Birger Dahlerus, a wealthy engineer whose identity was cloaked at the time under the title of 'Neutral D'. Dahlerus had no axe to grind. He merely wished to bring about peace between two countries he both knew and admired. Dahlerus had worked in both Germany and Britain during the First World War—as the employee of a Swedish firm's subsidiary near Hamburg in 1916 and 1917, and for another Swedish company, producing ball bearings, at Luton, Bedfordshire, in 1917–18. He thus had the unique experience of seeing both sides at war. His impressions in Britain, he wrote years later, were the same as they had been in Germany: 'The endless suffering to which the population of the warring nations was exposed seemed pointlessly cruel . . .'

Dahlerus had been trained from childhood by parents who travelled widely to take an international view of life and affairs. His successful business career in his native country, Britain and Germany, had developed this further and he was well placed to adopt the role of an honest, eager, if sometimes naïve, mediator in that summer of 1939. Friendship with Field Marshal Hermann Goering, Hitler's 46-year-old right-hand man and creator of the Luftwaffe, had been his passport to enter the school of international diplomacy. He had met Goering in 1935 when he appealed to the Nazi, then Minister of the Interior for Prussia, for help in sorting out some German property inheritance problems of Frau Elizabeth Nissen, the woman he planned to marry. In turn, Dahlerus had helped the business career in Sweden of Goering's stepson, Tomas Kantzow, and the two men had gradually grown closer together.

During the immediate pre-war years, Dahlerus had become both aware of the Nazi Government's grievances and motives, and of the lack of real knowledge it had of the outside world. By the summer of 1939 he had come to the conclusion that peace could only be preserved if the Nazi leaders could get to understand the allied, and especially the British point of view. So in the previous June he had begun arranging a top-level meeting of British and German industrialists and influential persons. In August, Goering had attended secret meetings with a group of seven leading British businessmen at Sonke Nissen Koog, a country house in Germany near the Danish border. That meeting had arranged to convene a four-power top-level conference to include representatives of France and Italy, too. It was scheduled to take place in Sweden, but it had been forgotten by Nazi leaders in the rush events in late August.

Since 24th August, Dahlerus had been engaged night and day in trying to find a formula to avert the war which seemed destined to engulf mankind and create the conditions for the spread of communism which Dahlerus particularly dreaded. Told by Goering that Germany wanted to reach a settlement with Britain, Dahlerus had flown to London on the 25th to confer with Halifax, Foreign Office officials, and business acquaintances. On the following day, he had told the British Foreign Secretary that the situation was serious and Goering was the only man who could prevent war. Halifax had then given him what the Swede called a 'frank and friendly' letter to take back to Goering. Returning to Berlin, Dahlerus had told Goering of Britain's dislike of German policies, but of the London Government's strong desire to come to a friendly agreement, as long as Germany refrained from measures that might trouble the peace of Europe. Dahlerus had also warned Goering—and therefore Hitler—that Britain would not fail to respect her agreement with Poland and would support that country against any aggression. On the 27th, he had made one last trip to London with a message from Hitler which he discussed with both Chamberlain and Halifax.

Now it was 3rd September and the war which Dahlerus had struggled so hard to avert seemed destined to break over their heads within a few hours. The earnest, anxious Swede was pouring his heart out to Sir George Ogilvie-Forbes and discussing with the British diplomat the events of the previous forty-eight hours. Dahlerus wrote later that the burden of their conversation was whether they could enforce the 'rightful demands of the British Government and what steps could be taken to persuade the Germans to accept them'.

Ogilvie-Forbes, the Swede recalled, was as calm and clear-sighted as ever as they discussed the situation until well past midnight. He told the Swede candidly that he was convinced the British policy was directed against the Hitlerian system and that the topical Danzig and Polish Corridor questions were of minor importance. The British Government, the diplomat told the amateur mediator, was obliged once and for all to show the persons who ruled Germany that they must make a radical change in their methods. The events of the past year, he added, were still a recent memory and the present ones were, Dahlerus quoted him as saying, patently an example of Hitler's delusion that he could continue with his unscrupulous policy precisely as far as it suited his book.

The two men reviewed the frantic efforts of the Swede for peace since the beginning of the German attack on Poland two days earlier. Goering, the vain, vigorous heavyweight whom Hitler had just officially named as his Number 2, had given early news of the German invasion personally to Dahlerus. According to the beribboned Field Marshal, Germany had been obliged to attack Poland and he quoted as evidence a Polish 'raid' on a German border radio station on the 31st. How could Germany be expected to remain impassive in the face of so much provocation? On the Friday, Goering had defended stoutly Germany's innocence and righteousness and had said the British must realize she had no other alternative. But he would do everything in his power to prevent the war from spreading.

From that meeting with Goering at the Luftwaffe Headquarters in Potsdam, Dahlerus had sped to a meeting with Sir Nevile Henderson, the British Ambassador. Henderson was pessimistic about the chances of an Anglo-American conference which Dahlerus proposed should take place in a neutral country, perhaps Holland. He felt things had gone too far and the situation was out of hand. The meeting had ended with the peace-loving and mild Henderson making a violent tirade against Hitler who was to blame for all that was happening. If the whole of Europe was to be plunged into war and untold misery, it would be Hitler's fault alone. Dahlerus had never seen Henderson like that before.

Following that 1st September meeting with Henderson, Dahlerus had been summoned to meet Hitler at the Chancellery. It was to prove a fantastic and horrifying session which shook the Swede's simple faith in the possibility of negotiating an honourable settlement with the Nazi chief. Goering, radiant at his new appointment as Hitler's Deputy, had taken him in to see the Führer. Hitler, who had just made one of his epic, rabble-rousing speeches in the Reichstag, had been pale but calm at the beginning of the interview. But soon it became very clear to the Swede that Hitler was boiling inside, like a volcano ready for eruption. The man's strange bearing, too, had an abnormal quality about it which the Swede sensed with concern.

Hitler had walked up close to Dahlerus and had spoken with the fixed stare of a man in a trance. 'His breath was so foul that it was all I could do not to step back,' Dahlerus recalled later. 'He was obviously determined to snatch at every argument, however far-fetched, that would serve to absolve him personally from the decision he had made.'

Hitler had then launched forth into bitter recriminations against Britain. He thanked Dahlerus for his efforts to promote peace and understanding between the two nations, but he had always known that England did not want peace. England was a nation of shop-keepers; her only concern was for her own selfish interests. She had no humanitarian considerations whatever. That was the real reason why Dahlerus's praiseworthy attempts to bring Britain and Germany together were doomed to failure. He no longer could hold out any hope of coming to an agreement.

Goering had remained in the background not saying a single word, but as Hitler paused for a moment to regain his breath, the Field Marshal chimed in. He said that in the Polish war it was essential that the German Army advance to certain specific points. But Goering had then been interrupted by Hitler who declared that he was now determined to crush Polish resistance and annihilate the Polish nation. 'And,' he yelled, 'if the British don't understand that it is in their own interest to keep out of a fight with me, they will live to repent their folly.'

Hitler had flushed, gazed about wildly and then begun to wave his arms like a madman as he shouted in the Swede's face: 'If England wants to fight for a year I shall fight for a year. If England wants to fight for two years, I shall fight two years.' He paused, seeking for words, then went on, 'If England wants to fight three years, I shall fight three years!'

His voice had risen to a shrill scream, his arms never stopped milling about wildly. His face had become suffused with hatred. His whole body vibrated and convulsed as he bellowed, '*Und wenn es erforderlich ist, will ich zehn Jahre kämpfen!*' His body was nearly doubled up and his tightly-shut fists almost hammered the floor.

Perhaps a more experienced and astute man than Dahlerus would have given up his efforts for peace after that experience with the Nazi dictator. But he had continued his efforts at mediation throughout Friday evening and Saturday, largely in the hope that Goering, Hitler's close friend and aide for seventeen years, could persuade his leader to make some gesture to win a settlement before it was too late. Even while the German forces were driving into Poland that first day, Goering had been eager for a peaceful settlement and had talked at length to the Swede on ways in which it could be achieved. (The sight of art treasures being hastily packed away at Goering's home, however, did not give Dahlerus an abundance of confidence.)

Later, Dahlerus had telephoned Sir Alexander Cadogan at the Foreign Office in London to inquire if there were any hope of accomplishing anything by direct negotiations between London and Berlin. Cadogan's reply had been short and concise: Britain was in no position to modify her stand. The prerequisite to any further talks was immediate cessation of hostilities and withdrawal by Germany of her troops.

Undismayed by the clarity of this information, Dahlerus had again seen Goering at his Luftwaffe Headquarters. Without mentioning his conversation with Cadogan, he had stressed the necessity for Germany to recall troops from Poland if a resumption of negotiations were to have the slightest chance of success. Goering had listened, nodded, smiled, but said nothing encouraging.

By Friday evening, Dahlerus had begun to lose faith in his friend Goering. The events of that day had produced a noticeable effect on the man. Having been appointed the Führer's successor and given a chance to show what the Luftwaffe could do in all-out warfare, he seemed to regard as of lesser moment the consequences of spreading the conflict. Within a few hours, the burly Field Marshal had become a man intoxicated with glory and ambition and, though still promising to do all in his power to localize the conflict between Germany and Poland, his general attitude had become vague and elusive. Dahlerus had stayed with Goering late on the Friday evening until he began to detect a hollow ring in the Nazi's repeated assurances, although he trusted that on reflection the German No. 2 would grasp the significance of the unwavering attitude being adopted by Britain.

At an early hour on the Saturday morning, Dahlerus had again called on Goering in the Field Marshal's private railway car at Luftwaffe Headquarters. Goering, fresh and rested and as usually dressed in a gorgeous uniform, was in great spirits. He had news for Dahlerus.

Mussolini had personally sponsored another peace move by Italy, and there now seemed to be some real hope of preventing the war from spreading. Goering had reliable information that France was very much in favour of the Duce's intervention and had declared her willingness to explore every avenue to reach an understanding.

Peace might yet be preserved if another 'Munich' could be staged. Dahlerus had been infected anew by the optimism of the Field Marshal who had also assured him that there was no need to reply to the allied ultimata of the previous day until it was known whether there was a possibility of arranging an armistice.

Following that meeting, Dahlerus had arrived at the British Embassy for a talk with Ogilvie-Forbes, who was sceptical over the prospects of Italian mediation so long as German forces remained in Poland. Then had followed another Goering–Dahlerus meeting, with the Nazi still in a highly optimistic mood about the prospects of the Italian manœuvres.

At 9 p.m. on the Saturday evening, Sir Nevile Henderson had dispatched a messenger to Dahlerus at his hotel, The Esplanade, with a copy of the statement Chamberlain had just made in the Commons. Dahlerus, dining with senior Nazi officials, had not been depressed by the tone of the British Prime Minister's remarks. The speech, he felt, merely emphasized what had been said before: that Britain was not willing to negotiate until hostilities ceased and Germany withdrew her forces. But Chamberlain's remarks were also 'permeated with the desire to try to prevent a catastrophe'. And Dahlerus and his German guests had come to the conclusion that it might 'still be possible to avoid a world war'.

Now it was well after midnight on the 3rd, and though Dahlerus and Ogilvie-Forbes did not know it, the die had been cast. Their earnest conversation could be to no avail. But Dahlerus bade farewell to the British diplomat still hopeful that something might be achieved, and looking forward to yet one more meeting with Goering that was to take place at 9 a.m. that day. The Field Marshal, however, was destined to have much more to think about at that particular hour than another round of platitudes with the well-meaning Swede . . .

Berlin, through the small hours of the morning, was a city blacked out as effectively as London, although the British capital had been engaged longer in its preparations. The danger of a Polish air-raid was remote, but no chances were being taken. Searchlights scanned the sky overhead and crews stood by their anti-aircraft guns.

Berlin was like a city mesmerized that Saturday night and Sunday morning. There was none of the nervous tension in evidence that characterized the western capitals and Rome. There was no patriotic fever, none of the bellicose exuberance that marked the outbreak of war in 1914. If it were mesmerized, and it seemed like that to independent eye-witnesses at the time, then Adolf Hitler was the hypnotist responsible. The founder of National Socialism and of the Third Reich, the 49-year-old ex-Austrian amateur painter was a man possessed. Nothing short of possession could explain the hold and the power he wielded over the German people in 1939.

The war with Poland had become quickly popular with Nazi political and military leaders. For them, there was hope of promotion, glory and possibly plunder. But the man in the street was like a person in a trance. He was a worried man, but only as worried as his state of hypnosis permitted. The Nazi propaganda machine, though neglecting no device for whipping up enthusiasm for Hitler's adventures, had not infected any but a minority of the young with war fever. The victories in the east were expected and were heard with, on the whole,

indifference. The news from the west—mobilization in France, ultimata from London and Paris—was ominous, but aroused no great
dread. The people had become used to crises since Hitler's advent
to power. Most Germans that night were behaving, in the words of
Dahlerus who had a warm, sympathetic feeling for them, like 'frightened animals before an approaching storm'.

Inside the German Foreign Office and the Service departments,
however, there was a sense of purpose and drive. All was enthusiasm
and efficiency, and messages and directives poured out from midnight
until dawn to the fighting units in the east and diplomatic and trade
missions all over the world. Von Ribbentrop had little sleep that
night and his last thought before retiring for a few brief hours was to
draft a memorandum warning diplomatic missions abroad that there
must be no weakening of the Berlin-Rome axis. His edict, issued from
Berlin at 4.50 a.m. on the 3rd, read:

'German-Italian policy is based on complete and clear agreements
between the Führer and the Duce. In case you are addressed on the
subject, you should adopt this point of view. There must be no criticism of the Italian attitude and, if made, it will be severely punished.
Subordinate officials are to be correspondingly instructed at your dis-
cretion.'

Von Ribbentrop, however, had another partner to think of when
he retired to bed that morning, an 'ally' more powerful than Italy,
but also untested and unpredictable: Soviet Russia. For, the previous
evening, ten days after the signing of a non-aggression pact between
fascist Germany and communist Russia, a Soviet military mission had
arrived in Berlin under the direction of General Maxim Purkajen.
With the mission was M. Chkvarzev, who had just succeeded M.
Merekalov as the Soviet Ambassador to Germany. History's strangest
bedfellows were about to lie down together . . .

VII

Warsaw at midnight was in a state of confusion bordering on chaos after a day in which the capital had felt a full taste of the might of the German air fleets. The impact of the city's first big air-raids was heightened at that hour by the arrival of the first trainloads of wounded, evacuated hastily from the hard-pressed Polish front line.

The advance guard of the trainloads of wounded began arriving in a quiet and blacked-out Warsaw around midnight. They continued to rumble in all through a night in which the dire nature of the country's plight began to sink deeply into the minds of everyone in the capital.

By the early hours of Sunday morning, the hospitals in Warsaw were already almost packed with casualties from the air-raids of the day. Soon there was no room for the new arrivals from the front. At first they were laid out in the hospital courtyards, in vestibules and corridors, anywhere space could be cleared. Later, the hospitals could take no more, and thousands of men had to be made as comfortable as was possible on the platforms of the city's railway stations.

The spectacle of those broken young bodies was particularly horrifying to the people of a city which only a few days earlier had been enjoying tranquil holiday weather. A woman eye-witness recalled later of the midnight scene in one of Warsaw's main line stations: 'The wounded men, looking very long and flat, lay on stretchers roughly covered with blankets. Horribly wounded. The first fruits of the Great Mechanized War.

'Their teeth were clenched, but they opened their eyes and looked up into the faces of those who were waiting to help them—all that night the women of Warsaw stood on the stations, hoping to give them at least a cigarette to smoke, something hot to drink. When they spoke they demanded news: "How are they fighting in the west? Are they bombing Germany? Is England in?" '

The wounded were more eager to ask questions than to tell stories of their own grim experiences on the battle front, how they had been ruthlessly pushed back by the irresistible German juggernaut rolling on in a column of steel and fire ten miles wide over terribly dry roads which were all in the enemy's favour.

All over Warsaw as 3rd September dawned, teams of firemen, soldiers and hastily-organized air-raid wardens were clearing away the debris of half a dozen bombing attacks during the Saturday. German ascendancy in the air had become firmly established during that afternoon and evening and the day ahead could only be expected to bring more attacks of greater intensity. But the capital was not alone in licking its wounds. Few towns of any size in Poland that afternoon had escaped air attack. A Government spokesman at midnight estimated that 1,500 civilians had been killed in the first two days of the German attack. The Nazi air-raids had been brutal and indiscriminate from the beginning. In the east, at any rate, Hitler had no intention of paying heed to the conventions of war.

Accounts of people who were in Warsaw that night all have a common theme: the nightmarish rapidity with which everything had happened. Only three days previously they had been at peace, albeit an uneasy one. The devout citizens of Warsaw had gone to attend mass on the Thursday and then flocked to an international soccer match to applaud a Polish team that beat the Hungarians 4–2. The city's streamlined cafés had been crowded with men and women sipping coffee and kummel. Now, they were scrambling through the rubble of collapsed houses and streets, with dust and smoke everywhere and the smell of death, destruction and ultimate defeat in the air . . .

The Government was still in Warsaw but plans for its evacuation to Lublin, about a hundred miles to the south-east, were already under consideration. Members of the Diplomatic Corps were getting ready to follow the Government. Trunks and valises were hastily being packed.

In the midst of all the turmoil and confusion, there was one very calm man near the head of affairs in Poland: Colonel Josef Beck, the country's imperturbable Foreign Minister. A striking figure, impeccably dressed and sporting a monocle in his right eye, the Colonel had refused to be rattled by the early German successes and the full blast of the Goebbels propaganda machine exploiting them. Dispatches filed to the overseas Press from Warsaw that night noted his calmness and refusal to lose his head in the crisis. He told one interviewer earlier in the evening that he was now sleeping more soundly in his Warsaw office than he ever had at home!

At midnight, the Foreign Minister was still engaged in a task which had occupied his attention for most of the day: the rallying of support from Poland's allies by appeals and bitter denunciations through his envoys in London and Paris. Only one hour earlier, Beck had sent urgent messages to his embassies in those cities which made his envoys scurry to the Foreign Office and the Quai d'Orsay to invoke, once more, the treaty clauses stipulating immediate military assistance in the event of aggression by another state.

The message addressed to Count Raczynski, the Ambassador in London, read: 'The Polish Government highly appreciates the formula used by Lord Halifax yesterday in his speech in Parliament that the British Government do not accept any conference whatsoever so long as the German invasion of Poland and Danzig persist.

'We are fighting now along the whole front with the main German forces, defending every foot of territory. Even the garrison in the Westerplatte is still putting up a fight.

'The hostile action of the bulk of the German air forces is assuming an increasingly brutal form. We had during 2nd September large losses of life among the civilian population.

'The Polish Government recalls Article 1 of the Agreement on Mutual Assistance between the United Kingdom and Poland in which each Contracting Party undertakes to give to the other Contracting Party, in case of aggression, at once "all the support and assistance in its power", and they are hoping to receive an immediate communication regarding the decision taken in this respect by His Majesty's Government.'

M. Léon Noel, the French Ambassador in Warsaw, began a long talk after midnight with the Polish Foreign Minister and Mme. Beck. In view of the day's happenings and the continued lightning advance of the Nazi troops, the Ambassador's visit was a painful occasion. He sensed his hosts' growing anxiety with which he could well sympathize, and was embarrassed by his own inability to reassure them, being himself without instructions, and almost without information, from Paris. He later recalled that he himself was not quite free of doubts as to the position his country would assume.

'Despite the general mobilization ordered in France,' M. Noel declared later, 'I was not free of apprehension. I knew the state of mind of several members of the Government and especially of M. Bonnet who, in accordance with his temperament, must have nurtured the *arrière-pensée* of finding *in extremis* some ingenious means of eluding the formal obligations to which the signature of France was appended. One can guess how I felt: anxious and sad, like all Frenchmen at the thought that war was coming down once more on our country, but fearing, on the other hand, lest it escaped that scourge by a shameful and inexcusable default.'

The Ambassador refrained from conveying his secret fears to his hosts, and was deeply moved and impressed by the Polish statesman's steadfastness in the face of events and the charming hospitality of the elegant Jadwiga Beck. But in his heart of hearts he was anxious, ill at ease, and overcome by an immense sadness at the thought of France being once more plunged into the misery and chaos of total war, and yet fearing the possibility of a last-minute manœuvre on the part of French political leaders to wriggle out of a solemn undertaking which would cover with shame the name of France.

VIII

Five o'clock in the morning marked not only the beginning of the third day of the German onslaught on Poland but a turning-point in the whole campaign. Dawn battle-front reports to headquarters from wearied and worried commanders told the same story of one German success after another. The pressure of the Nazi attacks had been stepped up during the night. Fresh motorized units had been thrown into the fray since the previous evening, making the contest between armour on the one hand and cavalry and infantry on the other all the more unequal. The last Polish forces were not to succumb until a month from 3rd September, but the effective end of the nation's resistance was already within sight on that grey dawn.

By that morning, the Germans had sixty-two divisions in the fight or waiting fresh behind the lines: twenty-eight infantry divisions, eighteen reserve and 'Landwehr', seven armoured, four motorized, four light motorized and one cavalry division. All had been concentrated in the east for weeks before Hitler had sent them into action and their movements had been planned ahead with meticulous German efficiency.

Poland was still suffering from a delay in mobilizing her forces, largely due to the insistence of her allies that she should do nothing that might be regarded by the Germans as an act of provocation. As a result, only three-quarters of the country's reservists had been called to the colours and the Polish Army was in dire need of those missing men all along the front. On paper, the Poles had forty infantry divisions in being to repel the invaders—thirty regular, nine reserve and three highland brigades which together comprised one more division. In addition, there were eleven cavalry brigades and two motorized brigades, but the latter had not been brought up to full strength.

Numerically, however, the Germans had been able by Sunday morning to bring a far greater proportion of their men to the front and outnumbered the Poles by some three to two.

Right from the firing of the first shots of the war at 4.40 a.m. on Friday morning, the German advantage in numbers had been surpassed by their superiority in armour and equipment. Forty-eight hours of bitter fighting had demonstrated clearly an enormous discrepancy between the fire-power of the German and Polish divisions. The German divisions had been shown to have four times as many light guns and three times as many howitzers and anti-armour guns.

In tanks, too, the Germans were vastly superior, both in numbers and quality. Poland did not possess any heavy tanks. Her light tanks, numbering 110, partly French-built, were proving to be slow, inadequately plated and insufficiently armed. Polish anti-aircraft and anti-armour guns, though of fairly recent make and good quality, were insufficient in numbers.

The really decisive factor, however, had been the crushing ascendancy enjoyed by the Germans in the air. Of Germany's 3,500 bomber and fighter aircraft more than 2,000 had been concentrated along the eastern frontier. Poland's Air Force, consisting of 400 largely obsolescent planes, was hopelessly outclassed by the Luftwaffe's operational strength.

All along the front that morning, as on the two previous days, German Messerschmitts were making short shift of slow and inadequately-armed Polish fighters trying to intercept the Nazi bombers. Poland had no heavy bombers and her small number of medium and light bombers had not weighed heavily in the balance of operations. The Nazis had also inaugurated a new technique of dive-bombing troop concentrations with their Stukas, a deadly innovation that spread terror and death among the Poles.

The war had come too early for Poland to have built up her industries to support a full-scale defensive effort. Since 1934, more than 40 per cent of the country's total budget had been spent on arms— but it represented only a fraction of what Germany had been able to lay out through putting 'guns before butter'. Anti-aircraft and anti-tank guns of high quality were being produced in Poland just before the German invasion, but many of these had been exported to earn direly-needed foreign exchange. The country had developed the Los

(Elk), a remarkable new type of medium bomber, put only thirty-six
had been delivered to the air force before the Luftwaffe razed the
factory to the ground that week-end. And only a prototype was available of the Jastrzab (Hawk), a really modern fighter aircraft.

Poland's Army was under the supreme command of 53-year-old, egg-
bald Marshal Edward Smigly-Rydz (meaning 'nimble-mushroom')
who painted in oils in his spare time. He was one of the ablest Polish
soldiers, trained—like Foreign Minister Beck—under the late great
Marshal Pilsudski's iron discipline. He was an excellent sharp-shooter,
and never wore more than one medal at a time.

The Marshal was struggling to cope with not only an incomparably
superior enemy but also the almost impossible strategical position of
Poland. Since Hitler's Munich coup, assuring German military control over Slovakia, Poland had been open to attack on three sides—
in the west, the north and the south. Apart from the chain of the
Carpathian and Tatra mountains, Poland's flat terrain made her easily
vulnerable to invasion.

The Marshal and his generals might have shortened their defence
line and gained the benefit of some sort of natural barrier by adopting
a line formed by the rivers, Narew, Vistula and San. But that would
have meant giving up the whole of Poland's richest western provinces
with their coal mines, industry and agricultural resources. Rightly or
wrongly, they had tried to defend the whole country—and that morning it was very clear they were going to pay the supreme penalty for
their decision.

Poland was doomed, therefore, before her allies had even decided
to take the field. Only massive military intervention by the French
on the western front might have saved the situation. France had agreed
to launch a mass attack of her troops not later than the fifteenth day
after the outbreak of a war with Germany and there were many Polish
officers in the field whose will to resist that morning was fortified by
this knowledge. But the French generals were in no mood to put the
strength of the German Siegfried Line to the test—and their nightmare was of a massed Nazi attack on their positions . . .

The morale of German troops that morning was high. For them it
was a just war of reprisal against the Poles. Hitler and his aides had
seen to that by manufacturing one of the most remarkable excuses for
conflict in human history. By the end of August, all the Nazi leader

had wanted was an excuse to mount an assault already planned down to the most minute detail. Some border incidents were necessary, acts of Polish 'provocation', frontier skirmishes and so on. If they refused to take place they had to be invented.

Inventing a formal cause for the invasion had not been a matter requiring much preparation. The Nazis, who had staged the Reichstag fire for similar propaganda purposes, were old hands at that sort of thing. The mere fact that it was transparent was irrelevant. The affair was never meant to go over big in the west, but Hitler could make good use of it to justify himself in the eyes of the German people.

The plot had been simple enough and consisted of a faked Polish attack on the southern Silesian border. Admiral Canaris, the German spy chief, supplied a few Polish uniforms which were required in a little play produced and directed by Himmler and Heydrich at a special request from 'higher up'. There were only two main actors—Heinrich Müller, a Gestapo officer, and an S.S. official by the name of Naujocks—plus a dozen or so expendable extras.

On 31st August, a small band of Germans disguised as Polish soldiers had made an abrupt appearance on the border, killing half a dozen Gestapo prisoners supplied by Müller under the appropriate cover name of 'canned goods'. Then the group under Naujocks' command had 'captured' the German radio station at Gleiwitz to enable a German linguist to broadcast in Polish the announcement of a Polish attack on Germany. There had been lots of noise, but no bloodshed, and the official German News Agency gave it all out with much detail and embellishment. It was a suitable prelude to sudden simultaneous attacks the following dawn on Polish airfields, military bases, railway junctions and main lines by aircraft, artillery and warships.

From the blowing up of a Polish ammunition dump at Westerplatte by the German battleship *Schleswig-Holstein* soon after 5 a.m. on the Friday there had been no slackening in the Nazi blitz. The German forces had quickly fanned out in all directions, some pressing south from East Prussia in the direction of Warsaw, others from Pomerania cutting the 'corridor' and thereby isolating the Polish forces in the Gdynia area from their main armies.

The Germans had made clear from the outset that their strategical plan was a quick and thorough defeat of the Polish forces before an organized retreat could take place. German strategy was based on a deep, swift thrust of their armoured spearhead through to Warsaw to break the back of the resistance.

The Nazi commanders had completely ignored the 'nose' of the Polish Poznan salient, but synchronized sweeping movements from the north and the south were aimed at outflanking and surrounding the bulk of the Polish forces massed on the left bank of the Vistula River. A second and wider 'pincer movement' from East Prussia in the north and from Slovakia in the south was designed to encircle the Polish forces on the right bank of the Vistula and the formations which might manage to escape from the encirclement of the inner pincers.

On the first day of the war, the German armoured divisions had succeeded in penetrating deeply into Polish territory between Lodz and Cracow, and on the Saturday had pushed forward as far as Pilitsa, more than fifty miles from the frontier.

Polish strategy that Sunday morning was still aimed at holding out against the attackers as long as possible, in the hope of being able to counter-attack when enemy pressure had weakened due to the entry into the war of the western allies. The Polish General Staff had on the whole anticipated the direction the German attack was to take and gathered fairly accurate information about the deployment and strength of the German formations. What had caught them by surprise, however, had been the unimaginable striking power of the Luft-waffe and the shattering effect of the panzer divisions on inadequately-equipped Polish forces. During the first two days, bombardments from the air had paralysed transport, disrupted communications and spread terror among civilians, whose hurried evacuation had further impeded the Polish troops.

At the start of hostilities, the Polish formations had been packed along the main defence line—from east to west, from west to south, and again to the east. These formations included the Special Opera-tional Narew Group and six armies bearing geographical names: the Modlin, Pomorze, Poznan, Lodz, Cracow and Carpathian armies.

The Narew Group was to ensure the defence of the northern flank running along the rivers Biebrza and Narew, while the Modlin Army's task was to cover the continuation of the northern flank. The Pomorze Army, wedged between German forces in Pomerania, was facing the enemy both in the west and in the east.

Separated from the Polish mainland, a special coastal defence group was operating to defend Westerplatte, Gdynia, and to hold the Hel peninsula. The Poznan Army was supposed to defend the western area along the Warta river, while the Lodz Army, which was soon to bear the brunt of one of the strongest German thrusts, was covering the approaches to Lodz and Warsaw. Further south, the Cracow Army stood in readiness to defend Silesia and the Cracow area. Troops of the Carpathian force, facing the German-held frontiers of Slovakia, were to prevent the enemy from rolling into southern Poland through the mountain passes.

In addition to her armies in the field, Poland also had four groups of reserve formations, the main group being concentrated south of Warsaw. Their aim was to reinforce the fighting formations to enable them to stage counter-attacks. The deployment of these reserve formations, however, had not been completed by early Sunday (and was later to be greatly hampered by the disruption of transport).

The Polish General Staff had entered the war expecting early withdrawals, but hoping that most of the front-line positions could be held for days or weeks. By the Sunday dawn, however, it was clear from almost every report that the German advance could not be more than momentarily stemmed anywhere, despite much gallant and dogged fighting. At points, the Nazi forces were being halted, but the main enemy thrusts were irresistible. Panzers could always break the Polish front line and wreak havoc among the rear formations.

Unable to check the waves of German tanks, wilting under the Luftwaffe dive-bombing and left flat-footed by the astonishing mobility of the enemy, Polish commanders were also cursing an unexpected natural ally for Hitler: the unseasonal dry weather. Had the rains come by 3rd September, there might have been some hope of a prolonged Polish resistance which could have been exploited by aggression in the west. The Poles still recalled the defeat of the Hindenburg Army in the First World War when German vehicles were caught in the Pripet Marshes and sank deeper and deeper above their axles. But this year the rains were very late. On hard ground, the fighting everywhere was proving disastrous for the Poles. The water level was so low that plans to flood certains areas in the northern sector of the Narew river to check the Germans had been abandoned. So it was no wonder that prayers for rain were being uttered that Sabbath morning by tough men who had never gone down on their knees before. . . .

IX

Six o'clock in the morning and Poland was hitting back hard at sea in the first naval engagement of the Second World War. The young and untried Polish fleet was establishing in blood and tears a tough fighting tradition which was to be carried on and enhanced even after the country's surrender on land. The scene of this sea fight was the harbour at Hel, Poland's naval base.

The Polish Navy had gone into action against the German Baltic fleet facing madly impossible odds and with almost no chance of escape. The total force it could muster at the time of the German invasion had been four destroyers, a small torpedo-boat, a minelayer, five submarines, eight trawler-minesweepers and a dozen river gunboats and small monitors. Against this, the Germans had been able to pit the old, but powerful battleships *Schleswig-Holstein* and *Schlesien*, a fleet of modern cruisers and numerous well-armed destroyers, submarines and lesser craft.

The Germans had also enjoyed from the beginning of hostilities almost complete superiority in the air along the Baltic coast, and it was from the Nazi bombers that the Polish naval units had experienced their baptism of fire. Within six hours of the launching of the German onslaught on Poland, bombing of some of the units of the fleet had begun in Gdynia Harbour.

In that first attack on 1st September, a bomb had hit the torpedo-boat *Mazur*, killing twenty men immediately. But the sailors still alive had gone on firing their guns at the planes with black crosses, even while the little warship was sinking into the still waters of the harbour. They had continued firing when the water was around their knees and had kept blazing away until it reached their waists and the guns would operate no more. Not until then had the *Mazur* been abandoned—the first ship to be sunk from the air in the war.

As the *Mazur* sank, the other units of the fleet in harbour had steamed out to sea, under constant attack from the air. All through Friday and Saturday they had been bombarded from the air. The minelayer *Gryf* had been attacked by twenty bombers at one stage and her captain killed by blast, although her cargo of mines had remained intact. The destroyer *Wicher* had survived repeated attacks, while a minesweeper, the *Mewa*, had been damaged but managed to reach Hel with the larger units on the Saturday. During Saturday night the bombers had returned again, but to no avail.

Now it was Sunday morning and the Germans had dispatched two heavy destroyers to finish off the *Gryf* and the *Wicher* in harbour. It was an unequal fight from the beginning. The Polish vessels were at anchor and some of their guns were out of action as the result of bombing. Their crews were weary from fighting and lack of sleep, but they had the courage of desperate men and of patriots and soon the German warships were taking a battering from the partly-crippled Polish units.

First, one of the German destroyers, though enjoying speed and freedom to manœuvre, was hit by a salvo from the Polish craft and turned, badly damaged, to make for Danzig. But she sank during the morning on the way to safety. The second German destroyer managed to inflict further damage on the Polish warships until she, too, was hit and withdrew under a heavy smoke screen.

It was the war's first naval engagement and a clear victory for the gallant, depleted band of Polish sailors who had defeated a fresh enemy after going through forty-eight hours of almost incessant attack. But it was a short-lived triumph. Within two hours the bombers returned and finished off both the little warships, as well as a pleasure steamer, the *Gdynia*, which the Polish Navy had hastily requisitioned.

The destruction of those units in Hel Harbour left the remainder of the Polish Navy divided into roughly three categories that morning: the minesweepers and other small craft, which could expect to survive only for a short period in the Baltic; the submarines; and the three largest destroyers.

Poland's five submarines had been stationed in Puck Bay between Hel and Gdynia on 1st September. Their first orders were to lie in the waters off the coast to guard against a thrust by the heavy German warships against Gdynia. But the German ships had kept clear of the area and in those shallow waters the submarines had been at the mercy of enemy bombers and anti-submarine planes since the Friday.

Now, in the early morning of 3rd September, it was the turn of one of these submarines, the *Sep* (Vulture), to come under a fierce rain of bombs. Her crew counted thirty-five exploding above the little craft before the Nazi bombers could be evaded. The damage was not great and could be repaired. But it was clear that the bombing had shortened the operational life of the *Sep*, and that her only hope would be to go on fighting the enemy until she became completely unmanageable. (In fact, the *Sep* stayed in action until mid-September when she entered internment in Sweden.)

The other submarines in action that morning in Puck Bay—the *Zbik* (Wild Cat), *Rys* (Lynx), *Wilk* (Wolf) and *Orzel* (Eagle)— faced a similar impossible future with no chance of fuel supplies, no base to use and no support from friendly aircraft. (*Zbik* and *Rys* were destined to be interned in Stockholm, but *Wilk* and *Orzel*, after surviving numerous attacks through courage and brilliant seamanship, made epic journeys to Britain, the latter after a spell of internment in Estonia.)

Co-operation with Britain had, in fact, been a basic tenet of the Polish Admiralty's war plan. And before 1st September, Poland had decided to sacrifice part of the safety of the Baltic coast in the interests of the wider war that seemed certain to come. In consequence, the three most powerful units of the fleet, the destroyers *Grom* (Thunderbolt) and *Blyskawica* (Lightning), both of 2,100 tons, and the *Burza* (Squall), of 1,540 tons, had left Polish waters on 30th August. On the morning of 3rd September, they were already in British waters, prepared to serve the allied cause anywhere in the world. Poland's surrender of part of her own protection that week-end must be counted among the heroic decisions of the early part of the Second World War.

PART TWO

6 a.m. to noon

I

Adolf Hitler was an early riser and the morning of 3rd September was no exception to his life-long rule. At 7 a.m. he had risen after only three or four hours' sleep and was ready to tackle the first military and diplomatic reports of the day: good news from the east, disquieting messages from the Chancelleries of the west.

The Führer, attired as ever during that period in his brown uniform, breakfasted on fruit, zwieback and a glass of milk. A vegetarian, non-smoker and non-drinker for many years, he was now eating more sparingly than ever. One of his great personal concerns was that he might have cancer of the stomach. This explained his frugal diet and, it has been suggested since, the aggressive policy he had been following. In a few years' time, he might be too ill to tyrannize Europe.

For almost a week Hitler had not left the Reich Chancellery, a superb building with marble chambers and vast, tapestry-hung walls. He had spent his days in endless conferences with Nazi leaders like Goering, von Ribbentrop and Rudolf Hess, interrupted only by meagre twenty-minute meals of bread and butter and vegetables and brief, hurried walks around the Chancellery garden. Now he was beginning the most crucial day of his life in the same austere, robot-like way.

The German people were able to enjoy a rather more substantial breakfast that morning than their leader—and better than some of the armchair strategists in the west believed. Germany was already living on a war economy, but the food situation was not as serious as sections of the British and French Press were asserting. The German *hausfrau* was still assured of adequate food rations for her family, although she had to show every scrap of feminine ingenuity to make her meals appetizing.

The rations available for the Germans compared roughly with those

in Britain in the last year of the First World War, although far
better than they had been in Germany in 1918. This table gives a
comparison between the home front situations in the two countries:

	Germany 1939	Germany 1918	Britain 1918
Meat (per week)	25 oz.	9 oz.	32 oz.
Fats	15 oz.	2.5 oz.	12 oz.
Sugar	10 oz.	5.3 oz.	8 oz.
Bread	Unrationed	4½ lb.	Unrationed
Milk	2½ pints	Very little	Unrationed
Potatoes	Unrationed	7 lb.	Unrationed
Jam	4 oz.	Very little	4 oz.
Tea	¾ oz. *ersatz*	Very little	2 oz.
Coffee substitute	1 oz.	—	—
Soap	1 oz.	—	—

Butter was scarce in Germany that morning. It had been rationed
for several years, as a result of the Nazi preference for guns. Such
luxuries as grapefruit, bananas, pineapples and other exotic fruits had
long been unobtainable by the general public because of the need to
conserve foreign exchange.

On the other hand, there were no restrictions on eggs, vegetables,
poultry and fish. Heavy workers were entitled to extra fats and almost
a double meat ration. Milk concessions were made to pregnant women
and breast-feeding mothers. There was enough to go round for everybody, except those in the concentration camps.

German newspaper articles on 3rd September, detailing rations
which had been introduced since the Polish campaign started,
stressed that there was no shortage of food. Rations had been introduced to ensure that there were 'fair shares for all', and to prevent
hoarding.

Wine lovers, turning away from the war news, were promised a good
harvest in the Rhineland. The grapes were reported in feature articles
that morning to be in good condition, thanks to the glorious summer
weather. The fruit was growing to good size and ripening well. A
vintage of very good quality was being forecast for 1939.

Petrol was severely rationed, and very few Germans got any at
all. The police had the power to stop cars and check on the necessity

of journeys. If these were not found to be absolutely vital, the car owners were barred from driving any more.

Germany had been economically at full stretch for more than twelve months. Both her population and her industry had been subjected to rationing systems which required little extension to make comprehensive. Nazi spending on arms had been so extensive that there was a shortage of both food and raw materials, but this was partly due to accumulation of large war reserves.

One of Hitler's headaches in preparing for a possible major war had been to make it as painless as possible for the civilian population. If there were enough food and if life behind the front could be kept relatively normal, the people would not worry too much about the future. Hitler could count on the bulk of the German youth; but he could not eradicate from the minds of those who had witnessed them the memory of the horrible days of 1918, when many had to eat turnips and sawdust bread and German mothers impotently watched their children dying of starvation.

Germany had never been entirely self-supporting in foodstuffs. For that reason, and with the lessons of the First World War in mind, the nation had done everything possible to increase agricultural output. Sugar and grain production had been stepped up and huge stocks of grains accumulated. Science had been pressed into the service of food production. Laboratories had devised artificial foods to survive sieges of almost any duration. While the outside world had smiled the German scientists had invented all kinds of vitamin concentrates and *ersatz* foods. IG Farben, the great German dye trust, had even produced a synthetic pepper and made something from coal tar which actually tasted like chocolate.

There was thus no immediate danger of famine as the Germans that Sunday morning settled down to breakfast and while nibbling their *brotchen* and sipping *ersatz* coffee perused their newspapers. The Germans are avid newspaper readers but there was not much to read apart from fresh edicts, restrictions, regulations. *Verbots* and wordy editorials plugging the von Ribbentrop foreign policy line were the staple reading that day. The news stories gave little indication of what was really happening in the outside world.

The *Deutsche Allgemeine Zeitung*, a daily of formerly high reputation which had now become a mere Nazi propaganda sheet, singled

out the British Prime Minister for a bitter personal attack. Dealing
with Chamberlain's declaration that Britain's quarrel was not with the
German people but with the Nazi régime, the newspaper commented:
'If Chamberlain holds to this position, every further word is superflu-
ous. One cannot deal with us in this sort of language any more. No
one is allowed to come to us with Versailles methods. Every criticism
of the German form of state and of the head of the Reich is a declaration of war on the whole German people and will be understood by
every German as an expression of the will to destroy the Reich and to
plunge the people in eternal misery.

'We leave to the others the joys of their democracies and do not
interfere in their internal affairs. But whoever thinks he can dictate
to the German people their political laws, betrays the intention of
pushing us back into the existence of slavery prepared for us at Versailles. We don't demand that anyone takes National Socialism as their
model. We don't even want anyone to. But we are of the opinion that
the principles that the Führer of the national socialist Germany laid
down years ago to settle international questions may have a claim to
be generally valid. It is just these principles, however, which have
been pushed to the side by the democracies because they obviously
haven't fitted into their aggressive plans . . .'

The *Völkischer Beobachter*, the Nazi Party daily, also made a bitter
attack on Britain, and indirectly on France: '. . . The peak of dis-
honesty and moral hypocrisy has been reached in recent history by
England's world war propaganda, which has been working with the
crudest methods of dishonouring and slandering its valiant opponents
but on the surface shrouded itself in the robe of scrupulous love of
truth and strict correctness.'

The editorial said that Imperial Germany tried to keep up the
people's spirits with 'completely unsatisfactory methods and false
promises', and tried to gloss over the situation. But the Nazi Reich
had avoided Imperial Germany's mistakes:

'From the clear recognition that in the last resort only a good cause
could be furthered by propaganda—propaganda of pure lies defeats itself with its own weapons—the German leadership has more than ever
in times of crisis taken care to provide complete information for the
nation about all important events in the surrounding world, for only
in this way can sudden bitter disappointments be avoided. More than

ever in the tense days and weeks which lie behind us the German Press and radio have carefully registered everything that happened in the camp of our opponents.'

Contrasting the British and French propaganda activities with the 'wise and sober' principles of the German Press and radio information, the editorial added:

'In the last few days the propaganda of the democracies has returned to the naked methods of a Northcliffe: crazy atrocity-mongering on reports from the Reich, mad deprecation of the strength and honour of their opponent, straight falsification of diplomatic events—that is the picture which speeches by English ministers, the democratic papers, and the west's radio have to offer today.

'What is written and said over there on the other side of the channel no longer serves the aims of practical policies, but only the arousing of low instincts and HATE.

'The Council of Ministers for the defence of the Reich has therefore taken only an obvious step by calling on the German people to seal its ear hermetically against this flow of propaganda.'

II

It had been an oppressively hot night of thunderstorms and drenching rains. Now the sun was shining brightly as the British people rose and breakfasted in dark apprehension of what lay ahead. Even the forecast of the weather for the coming day had been denied them as a security precaution. If the Meteorological Office had been able to disclose its forecast for the day to the Press and public it would have predicted 'showers, bright intervals, local thunderstorms, rather warm'. The closing words would have been 'Outlook: continuing unsettled'. But a firm censorship had been clamped down since the previous day on any information likely to assist enemy bombers in delivering a knock-out blow.

Preparations for a war of sudden and devastating attack from the air had been continuing all night throughout Britain, and evidence of the defence activity was everywhere. No one could glean any hope from the Sunday newspapers. They were full of detailed reports of savage fighting on the Polish front, moves towards war in London and Paris, and advice to readers on how they should behave under enemy attack. The British people were left in no doubt about the situation by their Press that morning: they could only count with certainty on a few hours of peace.

Civilians were exhorted in the newspapers to carry their gas-masks with them everywhere and to make sure of the exact location of the nearest air-raid shelter in case they were caught while shopping or on their way to work. In the absence of a public shelter, they should take refuge in the nearest basement or building. If caught in a raid while travelling by train, then lying down was recommended.

In the event of war, all theatres, cinemas and places of entertainment would be closed at short notice as a temporary measure to give the authorities time to gain experience of air-raids, their effect and extent. The warnings of the sirens were to be reinforced by repeated blasts of police and air-raid wardens' whistles.

As for food, the official advice to the public that morning was that there was no shortage whatever, and 'no reason for hoarding'. Meat, bacon, ham, butter, margarine, lard, other fats and sugars would be rationed. Application forms for householders to fill in had been pre-pared in readiness for issue as soon as the rationing plans were put into operation.

National registration, an essential preliminary to food rationing and other wartime controls, had not started by 3rd September. The Gov-ernment had avoided taking this measure largely because of its reluc-tance to do anything that might be interpreted as a preparation for war and therefore aggravate relations with Germany.

But the country was in an advanced state of readiness for air-raids which, understandably, troubled Whitehall that day far more than the maintenance of food supplies. Total war, it was generally believed, would begin with massive bombing of vulnerable points in the British Isles—the seaports, industrial areas and London. That was why the creation of a complete Civil Defence system had been made a top Government priority since the appointment of Sir John Anderson the previous November as the Minister responsible for the task. Now, an organization existed, without parallel anywhere in the world, to sup-port the efforts of the R.A.F. fighter squadrons, the anti-aircraft gun units and the balloon barrages.

By 3rd September, around £42 million had been invested within a year on air-raid precautions, and the nation had plenty to show for it. One million of the popular 'Anderson' shelters had been issued, mainly to householders in areas considered to be dangerous. People paid about £8 each for them and sank them about three feet deep in court-yards and suburban back gardens. Each 'Anderson' was protected by earth and sandbags, of which 207 million had been issued by the start of September. Employers had been obliged to provide shelters in base-ments and the parks and open spaces of most cities and towns were slashed with slit trenches to provide shelter for passers-by and those whom officialdom realized would consider themselves unsafe indoors.

Britain's preparations for Civil Defence, though far from perfect, were undoubtedly better than those of any other country. By Sunday morning, more than 1,900,000 civilian men and women out of two million required had enlisted for full- and part-time service in the A.R.P., including the auxiliary fire and police services. The entire population had been issued with gas-masks: thirty million in the September, 1938, crisis and a further twenty-two million since then. Emergency reservoirs of water had been established in the streets. Special squads equipped with hoses, chemicals and special clothing had been formed to deal with the aftermath of gas attacks. Voluntary ambulance services of private cars, first-aid posts and stretcher parties had also been organized in the past months of crisis. Five hundred thousand volunteers had responded to an appeal to undergo blood tests and to register as donors in case of war. And the police forces had been strengthened by the recruitment of 270,000 auxiliary policemen 'for the duration'.

Radio talks and Government leaflets had prepared the British population for air-raids, food shortages and dislocation of the public services. Every home had received leaflets giving advice on air-raids, gas attacks, blackouts, incendiary bomb raids, identity labels, food storage, evacuation, plans for food rationing and emergency first-aid. The last of these leaflets had just reached homes that week-end. It concluded with this warning: 'Do not take too much notice of noise in an air-raid. Much of it will be the noise of our own guns dealing with the raiders. Keep a good heart. We are going to win through.'

Evacuation—of children, elderly people and hospital cases—had been given priority in Government planning. Thirteen regional organizations had already been set up to carry on the nation's life if the central Government became disrupted. Many commercial and industrial firms had already set up country headquarters in case their premises in the major cities were destroyed. Large sections of Government departments were to be evacuated under conditions of great secrecy to safe havens in the provinces.

Evacuation of the children from the cities and industrial areas to new homes in the country was approaching completion that Sunday morning. In countless thousands of homes there was already the bewildering loneliness that was to stay with parents for most of the war. In thousands more, at breakfast time, suitcases were being packed, sandwiches cut, and gas-masks being slung over slight shoulders.

The movement of the evacuees from the presumed danger areas to rural districts had proceeded smoothly since the Friday. By Sunday morning, the last of 1,270,000 adults and children were being moved from eighty-one 'evacuation areas' to 1,100 reception areas. Almost three-quarters of a million of these were school children, many in school parties, and about one-third accompanied by their mothers. All available transport facilities, including ambulances and private cars, had been pressed into service to complete this mammoth movement before the outbreak of hostilities. The biggest bottlenecks had occurred in London, from where more than 366,000 children had been removed by train, car and steamboat. But, by Sunday morning, the operation was running quietly and smoothly. The then Mr. Herbert Morrison, Leader of the London County Council, spoke with pride of what the Council's organization had achieved by Sunday morning: 'All along, the L.C.C. had promised that if evacuation were ever necessary it would be an orderly operation. The promise has been kept. The planning has even included the collection of animals and school pets by the Royal Society for the Prevention of Cruelty to Animals.'

Officialdom could congratulate itself on a job well done. But numerous parents over breakfast that morning argued whether they had done the right thing. Was it right to have parted with the children? Shouldn't they stick together as a family, even if war was coming? Evacuation, after all, was not compulsory. Parents who had chosen to keep the children with them debated the same subject anxiously from their own angle. For most of the children, the movement to new homes that week-end was an exciting adventure as well as a sad break from parents and elder brothers and sisters. To some it was as good as a holiday, and years spent in the peaceful countryside of the west and south-west of England were to be the happiest of their lives. To others, the period as evacuees was to be bleak and lonely and even accompanied by physical suffering. And a handful were saying a final goodbye to parents who would disappear during the war, or conveniently forget them.

No one that morning could have forecast how long the evacuation scheme would be in operation. Most felt it would be only a matter of months when the 'scare' would be over, or the lightning war would have been won after a few massive air-raids on each side. In fact, the evacuation was to last almost nine years. The vast human upheaval which began in Britain on 1st September, 1939, was not to come to an end, officially, until 5th July, 1948 . . .

Evacuation was not restricted to human beings. Animal-loving readers of the Sunday newspapers were informed that the London Zoo authorities had completed their evacuation scheme without a hitch. All the rarer animals had been sent to rural Whipsnade. Among them were Tang and Ming, the giant pandas. But forty snakes, plus spiders and scorpions which could not be moved, had been destroyed. The Zoo might have to be closed for a few days but would then be reopened, unless bombing made that impossible.

London presented a strange, unfamiliar sight that morning. The sentries in Whitehall were in khaki battledress and helmets. Policemen were also without their traditional helmets, and looked as though they should be on point duty in some Middle European trouble spot with their 'tin hats' and gas-mask haversacks. A few of the newly recruited police were still in civilian dress, and only arm bands proclaimed their identity. But the criminals had made their task easier. The crime rate had sunk to its lowest level for five years and thieves were not robbing houses with the zeal they usually displayed during the summer holiday season.

Huge posters proclaiming 'We've got to be prepared' in Trafalgar Square and elsewhere looked already oddly out of date. Windows were still being barricaded and soon after breakfast gangs of men were back on the job stacking sandbags outside business houses. Signs everywhere called for volunteers to fill yet more sandbags. Zealous air-raid wardens were on the job early and newly-recruited auxiliary firemen were showing off their dark blue uniforms. One thousand London taxi-cabs had been equipped with trailers and transformed into fire-engines with pumps, ladders, ropes and axes. Every other car on the road appeared to be in the service of one or another of the newly-organized branches of Civil Defence. And, overhead, silver-grey barrage balloons glistened in the morning sunshine, a silent, static form of defence which made many people beneath feel strangely secure from attack.

In the windows of the travel bureaux in the West End, there were still incongruously alluring posters of holiday countries. 'Visit Sunny Jamaica', 'Go 1,000 miles up the Amazon', 'Ceylon offers you a warm welcome', 'Spend a month in Switzerland', or 'Take a crisis-cure at Butlin's Holiday Camps'. The German Travel Bureau was not to be outdone. 'Germany—Land of Healing Spas', the slogan in the window read.

The illusion given by the posters that things were normal was also conveyed by astrologers in the Sunday newspapers. None of the astrologers had detected in the stars and the planets signs that Britain would be at war that day and one leading newspaper even carried a confident 'no war' prediction by its astrologer that very morning. In another Sunday newspaper there appeared a review of a new work called *Hitler's Last Year of Power*, by Leonardo Blake. The reviewer explained that the author 'foretells further crises next year to culminate in a revulsion which removes Hitler. Hitler's function he sees as an attempt to arrest the progress of the Reich towards democracy, a progress which will be much expedited after his disappearance which will bring a new period of peace to Europe. Mr. Chamberlain's horoscope compares most favourably to Hitler's and entirely vindicates his policy. Despite terrible alarms there will be no world war.'

But even the most devoted followers of the astrologers had looked at the front pages first and decided that it was only a question of time. The realization that war was now inevitable caused no surprise, no shock, just a frozen feeling of relief that Britain was not going to shuffle back into appeasement. So the men who had not been caught up in Civil Defence work read their newspapers, mowed their lawns or washed cars which they knew would soon have to come off the roads because of petrol rationing. Motorists were advised that morning that petrol was to be debranded, pooled and distributed on a strict rationing basis.

By 9 a.m., the Ministry of Health was able to record that 80,000 hospital patients whose ailments or injuries were not serious had been sent home for care by relatives and friends. Evacuation of other patients to hospitals in the country had made a total of 150,000 beds available for casualties in England and Wales. Through far-sighted planning of that kind, the country had been prepared for war as never before in its history. Since January, the Government had been organizing conscription of young men for the fighting forces and for the reservation of occupations considered essential for the home-front effort. This was to create a strikingly different situation from the 1914 –18 war, when the varying temper of the nation, affected by victories and reverses, alternatively swamped and deserted the recruiting offices until the introduction of conscription in 1916.

All morning, the nation had listened avidly to the radio for news of the ultimatum to Germany. But all that came on the B.B.C.'s single emergency programme was light gramophone music. One person whose ears were glued to his set all that time has a recollection that nothing but 'Tales From the Vienna Woods' was played from breakfast time onwards! But there was a good reason for the monotony of the programmes. The B.B.C. was now broadcasting from emergency headquarters in the country and there was only one Home Service instead of eight separate programmes. The radio service had been designed so that the B.B.C. would not be knocked out by one massive blow at the beginning of war, ensuring that news and instructions to the public could be given quickly and efficiently by the authorities. As it turned out, the Corporation need not have reacted so quickly in the Polish crisis, but the preparations made with such care before the war were to pay dividends later.

While the nation waited for news and listened through one selection of light music after another, there was time for the middle-aged and the elderly who knew what war meant to lament the passing of the world they had known. Those thinking of a safe rural retreat from the bombs could contemplate the forthcoming sale of property in an area which was to acquire a far from peaceful significance in the years ahead. The Aldermaston Court Estate in Berkshire, consisting of a mansion, farms, cottages, land, smallholdings, licensed inns, a vicarage and a school, was to be sold in 388 lots on 20th and 21st September.

Cricket followers were wondering when Yorkshire, that summer's champions, would be accepting fresh challengers for the title. As R. C. Robertson-Glasgow wrote in *The Observer* that morning, 'It is idle to wander in the beauties that are born from cricket, vain to talk of its joys and friendships and strivings and triumphs. For a time they are gone, perhaps—who knows—for a long time . . .' A band of sportsmen, newly-arrived in Plymouth that day, were similarly concerned with what lay ahead for sport. The Australian Rugby Union team, about to start a tour of England, conferred that morning as to whether the tour should continue or whether it would be best for them to hurry home to volunteer for service as quickly as possible.

The likelihood of war within a few hours quietened and saddened those who had been pressing for a tough line as well as those who would have supported any further efforts to reach a peaceful settlement. Between 9 a.m. and 10 a.m., another meeting began of the Conservative 'rebels' who backed Winston Churchill. These M.P.s gathered at Mr. Ronald Tree's house in Queen Anne's Gate to review the political situation which would follow a declaration of war and talked of the need for Eden to be in any war cabinet as well as Churchill, but they, like all thinking Englishmen that morning, had no real heart for politics. They were meeting in an elegant, peaceful period home whose surroundings inspired higher thoughts.

Major-General Sir Edward Spears, one of those present, evoked the atmosphere later of the scene that morning . . . the sun shining in through the windows, the light sparkling on the crystal pendants of the chandeliers . . . tall clusters of flowers scenting the room. He recalled: 'I sat by a window looking out on St. James's Park, gazing up at the blue sky, and I wondered whether within an hour we should have lost the purest of all joys, that of breathing God's air in the sunshine and looking upwards to the serene expanse where countless generations had found peace and hope.

'The thought came to me that all of us, those burdened with years, and children with as yet no memories, might all quite soon step at the same second over the threshold of the pleasant world we knew into another where to look up to the sky would be only reaction to fear, a world where human beings could only relax in the dark safety of cellars. I felt no regrets for what we had done, but in that moment wanted to miss no glint of sunshine or of colour. People condemned for conscience's sake may have had similar feelings as they were led to their execution.'

Millions of Sir Edward's less articulate countrymen must have had similar feelings as they waited patiently through the hours of light operetta and Strauss waltzes for some firm news of their Government's intentions.

III

Breakfast in France, *le petit déjeuner*, has never been very important
to Frenchmen, and this Sunday morning it meant less than ever before as they leafed through their scanty newspapers, neglecting the
croissants and allowing the coffee to go cold. The intelligent newspaper reader could have no illusion that war might yet be averted, and
the press gave no clue to the extent to which the French Generals were
worried over the timing of a declaration of war. News of the increasingly bitter fighting on the Polish front dominated the front pages
and allowed of no complacent interpretation of the situation.

The French were as well prepared for the day as was possible with
a democratic and highly individualistic race. The mobilization was
going ahead slowly but purposefully. Three million men were in the
process of being called to the colours, to reinforce a similar number
already in uniform. Civilians being evacuated from the main cities,
industrial towns and front-line zones brought the total of adults and
children affected by war movements to almost ten million.

Like the British, the French population had been thoroughly briefed
by official leaflets, the press and the radio, as to what they must do in
an emergency. Parisians, like Londoners, had been warned not to go
out without their gas-masks and to ascertain the location of the nearest
shelter in case of air-raids. They had been told to conceal all lights at
night and householders had been instructed to fill bottles with clear
water in case the public supplies might be polluted by gas attacks.
Thousands of windows in the capital had already been criss-crossed
with sticky paper because this was considered to be a sensible precaution against the effect of bomb blasts.

The French people were generally calm and resigned to what was
inevitable. Like the Germans, they were not going to war with the

patriotic fervour of 1914. But they did have considerably more confidence in the outcome of another struggle with Germany. After all, there was no imminent danger of being slaughtered like the people of far-off Poland. This would be a very different kind of war. The flower of French manhood was not to moulder as it did between 1914 and 1918 in the trenches of Flanders and Eastern France, to be mown down in thousands whenever the Generals sought to advance their positions. This was also to be a static war, but behind the assault-proof Maginot Line which afforded France greater protection than at any time in her history.

As the British looked with confidence that morning to their battleships riding the seas, so did the French to their concrete battleships sunk deeply into the soil of their country. The Maginot Line was without question the most elaborate defensive scheme of its kind anywhere, and that morning fresh troops were arriving to bring the garrison forces up to full war strength. France had spent almost ten years in constructing this series of immensely powerful forts, sunk deep into the ground and armed with power-operated artillery. Each fort was linked by underground communications, and air-conditioning meant that they could be utilized as permanent living quarters. From the Luxembourg frontier to the meeting place of France, Germany and Switzerland close to Basle, the line appeared to give France complete protection against any attack from German territory.

On the opposite side of the border the Germans had erected their West Wall, or Siegfried Line, but its construction had only begun in 1937, by which time the Maginot Line had been almost completed. Germany had intended her defensive line, a system of blockhouses and pillboxes, to be manned as field fortifications only in time of war. The French, however, had designed the Maginot Line for permanent occupation by a force of specially trained troops who could be speedily reinforced on the outbreak of hostilities. The Siegfried Line was clearly inferior to the French fortifications and every armchair strategist in France could comfort himself with that fact as he read the war headlines. It was still too early in the war for amateur— or even professional—strategists to grasp the full significance of the war of movement the Germans were waging in Poland. Otherwise there might have been thoughts about the largely unfortified route into

France via the lowlands rather than of the theoretically perfect defensive line along the border with the Reich. . . .

Paris had a changed, slightly dishevelled look that Sunday and resembled, according to one resident foreign observer, a woman who had forgotten to put on her make-up after a bath. All the glamour of the city of lights appeared to have vanished overnight and there was nothing but her unadorned beauty to behold. In the very early morning, the city was bathed in pale sunshine which contrasted strikingly with the blackout of a few hours previously. The old buildings were outlined against the radiance of the blue sky with such clarity that it seemed as though nature had arranged it to implant the scene firmly in the memories of all who saw it that morning. By breakfast time, however, the skies had begun to darken and rain was starting to fall.

The newspaper kiosks sold out earlier than usual that morning, but there was really nothing in them that the nation had not already heard on the radio. The streets were already full of people by 9 a.m., but they were behaving differently from the usual Parisian Sunday crowds. Everyone seemed to know where he was going, and what he had to do. There was an air of quiet purpose discernible everywhere. The idlers appeared to have vanished overnight. So had the tourists, especially the Americans. An exodus by road and rail during the previous four days had removed hundreds of thousands of women and children, elderly folk, invalids and a fair proportion of the wealthy who had found pressing reasons to visit their estates on the Riviera. The people who had remained gave the impression of being ready for anything. The capital was beginning to take on a severe, warlike look and the tone of the morning press emphasized this.

Most of the papers were only of four pages, and were packed with news of official edicts and exhortations by political leaders. The Government offices were suspending their mid-week day off. Court cases against persons affected by mobilization orders were to be postponed. The underground railway service would be restricted to fewer stations, but would be open without interruption day and night. Police had listed eleven roads out of Paris which motorists were obliged to take as the authorities had closed all the others. Le Petit Parisien had twelve inches of headlines and a message from President Lebrun to Parliament: 'I salute our armies affectionately and give them the unanimous expression of trust of the country. Let us be united.' Among

news of personalities was an item about a man whose life had already
been turned upside down by a fascist dictator: King Zog of Albania,
who had been living in exile in France since his country's occupation
by Italy. He had announced that he was going to move with his Queen,
son and staff from Versailles to La Boule.

Le Figaro printed a letter from a schoolteacher in Strasbourg re-
porting on the state of morale of the people there on the border with
Germany: 'I would like you to know of the admirable attitude of the
population of this town. Everywhere I have only seen calm and kind-
ness. No discussions on the crisis; if one talks of it it is with good
humour. The trams are running, workmen are repairing asphalt in the
Place Broglie, others looking after the gardens at the University. At
the Botanical Gardens, gardeners are weeding. All this within a few
hundred metres of the Rhine.'

The editorial writers had given their pens free rein in describing
the nation's feelings on the eve of war. Le Figaro (Conservative),
commenting on Daladier's speech to the Deputies, said that Europe
was in its current position because of Hitler's repeated breaches of
his word, and added: 'France, which realized the tragic consequences
a general war would bring and which has respect for Christian civilization was, and remains, ready until the last moment to second all
efforts which have been made by the Holy See, the United States,
Belgium, the Netherlands and Italy, to avoid the cataclysm and assure
peace with honour and justice. But, as M. Daladier explained, she has
until now met intransigence, duplicity and silence—and, more, wilful
aggression.'

Le Figaro stressed that France was determined to carry out the
duties she had undertaken and spoke of the calm and admirable precision with which French mobilization was in progress. The newspaper
sought to dispel an impression abroad that the French lacked discipline. Though individualistic and impatient of authority, they yet
cultivated deep inside them 'the strongest and freest discipline'.
Le Figaro concluded: 'Never have we been more proud of our country. Never have we better understood what it represents. Never has
been better shown its purity, its moral strength, its energy. Never have
we felt nearer to one another.'

As in Britain, where the Labour opposition was just as strongly in favour of a showdown with Hitler as the Government party, the French Socialists unanimously subscribed to the action being taken by the French Government.

Le Populaire, Paris Socialist newspaper, published that morning an editorial signed by Leon Blum, the Socialist leader of the previous stormy decade. 'I will not seek laudatory adjectives for the speeches of Edouard Herriot and Edouard Daladier,' M. Blum wrote. 'I will simply say that they were worthy of the circumstances, worthy of the nation . . .'

Quoting a passage from Daladier's speech, in which the Premier deplored the fact that men who had devoted their lives to the cause and defence of peace were now compelled to reply by force to an aggressive adventurer, Blum commented: 'It is true that neither Daladier nor anyone else would have been able to mobilize France for the temptation of adventure or conquest. Never has a country been more profoundly imbued with the spirit of peace than France during the past twenty years and at the present moment. Never has a government promoted or welcomed more efforts of every kind to block the road leading to the catastrophe into which the mad pride of a despot threatens to plunge the human race. France did not want that; she has done everything to prevent it from happening . . .'

Rain was pouring down disconsolately as though Heaven itself were crying out its eyes over the follies of the human race heading towards another slaughter as devout Catholics went to mass. A *Paris-Midi* reporter, scouring the city for local colour, attended mass at the Sacre Coeur amid a silent crowd of soldiers, mothers, wives and sweethearts. He wrote in his notebook that morning: 'It was not the service, marked with peals of bells, of the great feast days. Never had a more silent assembly of the faithful entered the old church . . .

'Outside I saw, on the steps of the old building, sheltering under the same umbrella, a young man and a girl kissing each other before entering. And it was neither offensive nor ridiculous in such a place. He, though still in civilian clothes, carried a soldier's knapsack, she, sweet and resigned, gazed at him tenderly. No doubt her eyes had shed many tears but it was touching and most moving to see the obvious effort she made to remain calm and dignified.

'No, The Basilica had not an ordinary appearance. No sightseers, no strolling foreign tourists were there. Nobody offended against the placards asking for silence, for respect of the altar and the Divine Presence.

'The placard informing us that the crypt of the Basilica could not be used as a shelter against air-raids also seemed needless. The men and women who prayed relied on other help.

'Coming out of the Basilica, I followed the little alleys where shops selling holy articles stand. The shopkeepers did not serve many people. The restaurant owners on Montmartre hill did even less business. Their houses, with their curtained windows, had the appearance of provincial buildings. Montmartre, hidden by rain and mist, seemed to be waiting, under the protection of its highest church tower, for better days . . .'

At the Eglise Notre Dame des Victoires, a mass was held for the departing conscripts. Mgr. Touze, Archdeacon of St. Genevieve's, celebrated it in the presence of 100 young men, serious faced in spite of their extreme youth. Many were accompanied by their mothers, some widows from the 1914–18 war. And when the service was over the mothers clustered in groups in the precincts of the Church and talked sadly of other days and other masses said for the departure of fathers, uncles and brothers of the 1939 conscripts.

Montmartre seemed changed beyond all recognition, with all its customary noise and gaiety gone, its bars and restaurants almost deserted of patrons. Montparnasse had undergone a similar transition, as had Saint Germain-des-Pres, where uniformed intellectuals were bidding each other sad good-byes. Men like André Breton, the Pope of Surrealism, author of *Revolver à Cheveux Blancs,* were holding court for the last time in the literary cafés, surrounded by decimated groups of disciples who admired their uniforms and absorbed their last peacetime words of wisdom. 'When war goes away, poetry comes back,' another father of surrealism, Antonin Artaud, was heard to say to one such literary gathering. And one of his followers put in sagely, 'The reverse applies'.

A different type of break with tradition was evident at *Les Halles,* the central food market of Paris. Normally, the market, immortalized in the writings of Emile Zola, opened at night and closed during the day. But the blackout had forced new opening hours, which became effective as from the morning of 3rd September. The innovation brought order where there had been chaos on the Friday night, although fewer men were on duty than usually. Soon, the market was functioning as though it had always operated by day. Flowers and vegetables from the south, enormous sides of meat and dairy produce were handled speedily and efficiently by the reduced labour gangs. Within a few hours traders were able to announce 'very satisfactory' deliveries for a Sunday and officialdom could sigh with relief: Paris would have no food problems in the foreseeable future.

Not all the foreigners in Paris had packed their bags by Sunday and the recruiting offices for the Foreign Legion began to get a bigger than usual response as soon as they opened their doors. Self-exiled Americans in Paris were being invited to join their own unit to defend the soil of their adopted country. The Swiss Legation, anxious to pull home as many as possible of its nationals of military age, started to run special trains out of Paris for them soon after breakfast time. Switzerland, determined again on strict neutrality, was offering free travel home to any Swiss who might be tempted to take up arms.

Among the foreign nationals to volunteer in the early morning was Erich von Stroheim, the Austrian-born actor whom most film-goers regarded as the typically German 'villain'. Von Stroheim, holidaying at Etretat, near Le Havre, sent a telegram to the French War Ministry after breakfast offering his services as a soldier.

He had passed out of the Austrian Military Academy with the rank of lieutenant and had then served in Mexico as a captain under the orders of President Francisco Madera. Later, he served in the American Army and considered his military experience might be useful to France. 'I want to show my gratitude to the French people who received me so warmly on my return from Hollywood,' Von Stroheim said. 'If France does not accept my offer, I shall join the American Legion formed by Colonel Sweeny and General Reilly.'

IV

In Warsaw, breakfast—*sniadanie*—was a meal devoured hastily, fearfully, and under fire. The sirens began wailing around 8 a.m. as German bombers returned to give the capital another dose of low-level bombing, secure in the knowledge that there would be almost no opposition.

The Polish capital that morning looked pathetically for protection to her 'balloon barrage'. Had there been hundreds of balloons filling the skies, as over London and Paris, the attackers might have been forced high above accurate bombing range, or even tempted to disaster among their trailing wires. But by now there were only four balloons left, and the few Polish fighter aircraft were in demand elsewhere. So the Germans were able to raid almost at leisure.

One eye-witness of that raid recalls his cook running in and shouting: 'The air is burning! The air is burning!' Rushing out to see what she meant, he noticed that a balloon above his house had been set on fire by tracer bullets. As he watched, the balloon plunged earthwards, sputtering a long trail of smoke and fire. By the time it reached the ground it had burned itself out. Minutes later, the other three balloons suffered similar fates and Warsaw was completely at the German mercy for the first time. For one hour bombers roared over the city and suburbs at little more than rooftop level, dropping bombs as they pleased.

The German attack that morning was particularly indiscriminate, and just before 9 a.m. one of the Nazi pilots chased a strange objective which might have brought serious repercussions upon his masters in Berlin. The pilot chose for his Sabbath target a pleasant little summer resort known as Konstancin, about twelve miles south of Warsaw on the left bank of the Vistula river. It could not have interested him as

a military target, because there was no railway, factory or large building—just a collection of holiday villas scattered among the trees. The
nearest bridge over the Vistula was about five miles away.

Konstancin, however, happened to be the location of the summer
residence of the American Ambassador, Mr. Anthony J. Drexel Biddle Jun. He, his wife, their daughter and a woman guest were in the
garden when a German bomber appeared out of the clouds and dived
towards the holiday settlement. Five hundred feet above the villas it
dropped a pattern of six bombs, one of which hit a neighbouring villa
and another fell close to the official American residence. The Ambassador and his party were shaken but unharmed.

Here was the first diplomatic incident of the German attack to involve an American and Polish officialdom, though deploring the raid,
took satisfaction in having a crown witness for their case in such an
eminent neutral diplomat. The Poles could not have hoped for a better piece of propaganda in the United States. It would show the American people they had not been exaggerating when they saw the
Germans violating every paragraph of international law. Foreign correspondents rushed to Konstancin immediately the raid ended—here
was copy that would make even bigger headlines than the deaths of
thousands on the fighting front that day.

Mr. Biddle told journalists he was none the worse for his experience
and remarked: 'I am sure Hermann Goering knew my address but I
hardly believed he would send a calling card so soon. As an American husband and father I'm proud of the way the women with me
took the experience. They stood it like soldiers and never quivered.'

The Ambassador added that about a mile and a half from his villa
there was a small training airfield but he was quite sure that no mistake had been made because the bomber had come down so low he
was able to see the pilot's face. Therefore, he concluded, it was intended to make the group of country houses the target.

M. Léon Noel, the French Ambassador, commenting later on the
bombing, which might have cost the life of his 'likeable colleague from
the United States', said the Ambassador would be able to give President Roosevelt and his compatriots, 'personal witness of the German
methods of warfare which to shame and misery of humanity were to
characterize the war'.

While Warsaw was reeling under the new blows from the Luft-waffe, Cracow was getting a taste of an attack of similar savagery. That city had been partly devastated by raids the previous day, but then factories and railways had appeared to be the major targets. But this day, from 6 a.m. onwards, the raiders seemed to be concentrating on residential areas in the old city, which had neither adequate fighter defence nor Civil Defence arrangements.

Dominik Wegierski, an eye-witness of the Cracow bombing, later recalled the horrors of the early morning onslaught in a graphic account: 'The brutal savagery of the German airmen was fully displayed, for they bombed quarters without any military objective whatsoever. In Lobzowska Street there is a church and convent of the Carmelitan Sisters. German bombers aimed two bombs on the church, but missed it by a few yards. One of them made a huge crater next to the church and blew out its windows, while the other smashed to pieces a house just opposite.' When people began to run out of the church, frightened by the crash of the bombs and the house falling down, the German airmen turned back and deliberately machine-gunned the crowd, killing and wounding scores of innocent folk. The bombers attacked with special ferocity the residential quarter near the Krakowski Park. Although no house was hit, the explosions in the gardens and in the streets inflicted great damage to property.

'The streets of Cracow were full of the stifling, peculiar smell of high explosive, mixing with the smoke of burning houses. No large-scale fire-fighting was possible. The fire brigade had not enough engines and men, while the army was busy with other things. This made the situation even more terrible and heightened the feeling of being the defenceless prey of the enemy.

'The population of Cracow would surely have stood the bombardment well and managed its A.R.P. without any outside assistance if it had not felt helpless. People soon realized that the town was hardly protected at all, that there were only a few anti-aircraft guns, no fighters and no balloon barrage. Things would have been very different if we could now and then have seen a dogfight and a German raider brought down. But Cracow was defenceless, and we all knew what that meant . . .'

The press and radio that morning had news to both anger and hearten Polish readers. Warsaw's Sunday newspapers, much reduced in size, were filled with bitter reports of sabotage all over the country by minority German populations. These people, still loyal to the old Fatherland after almost a generation, were hampering the defence effort by giving away the position of Polish troops and cutting lines of communication. Some shops owned by Poles of German descent had been found to be harbouring ammunition and stores for use by the advancing Wehrmacht. Nazi parachutists were landing in places to find friends awaiting them on the ground. The Polish forces, already reeling under the German blows, were finding the presence of enemies behind the lines both dangerous and bad for morale.

Bitterness at the actions of these German patriots and Polish traitors could be slightly eased that morning by news of the gallant resistance of individual units all along the front, which the Warsaw newspapers asserted might lead to the stabilization of a defence line within a few days. But the special heroes of the press and the radio announcers were a group of men for whom there was not the slightest hope of survival: the garrison at Westerplatte. Repeatedly, Warsaw Radio broadcast the following message: "The Commander-in-Chief greets the brave defenders of Westerplatte and asks them to hold out . . .'

Westerplatte, a small flat peninsula belonging to the Free City of Danzig, had been turned into an arsenal in the pre-war years by the Polish authorities. When the Germans invaded Poland it was manned by just five officers and 265 men. Theoretically, the Westerplatte defenders could not have stood up to more than a few hours' fighting. They were crammed into a square kilometre on a flat coastal strip without natural defences or proper fortifications. From the first hour of the conflict, the defenders had been cut off from the world and under constant German bombardment by land, sea and air. But after forty-eight hours they were still holding out, though every building and every tree had been destroyed by the German bombs, shells and machine-gun fire. Somewhere among the ruins, the Westerplatte defenders were still entrenched, returning the German fire and writing themselves into the history books with an epic, vain, defence which was to continue for another five days until all the ammunition had gone and only fifty men were left.

Meanwhile, in Danzig itself, the authority of the League of Nations was finally being usurped by the Germans. Dr. Burckhardt, the

League's High Commissioner, was told that his duties had ended. He must leave his office within two hours, so that the swastika could be hoisted above the seat of government. The international civil servant packed hurriedly during the morning, but was unable to find room for his books and decided, reluctantly, that he would have to leave them behind with his furniture. Right on time, German police arrived to escort him to a car to take him away from the Free City. As he entered the car, an angry mob of young Nazis surrounded the vehicle shouting 'Kill the dog!'

All the violence throughout Poland that morning did not keep the people away from their Church. Those who can still recall the day speak with emotion of the full congregations, of the prayers said for Poland even as the air-raid sirens sounded. No service was interrupted by any of the bombing attacks, no one left to take shelter in the dugouts prepared hastily in the parks of every Polish town. Their refuge was in God.

The atmosphere of the Polish people at their devotions on 3rd September was evoked with great beauty and poignancy by the anonymous woman author of the 1940 book *My Name is Million*. She gave this moving description of the morning mass in a tiny chapel in Warsaw: 'Both chapel and courtyard were crowded with kneeling and weeping Poles. A Pole is not ashamed to shed tears before the catastrophe of his native land. Hearts were breaking with a sorrow that had little or nothing to do with personal loss. The soil of Poland, so often and so frightfully violated, is regarded by the Poles with a sentiment which has no counterpart here in the west. . . .

'The chaplain addressed the people. This, he said, was the third day of the war. We had suffered, but we must be prepared for suffering infinitely more great. Even the history we all knew so well could provide no parallel for what was now before us. The object of the German attack was the complete annihilation of Poland. Materially it was all too likely that they would seem to succeed. Every kind of frightfulness and horror, surpassing even our knowledge or imagination, would be employed. What an Army of Occupation under the orders of the Gestapo could mean, nobody needed to be in doubt. The Polish soil that we loved would be stamped into a bloody morass. Everywhere the lamp of freedom would be extinguished; men and women and even children would be tortured, maimed and executed for the crime of loving their country.

'The altars of Poland would be thrown down and her Holy of Holies desecrated by the foulest deeds . . . Poland, wiped from the map, must go on existing, where she had ever existed, in Polish hearts. The iron crown of martyrdom, which had ever been fitted to the bleeding brow of the nation, was being held out to us again. This was the traditional crown of Poland which, it had briefly seemed, a new generation was to be spared the wearing, and which our generation, and our fathers', had already worn. . . .'

The chaplain paused. The congregation was in tears, but his eyes were dry. He had reached a stage of prophetic insight in which tears were no longer a relief. With a gentle and sad voice, he concluded:

'It is part of our heritage. God has willed it so. God has called us once more to martyrdom. That is why the enemy has passed our frontiers, wasted our cities, and is rapidly approaching our capital. That is why, on the third day of the war, we have no sign from our allies. That is why such a country even as England is still waiting to fulfil her pledges. On the third day of the war, crushingly exposed and outnumbered, we are still alone.'

V

At 9 a.m. sharp, with diplomatic punctuality, Sir Nevile Henderson presented himself at the German Foreign Office to deliver the final British ultimatum. He had made his appointment a few hours earlier and was expected.

Von Ribbentrop was not there, but Sir Nevile had known that in advance. He was due to be received instead by Dr. Paul Otto Schmidt, the Foreign Ministry interpreter who had participated in all major international conferences at which Germany had been represented since 1923. But Dr. Schmidt, on that big day in his life, had over-slept and the British Ambassador was already entering the Foreign Office building when Dr. Schmidt's taxi arrived.

The interpreter, anxious not to lose face by being late, raced around to a side door and dashed through the corridors to von Ribbentrop's office to arrive a few moments before Sir Nevile. So their historic meeting began on time.

Sir Nevile and Dr. Schmidt shook hands solemnly, but the British diplomat declined the German's invitation to sit down. Instead, he stood and read his Government's ultimatum in serious, measured tones. Then he handed a copy to Dr. Schmidt. The two men had nothing further they could say to one another. The final curtain had fallen on the prelude to the drama which was to ravage the world for half a decade. Dr. Schmidt bowed and took the paper proferred by Sir Nevile, who then bade him farewell.

Sir Nevile had hardly left the precincts of the Foreign Office when Dr. Schmidt rushed to the Reich Chancellery to inform Hitler of the text of the British ultimatum. There was neither time nor need for him to prepare a translation of the document.

The Führer's ante-room was crowded as usual with a variety of people waiting to be received by the dictator. Dr. Schmidt knew them all. Most were members of the Cabinet, senior officers and high-ranking officials. They seemed to be aware that Dr. Schmidt had just seen the British Ambassador and assailed him with questions. But the Foreign Office official refused to divulge the news before Hitler had heard it. In response to their pleas, he merely said: 'There is not going to be a second Munich.'

Hitler was sitting at his desk and von Ribbentrop stood by the window. They had been in conference since early morning and seemed preoccupied. Both looked up expectantly as Dr. Schmidt entered. He stopped at some distance from the Führer's desk and, after a 'Heil Hitler', slowly translated the British ultimatum.

When he had finished there was complete silence. For a whole minute no one spoke. Hitler sat motionless at his desk, gazing into space. Von Ribbentrop did not move from his position at the window. Then suddenly Hitler turned on von Ribbentrop with a savage look in his eyes as though implying that his Foreign Minister had misled him about Britain's probable reaction. 'What now?' he asked. 'What is going to happen now?'

Von Ribbentrop considered the question for a moment. 'Now we can expect a French ultimatum any moment,' he replied blandly. Hitler and von Ribbentrop then began discussing the next diplomatic steps to be taken. The question of recalling this or that ambassador came up, but Schmidt did not linger. He had accomplished his duty as an interpreter and, with another 'Heil Hitler', left the room.

Dr. Schmidt was now at liberty to enlighten his audience in Hitler's ante-room. They already had an inkling of what was in the air and looked to him in apprehension.

'I saw by their anxious faces that my remark (that there would not be a second Munich) had been correctly interpreted,' he later declared. 'When I told them that I had just handed a British ultimatum to Hitler, a heavy silence fell on the room. The faces suddenly grew rather serious. I still remember that Goering, for instance, who was standing in front of me, turned round and said, "If we lose this war, then God help us". Goebbels was standing in a corner by himself and had a very serious, not to say depressed, expression. This depressing atmosphere prevailed over all those present, and it naturally lives

in my memory as being something most remarkable, for the first day
of war, in the ante-room of the Chancellery.'

Schmidt 'did not have the impression' that they had expected a
declaration of war. Neither had Hitler nor his Army and Navy chiefs.
None of the Nazi leaders, with the possible exception of von Ribbentrop, had expected that Great Britain and France would go to war for
Poland. Hitler's attack on Poland had been based on the firm assumption that they would not, and the German people had generally
shared their Führer's confidence that Germany would be allowed to
settle the Polish question on her own terms.

Within the next hour, the news of the British ultimatum had cir-
culated throughout Berlin government and service departments, although it was not to be given to the German people on the radio until
the propaganda experts had decided the proper slant the British action
was to be given. Top-ranking Wehrmacht officers were utterly dis-
mayed by the course of events, but kept their thoughts that morning
to themselves. Only in post-war recollections were the German service
chiefs to disclose just how shocked they were when Britain called
Hitler's bluff.

General Albert Jodl, for instance, had been so sure there would not
be a war that he had booked a Mediterranean cruise for himself,
leaving from Hamburg on 23rd September. Jodl, who had just returned from a command in Vienna to be promoted to full General
and prepare military operational plans, wrote later of the situation in
Berlin after 9 a.m.: 'I found a completely incomprehensible state of
affairs in Berlin. At least, it was incomprehensible to me. Nobody
knew what the truth was and what was bluff.

'The pact with Russia was feeding all our hopes for the preservation
of peace, hopes which were immediately increased and strengthened
by the surprise cancellation of the attack ordered for 26th August.

'None of the soldiers to whom I spoke expected a war with the western powers at that time. Nothing had been prepared except the attack
on Poland.

'There was only a defensive concentration of troops on the West
Wall. The forces stationed there were so weak that we could not man
all the pillboxes at one time . . .

'When the declarations of war were received from England and
France, their effect on us soldiers who had fought in the First World

War was like a blow from a cudgel, and I heard in confidence from the General Staff—today the matter is no longer confidential—that the Reichmarshal reacted in exactly the same way.'

The German Naval Command was even more shocked than the Wehrmacht Generals. The commanders of the Reich's modern, well-equipped, but small, fleet had every reason to dread the prospect of conflict with the immensely powerful fleet of Britain and her Empire. The submarine chief, Admiral Karl Donitz, was to reveal subsequently that Germany that morning had only seventeen U-boats operational in the Atlantic. He was at a complete loss on 3rd September to understand why Hitler had precipitated the war so prematurely. He was baffled all the more as his superior, Grand Admiral Erich Raeder, had just quoted the Führer as saying that in no circumstances must a war develop in the west because that 'would be the end of Germany'.

Raeder himself, who had been pacing Hitler's ante-room when Dr. Schmidt divulged the news of the British ultimatum, was flabbergasted. The Führer saw him later in the morning and confessed, 'I wasn't able to avoid war with England after all.' The Admiral found Hitler 'obviously ill at ease'. Raeder had been with the Führer on many occasions, but had never seen him in such a state of embarrassment.

Some of Germany's most experienced diplomats abroad were as equally disturbed by the presentation of the British ultimatum. As with the leading Generals and Admirals, most had assumed that the Führer would succeed once again in attaining his objects by a show of strength and bluff. Like Hitler, they had expected a final settling of scores with Britain one day—but not in 1939. Generally, they had regarded the Polish adventure as just the first move in a long-term struggle with the British and French, as a Nazi entrenchment in Eastern Europe would make Germany far less vulnerable to a naval blockade.

Franz von Papen, the German Ambassador to Turkey, was one of the diplomats who became convinced that morning that Hitler had blundered into a situation which would wreck his régime and bring disaster to Germany. As German Chancellor (in 1932) and the first Vice-Chancellor to Hitler after 1933, he was well placed to judge the effect the conflict ahead would have on the German state.

When the news of the British ultimatum and the inevitability of

1. Big Ben striking 11:00 AM—the hour of war. KEYSTONE PRESS AGENCY, LTD.

2. Crowds in Downing Street seconds after the declaration of war. KEYSTONE PRESS AGENCY, LTD.

3. Crowds in Downing Street awaiting the appearance of the Prime Minister. KEYSTONE PRESS AGENCY, LTD.

4. The Prime Minister, Neville Chamberlain, leaves No. 10. FOX PHOTOS, LTD.

5. The official declaration of war on the steps of the Royal Exchange, London. PLANET NEWS, LTD.

6. A police station in King's Cross Road, London, receiving reinforcement. FOX PHOTOS, LTD.

7. Londoners entering a trench in Hyde Park. FOX PHOTOS, LTD.

war reached Ankara that morning, von Papen could only stride up and down the Embassy garden, worrying about the future of his homeland. His private secretary said later that he looked 'extraordinarily agitated and seemed quite shattered'. Von Papen told her: 'Mark my words; this war is the worst crime and the greatest madness that Hitler and his clique have ever committed. Germany can never win this war. Nothing will be left but ruins.'

The senior Nazi diplomat wrote later: 'It was reliably reported that Hitler believed till the very last moment that the British and French threats were only a bluff and that he would be left to apply his solution of the Polish question alone. For my own part, I was certain that his attack meant the beginning of the Second World War, and when Britain declared war on 3rd September, I knew that it meant the eventual downfall of Germany.'

Von Papen spent most of that morning considering how he could best serve the interests of Germany as he saw them. Eventually, he decided that his best course of action was to remain in Ankara as Ambassador. He said subsequently that his reasoning had been as follows: 'Even without the documentary proofs which later became available, it was clear that Hitler had provoked the war and plunged Germany into nameless catastrophe. It seemed that I had three choices.

'I could direct a fierce protest to the world in general, which would indicate a moral weakening within Germany. To do this I would have had to seek asylum in Turkey and not return to Germany. Moreover, it seemed useless. The war proved that even the most burning patriots, once they became emigrés, were able to do nothing for their country which served to shorten the war and restore peace.

'I could have resigned. This would have meant my putting on uniform again and leading my regiment.

'My third choice was to remain at my post in Ankara, which seemed to offer the best chance of deflecting the coming catastrophe. The question whether I would be more use as a Colonel or as an Ambassador was easy to answer. Ankara would be the key post for anyone engaged in an attempt to limit the conflict. I decided to remain where I was, and in doing so accepted odds far higher than any I would have encountered as a refugee.'

Many Germans in authority had feelings identical to those of von

Papen that morning. But, like him, they decided, virtually unanimously, to 'soldier on'. Hitler so far had not lost a single trick in the international poker. Why should luck begin to desert him now? A mixture of patriotism, fear and respect for the strange little but successful rabble-rouser kept them loyal during those crucial morning hours.

VI

A desperate Birger Dahlerus began his last bid for a settlement just before 10 a.m., after a hurried conference with his friend Goering. They were together in the Field Marshal's mobile headquarters, a railway coach in a siding near Potsdam, where Prussia's ancient kings ruled.

The Swede had already been working for two hours in his amateur-ish, sincere way, to find some formula for peace. By 8 a.m. he had been informed of Britain's pending ultimatum by his contact, Ogilvie-Forbes, and had later left the Esplanade hotel for the railway siding in a Luftwaffe car placed at his disposal by Goering.

At Potsdam, Dahlerus, according to his account, had found the Nazi Number Two taken completely aback by the British action and had spoken in a fury about the proposed terms. 'Never in the history of the world has a victorious army been compelled to withdraw before negotiations have started.' Goering had gone on to remind Dahlerus of the Versailles Treaty which had only been concluded because Germany had stupidly laid down her arms and had thereafter to accept any conditions imposed upon her. That lesson had not been forgotten.

In the midst of his tirade, Goering had broken off to telephone von Ribbentrop for further news, and had then offered to get Hitler's opinion of the situation. But, with the minutes ticking by towards the 11 a.m. deadline, the Swede had become increasingly worried about the prospects of achieving anything through Goering. He had even started to become doubtful as to whether Goering seriously wanted peace and, if so, would risk his neck for it.

Now it was almost 10 a.m., and Goering was telling Dahlerus that he would do his best to try and persuade Hitler to make a courteous and obliging reply to the British ultimatum, stressing Germany's profound desire to come to an understanding. But the Swede suddenly realized that even if Goering drove immediately to see Hitler, it would be too late. So he decided to contact the Foreign Office in London direct.

There was a telephone placed between the kitchen and dining-car of the Field Marshal's special train, from which he decided to put through the call. He might have used the telephone in Goering's coach (which was equipped with every means of communication including wireless telephone, telegraph and wireless telegraph) but he preferred to speak from a place where he could be sure not to be disturbed.

Dahlerus spoke to the Berlin exchange but was told that telephone communication with London had been suspended. He pleaded with the operator to put him through, saying it was a 'matter of life and death'. His despair so moved the girl that, although it was *verboten*, she connected him with the London exchange. London, however, refused to put him through to the Foreign Office, and Dahlerus had to start pleading all over again.

Finally, at 10.15 a.m., he got a Foreign Office official on the line, a 'Mr. Roberts' as he remembered afterwards. Dahlerus knew that every word he said was recorded by Himmler's organization and would be reported subsequently to Hitler and von Ribbentrop. But there was no time to worry about that. He asserted that there would be a good chance of peace if the British Government would consider the German reply to the ultimatum, which he knew to be 'on the way' in the 'most favourable light'. He implored Roberts to see Chamberlain at once and tell him that in view of the situation in Germany he, Dahlerus, was convinced Hitler could not agree to more than a suspension of hostilities.

Roberts listened to Dahlerus's words without making any comments, and then promised briefly that the message would be passed on to the highest authority. There was not much encouragement for the Swede in the click that accompanied the replacing of the receiver in London, but at least he felt he had stressed the gravity of the situation.

Dahlerus then—according to his story—suggested to Goering that he should fly to London and try to undo the harm that von Ribbentrop had done. Goering agreed and Hitler's consent was quickly obtained.

Now there was little more than half an hour to the time when the great powers were destined to be at war again. Dahlerus urged on Goering the necessity for him to leave German soil before 11 a.m. Then he rang Ogilvie-Forbes to inform the British diplomat what he had done on his own initiative. Sir George told him that Britain could not approach the question of the desirability of a visit from Goering before the note was answered. He stated the demands of the British Government in three words—'assurance of sincerity'.

The stubborn Swede was not satisfied with this clear statement of the position, and a little later, at 10.50 a.m. to be exact, he again had Roberts of the Foreign Office on the line and made his proposal to him. At this point the plan broke down: from London came the uncompromising answer from Halifax that such a proposal could not be entertained. The German Government had been asked a definite question 'and they would presumably be sending a definite answer'. The British Government could not wait for further discussion with Goering.

Dahlerus told Roberts he would try to telephone him again at 11.30 a.m., by which time the German answer was bound to have arrived. He did not hear the reply, only the click of the receiver being replaced.

Goering was furious as the Swede informed him of the Whitehall reaction to his proposed visit to London. But while he ranted against the British, Dahlerus continued to urge him to see Hitler at once and to make sure that the German answer to the British note was couched in conciliatory terms. All hope was not over, Dahlerus repeated again and again. There was still a remote possibility of the Field Marshal making his trip to London, even though time was running desperately short . . .

The Swede remained an optimist to the end, but Goering abandoned the role of would-be mediator before the time-limit expired. At 11.15 a.m., the burly Field Marshal, his chest covered with medals gleaming in the morning sun, left for a secret conference with a band of senior Luftwaffe officers. Dahlerus returned to Berlin from Potsdam to disappear into the limbo of history after having held the centre of the stage for a few days in a bizarre, though honest, attempt to avert mankind's greatest catastrophe.

VII

France acted at 10.20 a.m. when Bonnet ordered the dispatch of an urgent message to M. Robert Coulondre, the Ambassador in Berlin. The Foreign Minister had been told by Daladier by telephone that the Army chiefs were now willing to commence hostilities at 5 a.m. the next morning, Monday. So Bonnet drafted the historic message, 'weighing each word', as he remarked later. He prefaced it with the instruction: 'To the French Ambassador in Berlin (via telephone and cable). Very Urgent. Absolute priority.' The message read: 'Last night, following a message sent by the British Government, and after the sitting of the French Chamber of Deputies, the French Government, meeting in Cabinet, took the following decisions on which it has charged me with informing you.

'You will go, today, 3rd September, at noon to the Wilhelmstrasse and you will demand the reply of the German Government to the note you sent it at 2200 on 1st September.

'If the reply to the questions set out in this note is negative, you will recall the responsibility laid on Germany during your last audience and you will notify the Reich Foreign Minister or his representative that the French Government is obliged, in view of the German reply, to fulfil as from tomorrow, 4th September, at 5 a.m., the engagements France has contracted towards Poland and which are known to the German Government.

'You may then ask for your passports.'

Bonnet declared later that his conscience was clear as he signed the document. Hitler's aggression had made entry into the war right and necessary. But he also reflected gravely on the action to which he had committed the French people. Towards what tragic future were they all heading? 'It seemed,' he wrote, 'that we had just decreed, brutally,

not only the deaths of millions of men, but that of precious ideas and
spiritual values and moreover that of a world in which we had lived
our best years and which we had loved dearly. I felt a few seconds of
intense emotion . . .'

Before dispatching the instructions to Berlin, Bonnet had been subjected to some plain speaking by Halifax from London. The British
Foreign Secretary had told him: 'I know why you can't send your
ultimatum before noon, but we have not made the same promise to
Count Ciano and we are obliged to send ours this morning. The
House of Commons meets at noon and if the Prime Minister appears
there without having fulfilled his promise to Poland, he may be overthrown by a unanimous movement of opinion.'

British annoyance at the French tardiness grew and soon after Bonnet's 10.20 a.m. telegram to Coulondre, the Ambassador in London,
M. Corbin, was on the telephone to his superior. He told Bonnet
that the news had spread that France was not going to war until
5 a.m. on the Monday and this had caused annoyance very prejudicial
to the allied cause.

Bonnet shrugged his shoulders. The timing of France's entry into
the war was up to the General Staff, and they were adamant. As it
was, France had already advanced her ultimatum to Germany by
twenty-four hours. He asked Corbin to make the British understand
that it would be criminal folly for France to risk German air-raids
by opening hostilities before the French Army was ready.

Bonnet rang off and waited. He knew that Daladier was making a
last desperate effort to get the Generals to change their minds. At
11.25 a.m. the Premier was able to report success. He shouted over
the telephone to Bonnet: 'We've made it at last, Georges!' Daladier,
in high spirits, added that he had made a fresh appraisal of the situation with the General Staff and it now seemed possible for the delay
to be reduced by a further twelve hours. Thus, the opening of hostilities could be fixed for 5 p.m. that afternoon.

'That's fine,' said Bonnet, replacing the receiver. He had no time
to lose. It was 11.30 a.m. and telephone communication to Berlin was
not as good as it used to be. It was important that he got M. Coulondre on the line before the Ambassador had left the Embassy for his
noon appointment with von Ribbentrop.

Bonnet contacted the Ambassador at 11.45 a.m. just as he was about to leave for the Wilhelmstrasse with the ultimatum, and dictated the short amendment to his previous telegraphic instructions: 'Hostilities will commence at 1700 hours today.'

This was clear and simple enough, but M. Coulondre was the kind of diplomat who refused to act on instructions unless he was quite sure who was giving them. He did not recognize his Foreign Minister's voice over the telephone and politely asked Bonnet to pass the telephone to one or two of his colleagues whose voices were more familiar to him. Bonnet laughed and congratulated the Ambassador on his presence of mind and then had two officials confirm the instruction verbally.

Bonnet next telephoned London joyfully to pass the news on to M. Corbin and through him to the British politicians who were besieging the Embassy with angry personal calls and telephone messages. Corbin, a tall, grey-haired man with a grey moustache and a perpetually sad expression, had taken the brunt of the British anger and had been trying to explain patiently his country's mobilization difficulties. Churchill's telephone calls had been most to the point that morning. In one of them, the British statesman had reacted to Corbin's talk of 'technical difficulties' by exclaiming, 'Technical difficulties be damned! I suppose you would call it a technical difficulty for a Pole if a German bomb fell on his head!' According to Brendan (later Lord) Bracken, Churchill had spoken to Corbin as 'though he were an old washerwoman'. Now the Frenchman was able to tell everyone that France was about to fulfil her promise to an ally within a few hours.

The first British politicians to whom Corbin was able to disclose the news were two Labourites, Mr. Hugh Dalton and Mr. A. V. Alexander. Corbin told them he was much concerned to hear that some M.P.s had cast doubt on the intention of France to honour her word. There was no truth whatsoever in those rumours, the Ambassador declared angrily.

It was a few minutes after 11 a.m. and Dalton glanced at his watch and told Corbin: 'My country is at war *now* in fulfilment of *our* pledge to Poland.' There was silence for a moment and then Corbin was able to say in triumph, 'And *my* country will be at war in a few hours' time.' The Frenchman added, 'France has already three million men under the flag. Soon she will have six million.' Even making al-

lowance for the immense power of the British fleet, and the most
valuable contribution Britain would make in the air and on land,
France was carrying a far heavier burden. 'It is upon my country that
the heaviest blows will fall,' Corbin told the Labour M.P.s.

In Paris, Bonnet immediately became caught up in a round of
meetings with foreign diplomats. The Portuguese envoy called to
discuss rumours that Britain and France were about to launch an
attack on Spain. Bonnet denied this stoutly. The Polish Ambassador
Lukasiewicz also called for news. He and the Foreign Minister had
recovered from their emotional outbursts the night before and now
tried to surpass each other in expressions of courtesy. Lukasiewicz,
nevertheless, reminded Bonnet that their alliance required France to
give Poland 'swift and effective' assistance. He asked him to persuade
Daladier to launch an immediate offensive on the western front.
Bonnet felt this request to be absolutely justified and promised to
support it.

Frenchmen were listening to the songs of Mlle. Yvonne Faroche
on the radio while these momentous events were in progress. Paris
was now usually quiet, even for a Sunday. The shops, with their grilles
closed and their awnings down, somehow looked as though they would
never open again. It had stopped raining, but the sky was murky.
Taxis and private cars were few in number. Convoys of lorries filled
with sand rumbled through the streets. Men were still painting on the
doors of buildings the word *Abri* (shelter) in white, and indicating
the number of places within. Only at the railway stations, where young
men were leaving to join their units, were there any signs of emotion.

The Chamber of Deputies was not due to meet that day as the
Government had already been authorized to take all necessary action.
The few Deputies present in the lobbies of the Chamber received
the news, according to Pressmen who interviewed them, with 'cool-
ness and calm'. Unlike their opposite numbers in London, the
French politicians expected no immediate ministerial reshuffle.

The early editions of the evening newspapers, on the streets of Paris
before 11 a.m., devoted columns of space to proving Germany's war
guilt. *Le Temps* told its readers: 'It is Hitler's acts which count and
not his words. It is on his acts, frightening for any human conscience,
that history will judge and condemn him.' *L'Intransigeant* commented: 'So many broken promises, so many dishonoured signa-

tures, so many "scraps of paper", so many breaches of their word do not allow us this time to hope for good faith.

'But we might still have hoped for a gleam of reason. We had the right to believe that on the edge of the abyss the odious person who alone is responsible for the catastrophe would draw back; that he would understand that he was condemning himself to death and dragging his country to final collapse. He did not understand. Or rather, perhaps, he could not see any solution other than war to escape from the terrible mess into which he had plunged the German nation.'

The newspapers also recalled that this was the 156th anniversary of the signing of the definitive Treaty of Versailles which gave America its independence from Britain. The treaty was signed on 3rd September, 1783.

VIII

Eleven o'clock. Downing Street was now packed with people who overflowed into Whitehall. They stood about, tense and silent, not knowing what to expect. Then, at zero hour, radio sets in parked cars were heard to announce that no communication had been received from Germany and war was inevitable. That broke the tension. The crowd's attitude changed swiftly to laughter and cheers.

One man produced a Union Jack and led a wild burst of cheering and the singing of patriotic songs like 'Rule Britannia'. Others vented their feelings by shouts and clenching fists in gestures of determination. Police had difficulty for some minutes in preventing the crowd from surging to the door of No. 10. Then, as though it had been stage-managed, the Prime Minister's chauffeur came out carrying his employer's gas-mask. He placed it almost with reverence on the back seat of the car and the grim symbol of the war that lay ahead stilled the songs and the cheering and the spectators began, slowly, to disperse.

At 11.10 a.m. Mr. Robert Dunbar, 44-year-old Head of the Treaty Department of the British Foreign Office, slipped quietly out of his office carrying a brief-case full of documents. None of his colleagues noticed his departure. He walked briskly across Horse Guards Parade, noting what a lovely morning it was, and then crossed The Mall. Mr. Dunbar was off to declare war.

The diplomat, who had won the Military Cross in the First World War and had then served in Foreign Office posts in Peking, Athens and Addis Ababa, cannot recall what he was wearing that Sunday morning. It might have been a black jacket and striped trousers, or a brown suit. But he knows he was 'not dressed up in any glad rags for the occasion'.

He climbed the Duke of York steps briskly, then turned into Carlton House Terrace, knocked on the door of the Embassy and asked to see Dr. Kordt, the *Chargé d'Affaires*. He was taken immediately to the German diplomat, a man he had known and worked with for some time and whose efficiency he respected.

Dunbar handed his communications to Dr. Kordt—Britain's declaration of war against Germany and the British Government's list of the people within the Embassy whom it considered were entitled to diplomatic protection.

'There it is,' said Dunbar. 'You know what it is.' Dr. Kordt replied, 'Yes, I do', and began reading the documents. Then the German diplomat began to challenge Britain's interpretation of the number and types of people in his Embassy who should be given safe passage home. The two men began to dispute courteously the details of the list of people who should get their 'passports'.

Their argument was broken by the sound of air-raid sirens wailing throughout London. The two diplomats listened to the sirens then, without comment, resumed their consideration of urgent matters of protocol. An 'all-clear' went minutes later but the two remained in earnest conversation until noon.

The talks had lasted about forty-five minutes, without any pause for refreshments, when Dunbar and Kordt decided they could achieve nothing more. The British diplomat wished Kordt 'good-bye' and recalls that he felt he must be careful not to add 'and good luck.' The German *Chargé d'Affaires* also said a plain 'good-bye'—and the two men who had seen so much of one another on official duties parted officially enemies.

Dunbar walked back to the Foreign Office by the same route, down the steps and across the Horse Guards Parade. Back at his desk, he went to work on the details of the departure from London of the German diplomats, relieved that his task had been made reasonably easy by the friendly and efficient Kordt.

Looking back on that incident he says: 'I could not have worked with a better fellow. He knew how everything should be done. With anyone who had been a Nazi and a fool it would have been a difficult business.'

Five minutes after Dunbar's departure from the Foreign Office, a broken-hearted Neville Chamberlain began a broadcast to the people of Britain, the Empire and the world, from the Cabinet Room in 10 Downing Street.

After referring to the ultimatum delivered in Berlin earlier, the Prime Minister said: 'I have to tell you now that no such undertaking has been received and that consequently this country is at war with Germany. You can imagine what a bitter blow it is to me that all my long struggle to win peace has failed.

'Yet I cannot believe that there is anything more or anything different that I could have done and that would have been more successful. Up to the very last it would have been quite possible to have arranged a peaceful and honourable settlement between Germany and Poland.

'But Hitler would not have it. He had evidently made up his mind to attack Poland whatever happened; and although he now says he put forward reasonable proposals which were rejected by the Poles, that is not a true statement. The proposals were never shown to the Poles nor to us; and though they were announced in the German broadcast on Thursday night, Hitler did not wait to hear comments on them, but ordered his troops to cross the Polish frontier next morning.

'His action shows convincingly that there is no chance of expecting that this man will ever give up his practice of using force to gain his will. He can only be stopped by force and we and France are today, in fulfilment of our obligations, going to the aid of Poland, who is so bravely resisting this wicked and unprovoked attack upon her people.

'We have a clear conscience. We have done all that any country could do to establish peace, but a situation in which no word given by Germany's ruler could be trusted and no people or country feel themselves safe has become intolerable. And now that we have resolved to finish it, I know that you will all play your part with calmness and courage.

'At such a moment as this, the assurances of support that we have received from the Empire are a source of profound encouragement to us.

'When I have finished speaking, certain detailed announcements will be made on behalf of the Government. Give them your close attention. The Government have made plans under which it will be possible to carry on the work of the nation in days of stress and strain that may be ahead. But these plans need your help.

'You may be taking part in the fighting services or as a volunteer in one of the branches of Civil Defence. If so, you will report for duty in accordance with the instructions you receive. You may be engaged in work essential to the prosecution of war or to the maintenance of the life of the people—in factories, in transport, in public utility concerns or in the supply of other necessaries of life. If so, it is of vital importance that you should carry on with your jobs.

'Now may God bless you all and may he defend the right. For it is evil things that we shall be fighting against, brute force, bad faith, injustice, oppression and persecution. And against them all I am certain that the right will prevail.'

The reactions to the Chamberlain broadcast in the reigning Royal House were typical of those of families all over the British Empire. King George VI, like so many other men who had known the First World War, had reason to view the future with fear and trepidation. But mingled with that feeling was one of relief that the nation had now embarked firmly upon a course of honour. Queen Elizabeth, as with so many other mothers of young children, thought anxiously of what might happen to them in the massive air-raids that undoubtedly loomed ahead.

The King and Queen were at Buckingham Palace that morning and listened to the Prime Minister in their private chambers. Their children, Princess Elizabeth and Princess Margaret, thirteen and nine respectively, were at the eighteenth-century manor of Birkhall, near Balmoral, and listened to the broadcast there. The widowed Queen Mary was at Sandringham, Norfolk, and heard the Prime Minister speak on a radio set installed specially in the nave of the little church of St. Mary Magdalene. Prince Philip of Greece, the future Duke of Edinburgh, who had already begun a boy-and-girl friendship with the future Queen, was on leave in Athens from the Royal Naval College, Dartmouth, where he was a cadet.

King George began keeping a diary the day war began. He summed up his feelings that morning in these words: 'As 11 o'clock struck that fateful morning, I had certain feeling of relief that those ten anxious days of intensive negotiations with Germany over Poland, which at moments looked favourable, with Mussolini working for peace as well, were over. Hitler would not and could not draw back from the edge of the abyss to which he had led us. Despite our protestations that the Polish question could have been settled without force, Hitler had taken the plunge, with the knowledge that the whole might of the British Empire would be against him to help Poland, our ally.

'France is our ally. Italy has declared herself neutral for the present.

'At the outbreak of war on 4th–5th August, 1914, I was a midshipman keeping the middle watch on the bridge of H.M.S. *Collingwood* at sea, somewhere in the North Sea. I was eighteen years of age.

'In the Grand Fleet everyone was pleased that it had come at last. We had been trained in the belief that war between Germany and this country had to come one day. We were not prepared for what we found a modern war really was, and those of us who had been through the Great War never wanted another.

'Today we are at war again and I am no longer a midshipman in the Royal Navy.

'For the last year, ever since the Munich agreement, Germany or rather its leaders have caused us incessant worry in crises of different magnitudes. Hitler marched into Czechoslovakia in March this year. Then Memel. We knew the Polish question would be the next on the list of Hitler's bloodless victories. The whole country knew it and had been preparing for it by making arms, aeroplanes and all the engines of war in record time to withstand the next real crisis.

'So today when the crisis is over and the result of the breakdown is war, the country is calm, firm and united behind its leaders, resolved to fight until Liberty and Justice are once more safe in the world . . .'

At Doorn, Holland, the former Kaiser Wilhelm II of Germany heard the Prime Minister's declaration of war on his fatherland with very mixed feelings. The 80-year-old, white-whiskered exile was one of the few Germans who could listen to Chamberlain without fear of a decree which forbade his countrymen from tuning in to foreign radio stations under pain of imprisonment or possible death.

The broadcast jolted the old man, once Emperor of Germany and King of Prussia, out of his life-end siesta. He called his wife, Hermine, and entourage into his modest living-room and led them in prayer. Then he went upstairs, knelt by the bed where his first wife, the Empress Augusta-Victoria had died eighteen years previously, and prayed again, alone.

Later he returned to the Great Hall of Doorn where a gigantic map of Poland had been hung on one wall. Methodically, and with the skill of one long versed in warfare, he began to arrange little pins along the battle fronts to indicate the positions of the opposing armies, their advances and retreats, the towns bombarded and the objectives which had fallen to German arms. It was to give the old militarist a new lease of life . . .

The Duke of Windsor, another Royal exile, was with the Duchess at La Croe, a handsome white villa at Cap d'Antibes on the Côte d'Azur. It was a hot and humid morning, even for the south of France.

All morning, the Duke had been listening to French radio broadcasts, broken only by farewell to two of his servants called up for military service. His one thought at the moment of Chamberlain's broadcast was how he could serve Britain and the Empire again, as he had promised to do at the time of his abdication as King Edward VIII three years earlier. But the French telephone circuits were hopelessly clogged by priority military calls. He could not telephone his brother or any of his friends in London to seek news and guidance on how, and where, he might serve his country again.

Just before noon, the Duke decided that there was no chance of getting through to London by telephone. He shrugged his shoulders and told the woman for whom he had given up the throne: 'There's nothing we can do from here right now. I'm sure that I will hear from my brother the moment any decision is taken. Let's go for a swim.'

As they walked down a lane towards a swimming pool by the blue Mediterranean, a servant hurried after the Duke to tell him that the British Ambassador was calling from Paris. He returned to the house while the Duchess and a house guest, Major Edward Metcalfe, continued on their way to the pool. Ten minutes later, the Duke rejoined them.

He walked to the edge of the pool and then said quietly: 'Great Britain has just declared war on Germany and I am afraid in the end this may open the way for world communism.' Then there came a splash as he dived into the pool . . .

IX

While Mr. Dunbar was strolling across St. James's Park in London's morning sunshine towards the German Embassy, Britain's Ambassador in Berlin was speeding through busy streets to a meeting with von Ribbentrop in the Wilhelmstrasse. The German Foreign Minister had sent him a message soon after 11 a.m. asking him to call 'at once'.

Sir Nevile Henderson arrived at the Foreign Ministry just before 11.30 a.m. Upon being shown into von Ribbentrop's room he was handed, after the opening formalities, not a new diplomatic note but a lengthy document. Henderson had time only to skim through what had been drawn up obviously with a view to publication and the history books.

It began with a refusal on the part of the German people to accept any demands in the nature of a British ultimatum and concluded by saying that any aggressive action by Britain would be answered with the same weapons and in the same form. The bulk of the document, the British envoy quickly concluded, was 'pure propaganda' written with the view, he declared later, of 'attempting to prove to the German people and the world generally that it was Britain alone who was to blame for everything which had happened'.

Henderson's only comment to the German Foreign Minister was that it would be 'left to history to judge where the blame really lay'. Von Ribbentrop replied that history had already proved the facts, and that nobody had striven harder for peace and good relations with England than Hitler himself.

The two men then parted on courteous and amicable terms. Von Ribbentrop told Henderson that he personally 'wished him good' and the British diplomat answered that he deeply regretted the failure of all his efforts for peace, but that he bore no grudge against the German people.

As they parted, members of the British Embassy staff were being received in the Protocol Section of the German Foreign Ministry where arrangements were to be made for their departure. Henderson was told later that his colleagues then were 'treated with every civility and consideration' and were informed that a special train would be placed at their disposal the following morning.

So Henderson returned to the Embassy to make the final arrangements for his return to Britain. In the car on the way home he was able to study in detail the unsigned memorandum presented to him by von Ribbentrop.

To him, as to any British reader, it was an astonishing piece of historical distortion, but phrased with sufficient skill to impress the German newspapers, for whom it would be a major news item the following morning, and some neutral opinion. The authorship of the last German peacetime message to Britain could not be ascertained that day or later, but it ranks as a prize item in any collection of Nazi literature:

'The German Government have received the British Government's ultimatum of 3rd September, 1939. They have the honour to reply as follows:

'1. The German Reich Government and the German people refuse to receive, or accept, let alone to fulfil, demands in the nature of ultimata made by the British Government.

'2. On our eastern frontier a virtual state of war has existed for many months. After the Versailles Treaty first tore Germany to pieces, every peaceful settlement has been refused to all German Governments ever since. The National Socialist Government also have, since the year 1933, tried again and again to remove by peaceful negotiations the worst violations and breaches of justice in this Treaty. The British Government have been among those who, by their intransigent attitude, took the chief part in frustrating every practical revision. But for the intervention of the British Government—of this the German Government and the German people are fully conscious—a reasonable solution doing justice to both sides would certainly have been found between Germany and Poland. For Germany did not intend, neither did she demand, the annihilation of Poland.

'The Reich demanded only the revision of those articles of the Versailles Treaty which, already at the time of the formulation of that dictate, had been described by understanding statesmen of all nations as being in the long run unbearable, and therefore impossible for a great nation, and also for the entire political and economic interests of Eastern Europe. British statesmen, too, described the solution in the east, which was then forced upon Germany, as containing the germ of future wars. To remove this danger was the desire of all German Governments and especially the intention of the new National Socialist People's Government. The blame for having prevented this peaceful revision lies with British Cabinet policy.

'3. The British Government have—an occurrence unique in history —given the Polish State full powers for all actions against Germany which that State might conceivably intend to undertake. The British Government assured the Polish Government of their military support in all circumstances, should Germany defend herself against any provocation or attack. Thereupon the Polish terror against the Germans living in the territories which had once been torn from Germany immediately assumed unbearable forms.

'The Free City of Danzig was, in violation of all legal provisions, first threatened with destruction economically and by measures of customs policy, and was finally subjected to a military blockade and its communications strangled. All these violations of the Danzig Statute, which were well known to the British Government, were approved and covered by a blank cheque given to Poland.

'The German Government, though moved by the sufferings of the German population which was being tortured and treated in an inhuman manner, nevertheless remained a patient onlooker for five months, without undertaking even once any similar aggressive action against Poland. They only warned Poland that these happenings would in the long run be unbearable and that they were determined, in the event of no other assistance being given to this population, to help them themselves.

'All these happenings were known in every detail to the British Government. It would have been easy for them to use their great influence in Warsaw in order to exhort those in power there to exercise justice and humanity and to keep to the existing obligations. The British Government did not do this.

'On the contrary, in emphasizing continually their obligation to assist Poland in all circumstances, they actually encouraged the Polish Government to continue in their criminal attitude which was threatening the peace of Europe. In this spirit, the British Government rejected the proposal by Mussolini, which might still have been able to save the peace of Europe, in spite of the fact that the German Government had declared their willingness to agree to it. The British Government, therefore, bear the responsibility for all the unhappiness and misery which have now overtaken and will overtake many peoples.

'4. After all efforts at finding and concluding a peaceful solution had been rendered impossible by the intransigence of the Polish Government, covered as they were by England, after the conditions resembling civil war, which had existed already for months on the eastern frontier of the Reich, had gradually developed into open attacks on German territory, without the British Government raising any objections, the German Government determined to put an end to this continual threat, unbearable for a great power, to the external and finally also to the internal peace of the German people, and to end it by those means which, since the Democratic Governments had in effect sabotaged all other possibilities of revision, alone remained at their disposal for the defence of the peace, security and honour of the German Reich. The last attacks of the Poles threatening Reich territory they have answered with similar measures.

'The German Government do not intend, on account of any sort of British intentions or obligations in the east, to tolerate conditions which are similar to those conditions which we observe in Palestine, which is under British protection. But above all the German people do not intend to allow themselves to be ill-treated by Poles.

'5. The German Government, therefore, reject the attempts to force Germany, by means of a demand amounting to an ultimatum, to recall their forces which are lined up for the defence of the Reich, and thereby to accept the old unrest and the old injustice again. The threat that, failing this, they will go to war with Germany, corresponds to the intention proclaimed for years past by numerous British politicians.

'The German Government and the German people have assured the English people countless times how much they desire an understanding, indeed the closest friendship, with them. If the British Government have hitherto always refused these offers and now answer them with an open threat of war, it is not the fault of the German people and of their Government, but exclusively the fault of the British Cabinet or of those men who for years have been preaching the destruction and extermination of the German people.

'The German people and their Government do not, like Great Britain, intend to dominate the world, but they are determined to defend their own liberty, their independence and above all their life. The intention, communicated to us by order of the British Government by Mr. King-Hall of carrying the destruction of the German people even further than was done through the Versailles Treaty, is taken note of by us and we shall therefore answer any aggressive action on the part of England with the same weapons and in the same form.' (Commander Stephen King-Hall's Newsletter, a private publication, was then being distributed in Germany.)

Back at the British Embassy, Henderson settled down to put the finishing touches to a note of exquisite diplomatic courtesy aimed at ensuring that Germany, like Britain, would observe the rules of modern warfare by banning the use of gas and germs. Soon, this note had been completed and was on its way to von Ribbentrop. It, too, is a collector's item for anyone young enough to regard the diplomatic doings of 1939 as having the charm of a period piece:

The message, written in English (a reminder to the Wilhelmstrasse that things were not as they were) read as follows:

'Your Excellency,

'I have the honour, by direction of His Majesty's Principal Secretary of State for Foreign Affairs, to inquire whether the German Government are prepared to give an assurance to His Majesty's Government in the United Kingdom that they will observe the provisions of the Geneva Protocol, signed on the 17th June, 1925, prohibiting the use in war of asphyxiating, poisonous or other gases, and of bacteriological methods of warfare.

'The German Government will be aware that His Majesty's Government in the United Kingdom are themselves party to this Protocol.

'I request that you will be so good as to communicate the reply of your Government to His Majesty's Government in the United Kingdom, through the representative in London of the Power taking charge of the German Government's interests in the United Kingdom.

'I avail myself of this opportunity to renew to Your Excellency the assurance of my highest consideration.

Nevile Henderson.'

Britain, too, had said her last polite word. And, just to ensure that the war game was played according to the best rules devised by the idealists of the past two decades, a note couched in similar terms and dealing with the bombing of places outside the direct area of hostilities was being relayed simultaneously from London to Berlin by the Nazi Embassy there.

X

The war's first 'atrocity', a bitter, bloody affair which was to figure in the Nuremberg Trials six and a half years later, began its ugly growth at 10.15 a.m. in the city of Bydgoszcz (Bromberg) in Central Poland. By 11 a.m., it had reached its peak of intensity. The Poles were to call it a German atrocity, the Germans were to make a similar allegation against the Poles. For both sides, the events around the town were to go down in history as 'bloody Sunday'.

The incident took place as the Poles were withdrawing from the western outskirts of Bydgoszcz. Members of the minority population began firing on the retreating Polish troops to speed the arrival of their 'liberators'. The Poles hit back hard, with the double intensity of men who felt they had been stabbed in the back by compatriots. But the local Germans had been well armed by agents from the Reich and desperate street fighting developed before the Poles were again in complete, though brief, command of the city. By then, according to an official Polish count, 238 Poles and 223 local Germans had been killed.

The Bydgoszcz fighting that morning, however, was destined to become a major propaganda issue between the two warring countries. For the Nazis, it was proof of Polish repression of the German minority, while the Poles could list it as one more example of the fifth column organized within their borders. So long as the German invasion of Poland continued, it was to be a major source of bitterness between the countries. And even when all Poland had been brought under the German heel, the bitterness felt by Germans against Poles in that city was to show itself in special persecution of the inhabitants. According to evidence at Nuremberg, 10,500 Polish citizens of Bydgoszcz were subsequently murdered by the Germans and a further 13,000 exterminated in concentration camps. So the Germans that morning who began to speed the retreating Poles on their way with a hail of bullets were starting a struggle which was to continue in one way or another throughout the whole war, and to result in 24,000 deaths. . . .

While the Bydgoszcz massacre was in progress, the German Third and Fourth armies were completing a link between their forces, and thereby sealing the fate of the Polish Pomorze Army. By noon, the German High Command was able to claim that 15,000 men had been taken prisoner and 90 field pieces and large stocks of material had been captured.

The position of the Polish forces in the Pomeranian province (Pomorze) had been precarious from the start of the fighting because German armies threatened them from both east and west. The Poles had stationed the Pomorze Army in the 'corridor' to the coast and the ports of Danzig and Gdynia largely for political reasons and to prevent a peacetime *putsch* in Danzig.

The Pomorze Army, consisting of five infantry divisions and one cavalry brigade, had been falling back from all positions ever since Friday morning. The German Third Army had assailed it from East Prussia, driving towards Grudziadz, a former German fortress on the Vistula. At the same time, the Fourth Army had attacked from the west, in the direction of Tuchola and Bydgoszcz. By Sunday morning, Grudziadz was certain to fall to the Germans within a few hours and the capture of Bydgoszcz was similarly assured. But crack panzer units led by General Heinz Guderian were finding in the defenders of Tuchola a near-fanatical bunch of infantrymen. The battle of the Tuchola Forests was at its height that morning. A large Polish force had been encircled and trapped by the swift panzer groups but the men were fighting on with a courage and a desperation that made their resistance one of the most dramatic and poignant aspects of the whole Polish campaign.

The Tuchola defenders were fighting like automatons. Shelled and bombed continuously throughout the morning, their morale was alternating between states of panic and reckless bravery. One sector along the Tuchola-Swiecie road, cluttered with upturned and smashed cars, carriages and guns and scattered with the bodies of dead men and horses, presented such a gruesome picture that it had already been dubbed the 'Road of Death' by the Germans. Repeated bayonet

8. Mounted police on patrol in London. FOX PHOTOS, LTD.

9. Londoners running to an air-raid shelter in Whitehall. KEYSTONE PRESS AGENCY.

10.-13. Four of the principal actors in the London diplomatic drama: *top left*, Count Raczynski, the Polish Ambassador; *centre*, M. Corbin, French Ambassador; *right*, Lord Halifax, British Foreign Secretary; *below*, Dr. Kordt, the German Charge d'Affaires, leaving the German Embassy under police escort. 10, ASSOCIATED PRESS, LTD.; 11, RADIO TIMES HULTON PICTURE LIBRARY; 12, FOX PHOTOS, LTD.; 13, ASSOCIATED PRESS, LTD.

14. Winston Churchill, the new First Lord of the Admiralty, leaves No. 10 Downing Street a few hours after war is declared. ASSOCIATED PRESS, LTD.

15. King George VI speaks to the nation, September 4, 1939. FOX PHOTOS, LTD.

16. Headline news in Times Square. PLANET NEWS, LTD.

charges by the Poles were preventing the Germans from sweeping through the forests and would continue to do so until as late as 15th September.

The linking of the two German armies that morning also isolated without hope of any relief the equally gallant bands of Poles fighting in the coastal area. The Coastal Defence Corps, entrusted with the protection of the ports, was still fighting hard and, contrary to all German expectations, was still in full possession of Gdynia. This mixed force of soldiers, sailors and marines was destined to hold out until 19th September, while the garrison at the naval base of Hel would remain unconquered for a further month.

At noon, the Pomorze Army had all but disintegrated and the Modlin Army, consisting of two infantry divisions and two cavalry brigades, was beginning to fare almost as badly. This Polish force had stood up well to the German drive towards Mlawa on the Friday and had survived considerable bombing and artillery fire. During the Saturday, however, German tanks had made numerous breaches in the line and infantrymen began to infiltrate to the rear of the Modlin Army. Now, the situation was deteriorating swiftly with a further increase in the German pressure. Liaison between the commanders of the Modlin Army and officers in the field was reported in the late morning to be disorganized, almost non-existent. Some of the Modlin troops were retreating for the first time by mid-day, and German light tanks and armoured cars were advancing swiftly through a breach in the defences towards Ciechanow.

In the north, the Polish Narew Group was less heavily pressed and no major front-line operations were in progress although the Luftwaffe, in complete control of the skies, was now bombing railway lines and towns with almost monotonous regularity. Cavalrymen of the Narew Group had enjoyed the satisfaction on the first day of the war of crossing the border into East Prussia and occupying temporarily a few small German localities. By Sunday morning a German drive in the direction of Myszyniec and Ostroleke had been checked at least for a time by the Narew forces. But a Polish effort to drive the invaders back from Myszyniec was being repulsed with heavy losses.

Poland's Poznan Army was largely uncommitted at noon and thousands of its troops were still waiting for the war to begin. This strong force of five infantry divisions and two cavalry brigades had been de-

ployed at the outbreak of fighting to cover the province of Wielkopol-
ska, but no major enemy force had been used against it in the first
two days. There had been a series of frontier clashes with shared
honours, but on the third morning the Poznan soldiers were still virtually fresh and untried. In view of the heavy fighting in adjacent sectors
—the Pomorze and Lodz Army operations—the situation was becoming
uncanny for the Poles, and by mid-morning many of the Poznan troops
were moved to new positions.

One of the strongest German drives was being directed towards
Lodz, along the front stretching between Kalisz and Czestochowa.
Here German armour and bombing was being directed with deadly
effect against the Polish force of five infantry divisions and two cavalry
brigades.

The position by late morning was that the Poles had begun withdrawing to fortified positions in the Warta and Widawka area after
two days of stubborn resistance which had resulted in the destruction
of many German tanks. The Polish line was still in good order, but
German armoured units were pushing forward on the flanks, especially
in the direction of Piotrkow. Polish aircraft were hitting back in this
area and made several morning raids on panzer units near Radomsko,
but their losses were heavy—not infrequently because their own ground
forces mistook them for German planes.

Disparity in strength between the German and Polish forces was
nowhere as it was along the front stretching from Czestochowa down
along the border of German Silesia to the Carpathian and Tatra mountains in the south. This front was manned on the Polish side by the
Cracow Army of seven infantry divisions, one cavalry brigade, one highland and one armoured brigade. It had been the largest Polish Army
at the time of the German attack, and some of its front was fortified;
but by Sunday morning it was clear that the forces were not adequate
to the task. The same pattern of events was being repeated as on the
other fronts: initial stubborn resistance, followed by the loss of individual positions, and now infiltration by the invaders everywhere.
The Poles had suffered heavy losses, but had gone down fighting. At
Wysoka, where their own armoured brigade had gone into action, fifty
German tanks lay destroyed that morning.

Since the previous evening, however, it had been clear to the Cracow
Army commanders that they could not hold their defence lines, and

a general retreat towards the river line of Nida-Dunajec was already in progress. This would mean the loss of the city of Cracow. Battlefield reports at noon indicated that the retreat was proceeding in an orderly fashion in the central sector, but a rout was developing in the north and the Poles along the southern part of the line were falling back under extreme pressure.

Cracow itself by noon was in imminent danger of occupation. The old part of the city was in ruins, the atmosphere filled with the pungent smell of high explosive mingling with the smoke and dust of burning buildings. Rows of trams lay gutted in the devastated streets. Direct bomb hits had brought down whole buildings. Fires were raging all over the city but serious fire-fighting was out of the question. The fire brigade had neither enough engines nor enough men, and appeals to the Army were in vain.

The movement of refugees was increasing from hour to hour and the streets were filled with people trying to escape the doomed city. Many of them were Jews. Out of a total population of 35,000,000, one of every ten in Poland was Jewish, most of whom were destined to perish in the Nazi gas chambers. They had never had a happy time in Poland and still wore the black coats, beards, skull-caps and haircuts forced on them by the Tzarist régime. Now they had every reason to fear a worse fate.

But all those fleeing from Cracow were not Jewish. Many were simply trying to get out of the city in the hope that the front line would be established a score or so miles beyond Cracow. They were still under the illusion that some sort of organized war life would be possible on the other side of that line, enabling the men to join the forces and the women to carry on some useful work.

The last Polish force, the Karpaty Army, was also fighting an enemy superior in numbers and in equipment. This group had been hastily organized the previous June, following the German occupation of Slovakia. Its task was to protect the southern frontier along the Carpathian mountains. Numerous valleys and passes made this a tough job for the two highland brigades and frontier guards who could be spared for this role. Since Friday, the Karpaty Army had been at grips with three German divisions and some detachments of Slovak troops. On the first two days, fighting had been limited to minor engagements. Now, on Sunday morning a major engagement with German troops and armour converging on Nowy Sacz was developing—and the Polish commanders were being asked to lend help to the harassed left wing of the retreating Cracow Army.

In the eyes of the outside world the German advance on all fronts that morning appeared to be the result of a well-prepared, perfectly co-ordinated and rapidly moving *blitzkrieg*, conducted almost without any kind of hitch. In fact, there were many weaknesses in the German war machine, which had already become evident to the Nazi High Command. General Guderian, the great specialist in tank warfare who was commanding the German XIXth Army Corps in Poland that morning, was later to give an account of various misadventures of his Corps that week-end. He enumerated faults which might have been fatal to the German advance had the Poles been able to take advantage of them. Guderian revealed instances where the German artillery fired into the fog, hitting advancing panzers. Attacks were stalled and troops were made to wait idly at critical moments for lack of orders or determined leadership. There were failures to transmit orders between higher units. And bridges were built and immediately dismantled because of conflicting orders.

But, apart from isolated instances, the Poles were in no position to exploit these faults, being outnumbered and virtually without air cover. And, due to the fact that Soviet Russia had been considered Poland's Number 1 potential enemy since 1918, the eastern frontiers had been far more effectively fortified than those facing Germany. There had not been time to complete fortifications in the west by 1st September, and any deficiencies in German command or equipment counted for little beside this lack of preparedness.

XI

A few minutes after Chamberlain had finished his broadcast to the British nation and the world, London's air-raid sirens wailed. The time was 11.30 a.m. There was no surprise, no panic. The population had been led by its political and military leaders to expect that the next war would begin with devastating attacks from the air, with the enemy attempting to deliver a knock-out blow at the outset of hostilities. Londoners moved swiftly and silently to the public shelters in buildings and parks, factories and offices, or to 'Andersons' and trenches in their own back gardens. Most were grimly resigned to the ordeal, although it was something of a surprise that the Germans had got their bombers over only half an hour after the war became official.

A crowd outside Buckingham Palace, focal point of London in any crisis, was shepherded quickly to nearby shelters and trenches by air-raid wardens and policemen. The space around the Victoria Memorial was cleared within a few minutes and the sightseers were soon crouching obediently in the park trenches.

Observers of that first alarm marvelled at the high degree of preparedness on the part of most of the public. Although the time that had elapsed since the Prime Minister's broadcast had been so short, many Londoners arrived at their nearest shelters complete with gas-masks, torches, cushions, rugs, camp stools, books, playing cards and supplies of chocolate for 'emergency rations'. The Government's campaign to make the nation air-raid conscious had succeeded to a remarkable degree.

Peers and commoners, gathering in Parliament for the session which was to begin at noon, proceeded in orderly fashion to shelters prepared for them, many carrying gas-masks slung over their shoulders. There was no distinction of class or rank. Tearoom girls and barmaids stood shoulder to shoulder with M.P.s. David Lloyd George, 76-year-old First World War Prime Minister, remarked affably as he descended the stairs that there was 'nothing new in all this' for him.

Labour's Parliamentary Executive was in session when the sirens sounded and members reluctantly obeyed a policeman who ordered them to take shelter. Some of the Labourites decided to go up top and admire the balloon barrage. One of the balloons was called the 'Herbert Morrison Special', after their fellow party member who led the London County Council. To the amusement of the M.P.s this enormous balloon anchored near County Hall across the Thames, failed to go up that morning.

Winston Churchill, awaiting the chance to speak in Parliament and then to return to office in the Government, was about to leave his Westminster flat when the alarm sounded. He and his wife commented calmly on the German promptitude and precision. Ex-Detective Inspector W. H. Thompson, of Scotland Yard, Churchill's newly-appointed bodyguard, recalled later that while the sirens were still wailing, Churchill stalked to the entrance of the flats and stared up into the sky like a 'war horse scenting battle'. But there were no aircraft to be seen in the clear, cool September light, only the silver-grey cylindrical balloons which reflected the brilliant sunshine.

The bodyguard had some trouble in persuading his charge to take shelter. Churchill was reluctant to move from his observation point and finally did so only because he realized that he was expected to set an example. He grabbed a bottle of brandy and other 'appropriate medical comforts' and set off, leading the little party a hundred yards down the street to the prepared basement. In the shelter, he prowled around like a 'caged animal', to use Thompson's words, but the Ex-Detective Inspector had a shrewd idea that Churchill was relishing every moment.

The shelter which received the Churchills on that first alarm of the war consisted 'merely of an open basement, not even sandbagged, in which the tenants of half a dozen flats were already assembled', as Churchill himself later described the place. The tenants were cheerful and jocular, but the man who was destined to lead the nation through five terrible years to victory, could then think only of the 250,000 beds the Government had ready for the casualties from the first air-raids . . .

At the United States Embassy, the shelter that morning was occupied by the Ambassador, Mr. Joseph Kennedy, his wife, and two sons. The 50-year-old Boston Irish Ambassador had already conceived a dread of the might of German arms which was to lead him into controversial pessimistic public comments a few months later. To him, the air-raid sirens were a swift indication of the might of the Nazi armed forces which he feared might prove too much for the western allies. One of his sons, however, was more impressed that morning by the determination of the British people. He was twenty-two years old and his name was John F. Kennedy.

The young man who was to become President of the United States two decades later summed up his 3rd September feelings in a book, *Why England Slept*, which he published as an extension of his Harvard thesis. Kennedy said he sensed the confidence on the part of the British in their new armed power, which gave the country an entirely new outlook on the situation. He added: 'The result was a feeling of grim determination among the Government and the people. Plans proceeded efficiently and with few hitches. The balloon barrage was complete, as were the anti-aircraft defences, and the evacuation plans went through on schedule. The result was that Britain felt secure in her defences and believed that if they could get through the winter without a knock-out blow, England would have so built up her defences that she would easily be able to outlast Germany.'

While the alarm was in progress, a call came through on the emergency switchboard of the Foreign Office from the German Embassy. The switchboard girls became excited and flustered. They knew that Lord Halifax was at a Cabinet meeting, but the various private lines had not been marked. So they tried them all in turn until they got through to the Cabinet Office.

By this time, Halifax had left the Cabinet Office. They explained this to the Embassy, and asked if the Under-Secretary or anybody else could deal with the matter.

'Yes, of course,' was the reply. They merely wanted to be sure that their old black dog (which used to be a London landmark, sitting on the Embassy steps) would be looked after, as they could not take him back to Germany with them.

When Halifax arrived, somebody told him about the incident, and tired and weary though he was he immediately gave instructions to have the dog cared for. 'This human touch at the beginning of the world's greatest conflict will always remain vividly with me,' recalls Mr. J. McLoughlin, a telephone operator who was on duty at the Foreign Office that day.

Another glimpse of the nation as it was during those few anxious minutes after 11.30 a.m. is given by Inspector Alfred Hailstone, of the Buckinghamshire Police. When the air-raid warning was transmitted to the County Police Headquarters at Aylesbury, the officer in charge had been so conditioned to German air might that he instructed all personnel to work with their gas-masks on immediately. One poor fellow had left his at home and a discussion ensued 'as to which was the riskier course: to allow him to stay under cover and perhaps be exposed to all the horrors of gas warfare or take a chance and run home for it'. When the police officer finally left for home, Hailstone relates, such was the effect of the A.R.P. propaganda that 'many of his colleagues thought they were seeing him for the last time'.

The British people were to become apathetic about bombing in the months ahead of the 'phoney war'. But that morning the un-certainty of the effects of a big raid weighed heavily on the public imagination. Bombs had been dropped in recent years in China, Abys-sinia and Spain, but not on such large cities as London or Paris. Scientists and novelists alike had prepared the population for slaughter on an enormous scale. Men like Professor J. B. S. Haldane had cal-culated that each 500-bomber raid would result in 20,000 deaths. Writers had published such prose as this descriptive piece by Neil Bell (who, incidentally, had predicted world war on 3rd September, 1940):

'In a dozen parts of London, that night, people died in their homes with the familiar walls crashing about them in flames; thousands rushed into the streets to be met by blasts of flame and explosion and blown to rags; they came pouring out of suddenly darkened theatres, cinemas, pubs, concert and dance halls into the dark, con-gested streets to be crushed or burnt or trodden to death. . . . And presently fire came to add a last touch of hellishness to that mad struggle, in which frenzied men, women and children wedged them-selves into ever thickening and deepening masses, that at last were motionless and silent except for hands that waved and clutched feebly, and intermittent choking cries. . . .'

Fed on this literature of the nineteen-thirties it was not surprising that on that Sunday morning a number of people were found in London and other cities wandering, unaware of their surroundings and in a state of distress. The *British Medical Journal* later reported the diagnosis made by doctors as being precisely the same as for shell-shock. The minds of the victims had been temporarily deranged as the result of 'catastrophic anticipation'. They were the war's first casualties in Britain.

The 'all-clear' went after only ten minutes, without any onslaught from the skies. Londoners wondered what had happened; rumours spread of heavy attacks elsewhere in the capital, or alternatively of a massive defeat for the German bombers. Some joked about it. William Barkley, the Parliamentary Correspondent of the *Daily Express*, quipped to his editor that the false alarm had been organized by Neville Chamberlain because he was afraid to face the House at noon!

A statement from the Air Ministry disclosed that the alarm had been sounded because an aircraft had been observed approaching the south coast. The statement added: 'As its identity could not be readily determined, an air-raid warning was given. It was shortly afterwards identified as a friendly aircraft and the all-clear signal was sounded.'

In fact, the plane contained two French officers bound for London to join the Allied Air Mission. They had been so keen to get to London quickly that they had forgotten to inform the proper authorities of their flight. The passage of their aircraft had completely mystified the nation's air controllers and plane-spotters.

Officialdom, however, was able to take some pride in the way the capital had reacted to the alarm. There had been few hitches in the air-raid precautions, apart from the fact that too many children had been out in the streets during the ten minutes. People who worried about how the nation's art treasures would have fared had there been a real raid were advised in a noon statement from the Tate Gallery that a massive evacuation of precious works of art to secret places in the country had been completed. More than 60 per cent of the Gallery's 2,600 paintings and 400 pieces of sculpture had been evacuated to their rural sanctuaries by that morning.

Eight minutes after the sounding of the all-clear—at 11.48 a.m.—Britain's first air operation of the war was launched from the Royal Air Force Station at Wyton. A Blenheim of No. 139 Squadron of

Bomber Command, commanded by Flying Officer A. McPherson and carrying a naval observer and an air gunner, took off in the direction of Germany. Its mission: to make a reconnaissance of the naval base at Wilhelmshaven, to prepare for a later bombing raid in force.

Attacks on the German fleet were felt in Whitehall to be the only use to which bombers could be put in the early days of the war, although official British policy was to conserve the bomber force for attacks on German industry. But the R.A.F. was ill-prepared for any serious attempt to attack the German Navy. Apart from the few squadrons experienced in bombing trials against a naval wireless-controlled target ship, no training in the search for warship targets, in their recognition, or in methods of attacking them had been carried out by Bomber Command.

Though unwilling to dissipate its strength by small-scale attacks on what it believed to be secondary objectives—with which British naval forces were prepared to deal—the Air Ministry was prepared to see what could be done against naval targets with a limited force. But the policy on air bombardment, agreed with the French Government, was designed to avoid incurring responsibility for initiating air attacks on civil populations. The most important shore targets could not, for this reason, be attacked.

Bombing the German fleet while at sea or in the open waters of its bases—but not while in dockyards—was, however, permitted. All these considerations had been carefully weighed in Whitehall before the Blenheim took off on its historic mission. . . .

XII

Coulondre left the French Embassy in Berlin a few minutes before noon to make his final *démarche* to the German Foreign Office. He had tried to make an appointment with von Ribbentrop but had been told the Foreign Minister would not be available and he would have to be received by Secretary of State von Weizsacker. Coulondre reflected that it did not really matter to whom he handed the French ultimatum, but etiquette had to be observed until the end.

A medium-sized crowd of people were standing outside the Embassy building as Coulondre left to drive to the Wilhelmstrasse. They had not come to stage a hostile demonstration. Most were just passers-by, puzzled by the smoke coming from the Embassy chimneys as secret archives were burned.

As Coulondre got into his car, a young boy of about fifteen broke away from a group and came towards him. Coulondre momentarily wondered if he were going to hit him. But the boy merely held out a postcard and a fountain pen and asked for the Ambassador's autograph. 'I gave it to him and patted his face,' Coulondre said later.

At the Wilhelmstrasse, Coulondre's solemn presentation of the French ultimatum to von Weizsacker almost turned into a farce. To his question whether the State Secretary had authority to give him a 'satisfactory' reply, Weizsacker answered that he could not give him any reply, 'satisfactory or otherwise'.

The Ambassador was nonplussed. He had not expected this kind of answer and it upset all his ideas of protocol and diplomatic procedure. When he tried to interpret von Weizsacker's response as a negative German reply, in which case he could have handed him the formal French ultimatum, the latter simply declined to accept it. Von Weizsacker could only suggest that the Ambassador 'be good enough

to be patient a little longer and see the Foreign Minister personally'.
Von Weizsacker acted apologetically but Coulondre nevertheless
felt the snub. It irked him to be made to wait. However, it was not a
long wait. Herr von Ribbentrop presently returned from the reception
to the new Soviet Ambassador, Alexander Shkvarzev, who had been
given an extremely warm welcome by Hitler.

Von Weizsacker immediately conducted Coulondre to the Foreign
Minister and the French envoy went straight to the point. Could von
Ribbentrop give him a satisfactory reply to the note he had had the
honour of sending him on 1st September?

Von Ribbentrop was not prepared to give a straightforward answer
and was not going to miss this last opportunity to give the Frenchman
a personal interpretation of events. 'The delay in replying was due to
to Mussolini's initiative taken on 2nd September,' he began to explain. 'The Duce had offered to mediate,' he went on, 'and we were
prepared for a compromise if we had French agreement. Later Mussolini informed us that the compromise had failed owing to British
intransigence.

'This morning, the Ambassador of Great Britain gave us an unacceptable ultimatum which was rejected. If the French Government
considers itself bound, because of its engagements towards Poland,
to enter the conflict, I can only regret it. We shall only fight France
if she attacks us and it would be on her part a war of aggression.'

Coulondre listened to the rigmarole in silence, then asked: 'Must I
conclude from this that the German Government's reply to my letter
of 1st September is negative?' Von Ribbentrop replied 'yes', where-
upon the Ambassador read to him the content of the French ultimatum. 'Very well,' said the German in a cold voice. 'France will be
the aggressor.' Coulondre replied: 'History will be the judge of that.'

At 12.40 p.m., Coulondre handed to the Reich Foreign Minister
the same sort of courteous note that his British colleague, Henderson,
had delivered earlier. Written in French as a gesture fitting the mood
of the day, it said:

Your Excellency,

Not having received by noon on 3rd September a satisfactory reply
from the Government of the Reich to the letter which I presented to
you on 1st September at 10 p.m., I have the honour, on the instruc-

tions of my Government, to make the following communication to you.

The Government of the French Republic consider it their duty to point out for the last time the heavy responsibility assumed by the Government of the Reich in opening hostilities against Poland without a declaration of war and in not taking up the suggestion made by the Governments of the French Republic and of His Britannic Majesty to suspend all aggressive action against Poland and to declare themselves ready promptly to withdraw their forces from Polish territory.

In consequence, the Government of the Republic have the honour to inform the Government of the Reich that they find themselves obliged to fulfil, as from today, 3rd September at 5 p.m., the obligations which France has entered into towards Poland and which are known to the German Government.

Pray accept, Your Excellency, the assurance of my highest consideration,

Coulondre.

Von Weizsacker, who was present at the meeting, shook the Frenchman's hand firmly. But Coulondre did not proffer his hand to von Ribbentrop. Instead, he and the Foreign Minister looked into each other's eyes and the French diplomat got the impression that the German had not wanted the situation to develop in the way it had.

Coulondre returned to the Embassy feeling 'a little like a robot'. Now he was no longer involved, he felt a strange sense of detachment from himself and events around him. He was indifferent, 'a stranger to everything'. Back in his office, he stood for some time with his forehead pressed against the cold glass of the window, looking down at the amorphous, almost unmoving crowd of his new enemies down below. He felt heavy and solid, 'like a pebble rolled in a torrent for a long time'.

The Germans outside did not seem to Coulondre to be a people eager for war. There was 'no patriotic fever, none of the bellicose enthusiasm which accompanied the war of 1914. If the war with Poland was popular among the Nazi and military leaders, it did not seem to be with the man in the street . . .'

Coulondre reflected on the difference in wording between the allied ultimata. He did not accept then, or years later, criticism of the French for being 'afraid' to make a straightforward declaration of war on

Germany. Coulondre explained the terms of the French *démarche* in these words: 'The Polish-French defensive alliance was meant to come into effect automatically in the event of aggression on either country, this automatic effect having been solemnly and on several occasions brought to the notice of the German Government. Germany had put itself into a state of war with France and not France with Germany at the moment when, as my note formally stated, aggression took place.

'One will say that, even so, it was up to France and not Germany to decide on and decree a state of war. That is so, and internally the Government had to take into account the moves laid down in the constitution. But externally it was enough to state that our automatic alliance with Poland had come into effect.

'If, for example, the French Parliament had refused to follow the Government it could only have prevented France's entry into war by declaring that conditions foreseen as bringing about the operation of the Franco-Polish alliance, which in its own time it had ratified, had not been fulfilled.

'In these conditions, why aid von Ribbentrop's propaganda when he was trying to convince the German people that they had been unjustly attacked by the Western Powers? It is possible that certain French ministers may have sought, until the end, a way out even while our ally's blood was flowing, but he who wants to prove too much ends by proving nothing.'

XIII

Within minutes of Britain's declaration of war, messages of support and allegiance to the mother country poured in from every corner of the Commonwealth. Before Big Ben struck noon, reports from Ottawa had clearly indicated that Canada's entry into the war was imminent. On the principle that 'when Britain is at war, Canada is at war', first laid down by the great French-Canadian Prime Minister, Sir Wilfrid Laurier, Canada automatically entered the struggle against Hitler at 6 a.m. (Canadian time) when the British ultimatum to Berlin expired.

Canada's entry had been all but a foregone conclusion since the country's French-Canadian chief representative in the Government, Minister of Justice Ernest Lapointe, told Parliament in March that neutrality would be impossible for the Dominion in practice if the mother country were engaged in war. It had become certain on 1st September when the Prime Minister, Mr. W. L. Mackenzie King, sent a message to Chamberlain that his Government would recommend effective wartime co-operation with Britain to the Dominion Parliament.

Thus, at the outbreak of war, only the degree of Canada's participation remained to be decided. This decision, it was felt in Ottawa Cabinet circles, would largely be determined by the wishes of the British Government, but it was considered unlikely that Mr. King's recommendations to a special session of Parliament, called for 7th September, would include the immediate dispatch of even a volunteer expeditionary force.

'Our first concern,' the Prime Minister said that day in a broadcast speech, 'is with the defence of Canada. To be helpful to others we must ourselves be strong, secure and united. Our effort will be voluntary. In the process of defending herself, Canada will recruit new soldiers and train them. Later, if and when the British Government indicates the need for an expeditionary force and it becomes apparent that Canada is in no great danger of attack, there is no doubt that such a force will be sent.'

At 9 a.m. (Canadian time), the Cabinet met to put Canada for the second time in twenty-five years on a war footing. Later it was announced that 'in the effort to resist aggression, the Government of Canada had unanimously decided to seek its authority from Parliament for effective co-operation by Canada on the side of Britain'.

In Australia, nine hours ahead of British time, the declaration of war became known at 8.15 p.m. Mr. Robert Menzies and his ministers were at the Commonwealth Offices in Melbourne. The news reached them first not in the form of the official telegram which they had expected, but through short-wave radio reception of Chamberlain's broadcast. For a while there was some confusion, as the Australian leaders wondered whether to accept the broadcast in Chamberlain's voice as official news that Britain was at war.

Finally, they decided to take it as an official declaration, and their doubt was resolved shortly afterwards by a British Admiralty telegram announcing the commencement of hostilities against Germany. This message, received at the Navy Office in Melbourne, was passed on to Menzies. He at once summoned the Executive Council, which approved a prepared proclamation declaring a state of war to exist. Then the Australian leader prepared to broadcast to the nation. Menzies' view, widely known and supported in Australia, was that the British Commonwealth rested in unity on a common loyalty to the Crown. He had gone so far as to declare that any idea that the King could be at war in one part of his Empire and at peace in another was 'a metaphysical notion that quite eludes me'.

There were further reasons which hastened Australia's leader to move smartly into line with Britain. The great body of public opinion in the country clearly desired it, and Mr. Menzies and his ministers felt that a decisive show of united strength in the Commonwealth would have the effect of rallying resistance throughout the world against the latest German encroachments. The readiness of the Australian Government for the turn of events in Europe was to be clearly revealed on 15th September, when decisions which had in fact been

taken secretly in August were announced. These were to call up the
entire militia in two drafts of 40,000 men for a month's training,
and to enlist an expeditionary force of 20,000 which could be called
to service at home or abroad at any time. The Australian man-in-the-
street received the war news—through Chamberlain's broadcast—
calmly. Within a few minutes of receiving it, he heard his own Prime
Minister declare that Australia stood squarely beside Britain.

At 9.15 p.m. Australian time—just after noon in Britain—listeners to
every national and commercial broadcasting station in Australia heard
Menzies, speaking from the Postmaster-General's room in Melbourne's
Commonwealth Offices, declare: 'It is my melancholy duty to inform
you that, in consequence of a persistence by Germany in her invasion
of Poland, Great Britain has declared war upon her and that, as a
result, Australia is at war. No harder task can fall to the lot of a democratic leader than to make such an announcement.

'Great Britain and France, with the co-operation of the British
Dominions, have struggled to avoid this tragedy. They have, as I firmly
believe, been patient. They have kept the door of negotiation open;
they have given no cause for aggression. But in the result their efforts
have failed and we are, therefore, as a great family of nations involved
in a struggle which we must at all costs win, and which we believe in
our hearts we will win.'

The Prime Minister then reviewed the events of the preceding days,
making it clear that Hitler had been determined on war, and his proposals for a settlement had been merely a bid for world opinion before
he set his armies on the move. Menzies added: 'It is plain, indeed it
is brutally plain, that the Hitler ambition has been, not as he once said,
to unite the German peoples under one rule, but to bring under that
rule as many European countries, even of alien race, as can be subdued by force. If such a policy were allowed to go unchecked there
could be no security in Europe and there could be no peace for the
world.

'A halt has been called. Force has had to be resorted to, to check the
march of force. Honest dealing, the peaceful adjustment of differences,
the rights of independent peoples to live their own lives, the honouring
of international obligations and promises—all these things are at stake.
There never was any doubt as to where Great Britain stood in rela-

tion to them. There can be no doubt that where Great Britain stands, there stand the people of the entire British world.

'Bitter as we may feel at this wanton crime, this is not a moment for rhetoric. Prompt as the action of many thousands must be, it is for the rest a moment for quiet thinking, for that calm fortitude which rests not upon the beating of drums but upon the unconquerable spirit of man, created by God in his own image. What may be before us we do not know, nor how long the journey. But this we do know, that truth is our companion on that journey, that truth is with us in the battle, and that truth must win.

'Before I end, may I say this to you: in the bitter months that are to come, calmness, resoluteness, confidence and hard work will be required as never before. The war will involve not only soldiers and sailors and airmen, but supplies, foodstuffs, money. Our staying power, and particularly the staying power of the mother country, will be best assisted by keeping our production going; by continuing our avocations and our business as fully as we can; by maintaining employment, and with it our strength. I know that, in spite of the emotions we are all feeling, you will show that Australia is ready to see it through. May God in his mercy and compassion grant that the world may soon be delivered from this agony.'

Within an hour, Lord Gowrie, Australia's Governor-General, had signed the country's official proclamation of war, and immediately after that Sir Harry Brown, Director-General of Australian Posts and Telegraphs, ordered all radio amateurs off the air and told them to dismantle their equipment. The tough little Australian fleet also put to sea immediately in search of German merchant craft known to be in Australian waters, and possibly armed commerce raiders. Four cruisers, five destroyers and two sloops were soon at sea or making ready to leave harbour.

Some of the reservists who had been hurriedly called to the colours during the crisis of the previous few days were completely fresh to sea-going routine. The official Australian war history relates this classic story of an incident aboard the destroyer *Vampire* on that first night: the *Vampire*, after taking on reservists hurriedly in Port Melbourne, was passing through Port Phillip Heads when one of the shore batteries called her on a signalling lamp. The *Vampire*'s captain ordered a reserve signal rating: 'Answer the fort.' The rating replied: 'What do I do, sir?' The captain turned, astonished. 'You're a signalman, aren't you?' he asked. 'Well sir,' the man explained, 'they asked me at the depot what I was in civil life, and I said I was a signalman on the railways, and they said, "Right! You're a signalman." '

Within a few hours of hostilities commencing, at 1.50 a.m. Australian time on the 4th (4.50 p.m. the previous day in Britain) Australia's first shot of the war was fired from a fort at Port Phillip Heads across the bows of a small coastal steamer which failed to stop for examination. The captain explained later that he had given the name of his ship and thought he could enter without heaving to. The incident was one of the many historical echoes of the first days of the war, for the very same fort at Port Phillip Heads had fired Australia's first shot of the First World War on 5th August, 1914, across the bows of the German steamer *Pfalz*.

From New Zealand the same swift support for Britain followed within minutes of the news from London. Mr. Joseph Savage, the Prime Minister, said in a message of solidarity to the British Government that New Zealand fully concurred with Britain's action, which he regarded as 'inevitably forced upon the British Commonwealth if the cause of justice, freedom and democracy is to endure in this world'. Savage went on to declare: 'With reference to the intimation just received that a state of war exists between the United Kingdom and Germany, His Majesty's Government in New Zealand desire immediately to associate themselves with His Majesty's Government in the United Kingdom in honouring their pledged word . . .

'The existence of a state of war with Germany has accordingly been proclaimed in New Zealand, and H.M. New Zealand Government would be grateful if H.M. Government in the United Kingdom would take any steps that may be necessary to indicate to the German Government that H.M. Government in New Zealand associate themselves in this matter with the action taken by H.M. Government in the United Kingdom. The New Zealand Government wish to offer to the British Government the fullest assurances of all possible support. They are convinced that the step that has been taken will meet with the approval of the people of this Dominion and they will give the fullest consideration in due course to any suggestions of the British Government as to the methods by which this Dominion can best assist the common cause.'

Of the Dominions, only South Africa's position remained to be clarified. During the critical days before 3rd September there had been open discussion as to whether material assistance would be offered to Britain in the event of war. On the previous day the Prime Minister, General J. B. M. Hertzog, had told his Parliament that he would be making a statement shortly on South Africa's attitude 'in connection with the possible war position'.

The situation in South Africa had been coloured by five years of intensive Nazi propaganda, bribery and intimidation in the fertile soil of the many German pockets of population in the Union. From 1935 onwards, Germany had been carrying on a campaign to influence local opinion, and members of the Gestapo had been attached to German consulates to spread the Nazi gospel and put pressure on South Africans of German descent. By boosting trade, the Nazis had made many South African traders dependent on German purchases. Early in 1939 the German radio station at Zeesen had begun pumping out English and Afrikaans propaganda programmes, anti-semitic in tone and taking full advantage of the Afrikaaners' strong belief in white supremacy.

But Munich had already shown South Africa the danger signal and impressed the Government with the Nazi technique of intervening on behalf of 'repressed' German minorities. The damage to Hitler's image had been increased when the Germans entered Prague and the Nazis had lost much of South Africa's sympathy by the time a former German consul, Dr. von Oelhaven, told a Windhoek meeting of German youth in April, 1939: 'If you trust the Führer and rely on him, he will keep his pledge and liberate us in south-west Africa.'

Even so, the British declaration of war found South Africa unprepared and undecided, and the position was complicated by the fact that at midnight on 5th September the terms of office of a majority of the South African Senate were due to expire and there would then be no legal quorum to take decisions. So the stage was set for a political battle which was to split the Union Cabinet from top to bottom. A special Parliamentary session called to prolong the Senate's life had met on Saturday. Three p.m. on the 3rd found the Cabinet meeting at Groote Schuur, the magnificent old homestead bequeathed by Cecil Rhodes for the use of South Africa's Prime Ministers when they were in Capetown.

While the Cabinet argued fiercely, the Opposition's chief whip made a dramatic car dash from the city, shooting traffic lights, to give General Hertzog a message assuring him of the Opposition's support for any South African declaration of neutrality. But by the time he arrived, an irreparable rift had already occurred in the Cabinet. Seven of the thirteen ministers called for a declaration of war against Germany, both as a duty and in the country's own interest. Six, led by Hertzog, insisted on neutrality, while at the same time fulfilling South African obligations by defending the British naval port of Simonstown. Those for war were: General J. C. Smuts, Colonel Deneys Reitz, Mr. R. Stuttaford, Mr. H. G. Lawrence, Colonel W. R. Collins, Mr. R. H. Henderson and Mr. C. F. Clarkson. Those for neutrality: General Hertzog, Mr. N. C. Havenga, Mr. Oswald Pirow, Mr. A. P. J. Fourie, Mr. H. A. Fagan and General J. C. G. Kemp.

The next day the Union Parliament was to meet, passing in minutes the Bill prolonging the Senate's life and then witnessing Smuts and Hertzog firing their political broadsides for and against South Africa entering the war. Then the House was to divide in a strange political transmigration, leaving Hertzog with the entire Opposition behind him but only about thirty of his own supporters and resulting in his defeat by eighty votes to sixty-seven. Only then was the Prime Minister to see that he had lost the leadership of the country by staking it on South African neutrality, leaving Smuts, at the head of a new Government, to declare within hours the Union's solidarity with the powers at war against Germany.

South Africa's final entry into the war was to underline the overwhelming superiority in manpower and resources of the British and French Empires. Britain had only 600,000 of her forty-five million population under arms at the outbreak of war, and she produced just coal, iron ore and nitrates among the raw materials of war from her own resources. She depended entirely on imports for the rest—and four-fifths of her food. But these deficiencies were largely made up by the Commonwealth and Empire which also had an enormous potential military manpower.

Out of a total population of nearly 10,500,000, Canada's potential manpower was more than 2,750,000. Already the 50,000-man militia and the naval and air force services had been mobilized. Canada was also in a position to supply Britain with a steady flow of vital food-stuffs and various war materials including aircraft and munitions. Australia could also make a valuable contribution. With a population of nearly 7,000,000, her potential manpower was 1,900,000, but Australia's chief importance to the Empire was that she constituted both a food larder and a potential arsenal of the Pacific; twenty-three munitions annexes were to be in operation by the end of the year. New Zealand's population of 1,600,000 was able to muster a potential manpower of 400,000. A 16,000-strong militia was ready and fully equipped when the war broke out. From her total population of 10,-000,000, South Africa could produce a possible European force half a million strong. Only 15,000 were under arms on 3rd September. The country was capable of taking care of her own defence and could produce foodstuffs, clothing and some munitions for the Empire effort.

As the Dominions' pledges of allegiance flooded into Whitehall, nearly fifty of India's most powerful potentates also gave their support, and within a few hours others were expected to follow suit. India, on her way to becoming a Dominion, had the largest garrison and field force of any single unit of Britain's overseas Empire. It consisted of 55,000 men of the British Regular Army plus 160,000 of the Indian forces. Moreover, many of the Princes of the Indian States maintained private armies, some of which were likely to be offered for active service. In the First World War, India had sent 800,000 combatants and 400,000 non-combatants to Europe and had also supplied vast quantities of food and war materials.

France, with a population of 42,000,000, had 3,000,000 already under arms on 3rd September and was in the process of doubling that total. Her potential manpower was estimated at roughly 10,000,000. The Republic was almost self-sufficient in food production but of the necessary raw materials produced only iron ore, nickel, antimony, potash, phosphates, aluminium, coal and nitrates. The French Empire's population of 65,000,000 also constituted a vast reservoir of manpower. Moreover, the Empire abounded in vital war materials—coal in Indo-China, oil in North Africa, minerals and agricultural products elsewhere.

The Anglo-French declaration of war had brought Nazi Germany in conflict with two Empires which could summon economic reserves and additional manpower from every corner of the world. In reply, Greater

Germany, with a total population of 88,000,000, had 2,000,000 men under arms, with another million hastening to join them. The remaining trained reserve amounted to approximately a million. Total potential manpower was 17,500,000. In a military sense, however, Germany's central position to a considerable extent made up for the superior total manpower and resources of its enemies.

Of the twenty-two raw materials considered vital for the conduct of war, Germany produced in sufficient quantities only potash, zinc, coal and nitrates. The country was dependent on imports of iron ore, oil, copper, lead, sulphur, cotton, mica, rubber, aluminium, wool, manganese, phosphates, mercury, tungsten, tin, antimony and nickel. Large quantities of foodstuffs had also to be imported from abroad to supplement the insufficient German production.

During the early afternoon of 3rd September the ranks of the allied forces continued to grow. Newfoundland, Palestine, even remote Tonga in the mid-Pacific, were among those to declare support for the action against the Reich. Egypt also embraced the allied cause, and according to noon Press reports from Cairo, severed relations with Germany immediately after the Anglo-French declaration. The German minister in Cairo was to be handed his passports and the Egyptian Minister in Berlin recalled.

At the same time, the world's uncommitted nations were expressing varying degrees of neutrality. An urgent Cabinet meeting was held in Tokyo, in the course of which the Japanese Government decided to 'watch European developments and preserve freedom of action'. This decision was to be interpreted as 'undeclared neutrality' by the Press, and it was widely asserted that Germany's violation of the anti-Comintern Pact with Italy and Japan had placed Japan in a position of complete freedom.

Renzo Sawada, Japanese deputy Foreign Minister, in outlining the situation, explained that the former Cabinet's plans to strengthen the anti-Comintern Pact had been abandoned as a result of Germany's agreement with Soviet Russia. He then gave his colleagues an account of the present position in Europe from the latest dispatches of Japanese ambassadors. It was on the basis of this account that the Cabinet decided on its policy which, though qualified for the present by its intention to 'wait and see', was believed to envisage complete neutrality.

The Cabinet next considered the economic effects the European war was likely to have on Japan's industrial expansion and 'mobilization of materials', which were vital to the New Order Japan was attempting to create in China. It was to be anticipated that all Japan's military supplies from Europe would cease and that, moreover, Europe would absorb America's surplus. Japan would have to resign herself, it was felt, to a slowing down of the pace of both the war and reconstruction in China.

In Hong Kong, German residents were rounded up for internment in a requisitioned Catholic Church school around which a barbed wire fence was stretched. Several were reported as saying that they would 'rather get two meals a day in a Hong Kong prison camp than return to the Fatherland'. The Hong Kong authorities appealed for 2,000 volunteers to take training as wardens in A.R.P. work, in addition to several hundred already qualified. Hong Kong was put on a complete wartime basis that day. Decrees were announced regulating the conduct of individuals, the movement of ships and aircraft, and the operation of communications. British warships took up positions at the entrance to the harbour through which all other vessels would have to pass. Civil aircraft operators were warned that any plane contravening the new regulations was liable to be shot down by Hong Kong's guns. A strict censorship was imposed immediately on all telegraphic and radio communications, and the licences of Hong Kong's ten amateur radio broadcasting stations were revoked.

In Chungking, the Indian Nationalist leader Jawaharlal Nehru decided to cut short his visit to China and hurry home to summon the all-India Congress at Calcutta to decide the Indian attitude towards the European war. Chiang Kai-Shek, the Chinese Generalissimo with whom Nehru had been conferring, immediately placed a special aircraft at his disposal. Chungking Sunday newspapers, reflecting all shades of political opinion, generally spoke in favour of a 'sympathetic' attitude towards Britain and France.

The Chinese Communist Press, however, condemned the western allies as 'imperialist war-mongers', attacked the Chiang Kai-Shek administration for its co-operation with the United States and Britain and issued fresh calls for alignment with Soviet Russia. Mao Tse-tung, the Communist leader then linked to Chiang Kai-Shek in an uneasy alliance against the Japanese invaders, had resolved that week-end his embarrassing problems posed by the Russo-German Mutual Assistance Pact. In a statement to the *Hsinhua Daily News*, a Communist organ, he explained the new Party line in these terms: 'The said Pact upsets the intrigue of Chamberlain and Daladier and the international reactionary capitalist class to provoke a war between Soviet Russia and Germany, upsets the encirclement of Soviet Russia by the reactionary *bloc* of Italy, Germany and Japan, and solidifies the peace between Soviet Russia and Germany and secures further progress of Socialist reconstruction in Soviet Russia.'

Sweden, Norway, Denmark, Finland, Belgium and Iceland all declared their neutrality within hours of the British and French war declarations, but at the same time blackout preparations went on in many Scandinavian cities. In sunlit Copenhagen, however, the Danes continued with the preparations for the fiercely contested cycling sprint championships. In Denmark, despite neutrality, mobilization began, though the population was hopeful of avoiding involvement in the conflict. In Sweden, private car traffic was officially curtailed that day and the sale of petrol to private car-owners forbidden.

In Bratislava, War Minister General Ferdinand Csatlos told the fully mobilized Slovakian Army of 300,000 that Slovak interests had become 'allied to the German Army and in hostile relationship to Poland'. Premier Josef Tiso made a speech declaring that his Army 'will defend our independence and recover our historic territories from Poland'. So, the little country under German 'protection' since the previous year, became an ally of Berlin in the middle of 3rd September—to nobody's surprise.

PART THREE

Noon to 6 p.m.

I

Modern history's most cynical alliance was being strengthened at the very moment that M. Coulondre was cooling his heels at the German Foreign Office. However much he may have desired to play the correct Foreign Minister until the bitter end, von Ribbentrop had a very pressing reason for keeping his visitor waiting: the Führer was receiving the new Soviet Ambassador, M. Alexander Shkvarzev. He and the new Soviet Military Attaché, General Maxim Purkajev, had flown into Berlin the previous day in a Russian military aircraft.

All the trappings of Nazi military might were paraded for the Russian V.I.P.s. A hand-picked guard of honour, larger than would normally be on duty, greeted the Soviet diplomats as they arrived at the Chancellery. Inside, the new Ambassador presented his credentials and then all four men began a highly secret discussion from which secretaries and aides were excluded. Von Ribbentrop stayed for only a quarter of an hour, but the Russians remained with Hitler until well past 1 p.m. for what an official communiqué said later was a 'lengthy talk'.

The Führer had plenty to discuss with the Russians, and he can be assumed to have used all his charm on the newest and most highly regarded members of the Berlin Diplomatic Corps. They had one major item on their agenda: the fourth partition of Poland. For, since 23rd August, Communist Russia and Fascist Germany, bitter enemies for the greater part of a decade, had been signatories to a ten-year non-aggression pact. The agreement had been negotiated in Moscow by von Ribbentrop, so this was Hitler's first opportunity to sound out Russian views on the future of the alliance at first hand. No record exists of what transpired at the Chancellery from noon onwards, but from public attitudes then being adopted by the totalitarian states towards one another it can be inferred that it was as cordial an affair as could be imagined. The Press of Moscow and Berlin were cooing at one another that day and Hitler, his biggest headache solved at least temporarily by the willingness of the Russians to share in the plunder of Poland, could easily and profitably turn on the smile and friendliness that he normally reserved for blonde aryan women or foreigners likely to be useful to him.

The 23rd August Pact, following a trade agreement between the two countries highly advantageous to Soviet Russia, had been effective from the hour of signature. Both partners guaranteed each other absolute neutrality if either were attacked by a third party. Provision was made for regular consultations on questions of mutual interest and friendly discussions in case of disagreement. But the world was not to know until much later of secret codicils to the Pact, laying down the division of Poland with the rivers Narew, Vistula and San as the demarcation line. The question of an independent Polish State was left open in the agreement, to be decided by Russia and Germany later. Division of the Baltic states was also settled in the codicils, according to spheres of interest. Estonia and Latvia were allotted to the Soviet Union, Lithuania to Germany. Finally, in south-eastern Europe, the Russians emphasized their interest in Bessarabia which the Soviet Union had lost to Rumania in 1919 and the Germans declared their disinterest in the territory—a concession the Reich was later to regret.

Since the announcement of the general outline of the agreement had burst on the world like a bombshell, all hostile propaganda between the two states had ceased, thanks to the total control in Moscow and Berlin of all organs of public opinion. The newspapers in both capitals had been engaged now for days in mutual declarations of everlasting friendship and in publishing editorials giving an historical justification for the new friendship with remarks about the Nineteenth-Century Prussian wars of liberation, Bismarck and Rapallo.

All over the world, Communists had been shocked in varying degrees by the *volte-face* of their masters in Moscow and were trying, without much success, to explain the new Kremlin policy to followers and friends. Many, sickened by the obvious cynicisms of the deal, had already quit the Party. Stalin, the tyrant and realist in the Kremlin, had taken the step out of pure self interest and because he was confident that the western powers would desert Poland as they had abandoned Czechoslovakia to her fate. Britain and France had made half-hearted and tardy overtures to Russia in the summer of 1939, but the manner of the western approaches convinced Stalin that he could do far better for himself through even a temporary arrangement with Hitler. On top of that, Hitler had shown himself willing during August to concede to Russia an increase in her sphere of influence in Eastern Europe.

Stalin was to justify his conduct after the German attack on Russia in July 1941, by declaring that the Pact had secured peace for Russia for eighteen months and thereby enabled her to complete military preparations. But the Soviet dictator would not mention the immense territorial gains the agreement brought to the Kremlin, which proved to be important not only for defence but as an avenue for political infiltration into Europe. In all, Russia was to gain 200,000 square kilometres of territory and thirteen million inhabitants by the fourth division of Poland, which was then exactly a fortnight away.

On 3rd September, therefore, the Pact with Germany must have appeared to Stalin to be a definite gain for the Soviet Union. Even Churchill was later to concede that it was at the time 'realistic in a high degree'. But the Russian dictator was not to know that within a year the French would be vanquished, the British swept from the Continent and no chance of a 'second front' on land against Germany until 1944. Russia was going to need every minute of the breathing space she had bought so dearly from the people reviled so long from every Communist platform as 'fascist beasts'. . . .

Just before Hitler had greeted the new Soviet envoy in Berlin, a short interview had been granted in Moscow by the Russian Foreign Minister, Vacheslav Molotov, to the Polish Ambassador to the Soviet Union, Waclaw Grzybowski. The latter had officially informed Molotov the previous day of the German aggression and of the fact that his country was at war. Late on Sunday morning he returned to Molotov to describe the situation in more detail and to attempt to clarify Russian intentions towards his own country.

Molotov did not question the Polish diplomat's statement that the German attack was a case of 'unprovoked aggression committed without previous declaration of war, by a surprise attack during negotiations'. He agreed, Grzybowski reported to his government later, in recognizing Germany as the aggressor. And the Soviet Foreign Minister even reacted favourably to the idea of giving indirect aid 'in economic guise' to Poland. Molotov then asked whether Poland counted on the intervention of Britain and France, and whether they expected any time limit. The Pole told him he had no official information, but anticipated the western declarations of war would follow the next day, 4th September. Molotov 'smiled sceptically', and then replied to the anxious Pole: 'Well, we shall see, Monsieur l'Ambassadeur . . .'

Molotov had his answer within an hour of making that cynical remark. He was obviously as surprised as most Russians by the British declaration of war, which caused a sensation in the Soviet capital. From noon onwards, western correspondents in Moscow began cabling thousands of words describing the Russian bewilderment at the sudden ending of appeasement. The *Havas* correspondent reported that Russians had laughed and shrugged their shoulders whenever foreigners told them that the British and French would fight. 'News of the war,' the *Daily Telegraph* correspondent wrote, 'astonished the Russians. They expected a compromise.'

A reporter for the *Posledniya Novosti* in Paris sent the following Moscow reaction story to his newspaper that afternoon: 'Events in Europe have completely stupefied the Russian people. Up to 1st September everyone in the Kremlin was certain that the democracies would not declare war on Germany; that they would capitulate to Hitler; and that the German-Polish conflict would end in a conference patterned after Munich. Hence they considered it advantageous to be on the side of the strong rather than the weak. Molotov and particularly Zhdanov had no doubt but that the new European conflict would result in another bloodless victory for Hitler and von Ribbentrop.'

The Soviet Ambassador in London, Maisky, a well known and widely liked figure in many walks of British life, was bearing the brunt that afternoon of much bitter criticism of his country's alliance with Nazi Germany. Many friends turned their backs on him as he arrived at the House of Commons for the noon session of Parliament. Hugh Dalton thought that Maisky looked 'tense and unhappy' at the House and told the Russian: 'Your Government has greatly disconcerted us. But I hope that some of us will still keep in touch with you from time to time.' Maisky replied that he hoped so, too, and added: 'Don't believe everything you read about our Pact with Germany. We are neutral now. All our future actions will be guided, not by sentiment, but by self-interest.'

A little parlour game which had suddenly become popular in Britain, echoed that view. Many people were joking about it the day war started. One wrote the following words one under the other:

Mussolini
Hitler
Chamberlain
Daladier
Which
Wins?

One found the answer by drawing a line through the third letter in each word. It spelled out: Stalin.

II

At noon in London the House of Commons began a session in a brisk, determined mood. The benches were packed with quietly determined legislators. Party loyalties had clearly been submerged in the common interest and the frustration and unrest of the previous day's sitting had dissolved almost miraculously. The House had met on Sunday only on three previous occasions in British history, each time immediately following the death of a monarch. The last Sunday sitting had occurred 119 years previously on 30th January, 1820, on the accession of George IV following the death of George III.

But never before had the Commons met on a Sunday to learn that Britain was at war. In one of the most dramatic Parliamentary sessions of the century, spokesmen for the Opposition and First World War leaders like David Lloyd George and Winston Churchill pledged their support for the Government's action. The sitting began with messages from the House of Lords that the Peers had agreed to certain priority bills designed to gear the country's armed forces and civilians for war. They included provisions to extend the service of Royal Marines and to impose penalties for trading with the enemy.

The Prime Minister hurried into the House at 12.05 and rose to speak at once. He was greeted with cheers by colleagues who would have swept him out of office in minutes if the events of the past few hours had taken a different turn. As he glanced briefly around, familiar faces caught his eye. Just across the gangway from the Government Bench, Churchill sat with shoulders hunched forward determinedly and Lloyd George with bowed white head, his hands characteristically crossed on his broad chest.

Both had sat in the same House, twenty-five years and one month previously to hear that earlier declaration of war on Germany.

'Jimmy' Maxton, the Independent Labour Leader, made plain he did not like what was going on, and one American Correspondent John Gunther, noted from the Press Gallery that Maxton looked like a Dante who 'had just had a bad dream'. The first bout of cheering died and Chamberlain began to speak in a slow, weary voice that faltered sometimes.

'When I spoke last night to the House,' he said, 'I could not but be aware that in some parts of the House there were doubts and some bewilderment as to whether there had been any weakening, hesitation or vacillation on the part of His Majesty's Government. In the circumstances I make no reproach, for if I had been in the same position as Hon. Members not sitting on this Bench and not in possession of all the information which we have, I should very likely have felt the same.

'The statement which I have to make this morning will show that there were no grounds for doubt. We were in consultation all day yesterday with the French Government and we felt that the intensified action which the Germans were taking against Poland allowed no delay in making our own position clear. Accordingly, we decided to send to our Ambassador in Berlin instructions which he was to hand at nine o'clock this morning to the German Foreign Secretary.'

Chamberlain then read the text of the British ultimatum to Hitler to a hushed House. He finished, and looked up. 'That was the final Note,' he declared firmly. 'No such undertaking was received by the time stipulated, and consequently this country is at war with Germany.

'I am in a position to inform the House that, according to arrangements made between the British and French Governments, the French Ambassador in Berlin is at this moment making a similar *démarche*, accompanied also by a definite time limit. The House has already been made aware of our plans. As I said the other day, we are ready.

'This is a sad day for all of us, and to none is it sadder than to me. Everything that I have worked for, everything that I have believed in during my public life, has crashed into ruins. There is only one thing left for me to do; that is, to devote what strength and powers I have to forwarding the victory of the cause for which we have sacrificed so much. I cannot tell what part I may be allowed to play myself; I trust I may live to see the day when Hitlerism has been destroyed and a liberated Europe has been re-established.'

The Prime Minister had spoken for five minutes. Five minutes that had kept himself and his Government in office, and which had also altered the course of world history. He was greeted with subdued but moving cheers, and Arthur Greenwood, deputy leader of the Labour Party, quickly took the floor, in the absence through illness of his leader, the then Mr. Clement Attlee.

He did not deny himself a reference to the previous night's fears that 'delays might end in national dishonour and the sacrifice of the Polish people to German tyranny'. But Greenwood then continued: 'This morning we meet in an entirely different atmosphere—one of relief, one of composure, and one of resolution. The intolerable agony of suspense from which all of us have suffered is over; we now know the worst.

'The hated word "war" has been spoken by Britain, in fulfilment of her pledged word and unbreakable intention to defend Poland and so to defend the liberties of Europe. We have heard more than the word spoken. We have heard the war begin, within the precincts of this House.'

Paying tribute to Poland—'who for fifty-four hours had stood alone, at the portals of civilization, defending us and all free nations'—Greenwood declared: 'Nazism must be finally overthrown.' He went on to pledge his party's 'wholehearted support to the measures necessary to equip this State with the powers that are desired'. But he also issued a grave warning to Chamberlain and his Government that should there be 'inefficiency and wavering' then 'other men must be called to take their place'.

Sir Archibald Sinclair, the Liberal leader, followed Greenwood with a declaration of his belief that at the moment France was ahead of Britain in her preparations for war. 'Great advances have been made in our organization for war, but in individual preparation, in the contributions which the men and women of the two countries are making to the common cause, I say that France at this moment is ahead of us. If you go to France and meet ten people in the streets you may be sure that eight of them have their places and their parts to play. Our people will do the same as time goes on, but let us have no doubt as to the determination with which the French people are facing this crisis.

'Let me only say in conclusion: let the world know that the British people are inexorably determined, as the Prime Minister said, to end this Nazi domination for ever and build a world order based on justice and freedom.'

With the basic solidarity of the House and the nation established with these three speeches, Winston Churchill rose to add, in a five-minute speech, his unparalleled oratory to the cause.

'In this solemn hour,' said Churchill, 'it is a consolation to recall and to dwell upon our repeated efforts for peace. All have been ill-starred, but all have been faithful and sincere. This is of the highest moral value—and not only moral value, but practical value—at the present time, because the wholehearted concurrence of scores of millions of men and women, whose co-operation is indispensable and whose comradeship and brotherhood are indispensable, is the only foundation upon which the trial and tribulation of modern war can be endured and surmounted.

'This moral conviction alone affords that ever-fresh resilience which renews the strength and energy of people in long, doubtful and dark days. Outside, the storms of war may blow and the lands may be lashed with the fury of its gales, but in our own hearts this Sunday morning there is peace. Our hands may be active, but our consciences are at rest.

'We must not underrate the gravity of the task which lies before us or the temerity of the ordeal, to which we shall not be found un-equal. We must expect many disappointments and many unpleasant surprises, but we may be sure that the task which we have freely accepted is one not beyond the compass and the strength of the British Empire and the French Republic.

'The Prime Minister said it was a sad day, and that is indeed true, but at the present time there is another note which may be present, and that is a feeling of thankfulness that, if these great trials were to come upon our island, there is a generation of Britons here now ready to prove itself not unworthy of those great men, the fathers of our land, who laid the foundations of our laws and shaped the greatness of our country.

'This is not a question of fighting for Danzig or fighting for Poland. We are fighting to save the whole world from the pestilence of Nazi tyranny and in defence of all that is most sacred to man. This is no war for domination or imperial aggrandisement or material gain; no war to shut any country out of its sunlight and means of progress.

'It is a war, viewed in its inherent quality, to establish on impregnable rocks the rights of the individual, and it is a war to establish and revive the stature of man. Perhaps it might seem a paradox that a war undertaken in the name of liberty and right should require, as a necessary part of its processes, the surrender for the time being of so many of the dearly valued liberties and rights. In these last few days the House of Commons has been voting dozens of Bills which hand over to the executive our most dearly valued traditional liberties.

'We are sure that these liberties will be in hands which will not abuse them, which will use them for no class or party interests, which will cherish and guard them, and we look forward to the day, surely and confidently we look forward to the day, when our liberties and rights will be restored to us, and when we shall be able to share them with the peoples to whom such blessings are unknown.'

A few minutes after Churchill, Mr. David Lloyd George, one of the last living giants of the First World War, rose to draw on his experience to encourage the House. In a brief, lucid speech he said: 'The Government are now confronted with the latest, but I am afraid not the last, of a series of acts of brigandage by a very formidable military Power, which if they are left unchallenged will undermine the whole foundation of civilization throughout the whole world.

'The Government could do no other than what they have done. I am one out of tens of millions in this country who will back any Government that is in power in fighting this struggle through, in however humble a capacity we may be called upon to render service to our country. I have been through this before, and there is only one word I want to say about that.

'We had very bad moments, moments when brave men were rather quailing and doubting, but the nation was firm right through, from beginning to end. One thing that struck me then was that it was in moments of disaster, and in some of the worst disasters with which we were confronted in the War, that I found the greatest union among all classes, the greatest disappearance of discontent and disaffection, and of the grabbing for rights and privileges. The nation closed its ranks then. By that means we went through right to the end, and after four and a half years, terrible years, we won a victory for right. We will do it again.'

General Sir Edward Spears, an observer of the proceedings, commented later that 'Lloyd George, in a three minutes' speech, did best of all'. Sir Edward added: 'We realized that we had heard a great and comforting truth and we knew that it would be exactly the same this time, though the ordeal might be far worse. The serenity flowing from words which voiced so accurately the inner feelings of everyone gave reality to the confidence each of us had in our country, of which we felt so completely, so warmly, so cosily a part. I felt, as so many must have, positive relief in the clear and quite sudden realization that all inhibiting social barriers had fallen away.'

When the cheers for Lloyd George had subsided, Brigadier-General Sir Henry Croft spoke up on behalf of the 'old Tories'—the Government's right-wing supporters. In ringing tones he told the House: 'I hope that we shall all be heartened with the knowledge that in the great Dominions overseas today hearts are pulsating for liberty and freedom in precisely the same way as in the old land. It was my supreme privilege, in many bloody battles, to stand with Australians, New Zealanders and South Africans in the Great War, and there can be no doubt whatever that the coming of those mighty hosts from overseas turned the scales in favour of victory. I should like, as a private individual, to say to the Dominions that we have confidence that in this struggle, however dire and long the fight may be, they will be with us right to the end.'

The veteran Labour leader, Mr. George Lansbury, spoke with apprehension of the possibility of massive air-raids and the effect of total war on the British population. He declared: 'I want to ask the Prime Minister and the Government when they are considering the question of aerial warfare as they have considered it once, and may consider it again, whether even now it would not be possible to make a proposal to Germany and the world that we would be perfectly willing to abolish aerial warfare in its entirety.'

Mr. Lansbury added that he had just come from an air-raid shelter and while he was struck by the calmness of the people he felt there was an underlying feeling that it was terrible to think that 'either young people or old people should have lived to see the day when those foul weapons are being used'. Repeating his request that the Government should consider his suggestion, Lansbury said: 'I hope that out of this calamity there will arise a real spirit, a spirit that will compel people to give up reliance on force, and that perhaps this time humanity will learn the lesson and refuse in the future to put its trust in poison gas, in the massacre of little children and universal slaughter.'

Anyone watching the Prime Minister closely as Mr. J. P. Morgan rose to speak, might have noticed a hint of impatience in his mien. He had had ample opportunity to gauge the mood of the House which was one—on matters of principle—of strong unity. Chamberlain was now anxious to speed through the Commons the flood of legislation urgently needed to mobilize the forces and prepare for the ordeal ahead. Mr. Morgan had done little more than express his 'admiration' for the Prime Minister, the deputy leader of the Opposition and most of the other speakers, when Chamberlain rose and appealed to the House to bring the proceedings to a close.

A sense of urgency returned to the Commons with his words: 'There is an immense amount of work to be done, and I am extremely anxious to get it through.' But the Communist member, Mr. William Gallacher, had a 'necessary and desirable' statement to make in which he called for the 'speedy and effective defeat' of the Nazi régime. 'In taking that stand,' he added, 'I want to declare here with the utmost confidence, from experience and from knowledge, that I will not come into conflict with the policy of my working-class comrades of the Soviet Union.'

The entire House of Commons then went into Committee to consider the National Service (Armed Forces) Bill. It immediately became apparent that though the House was united on the need for war, and supported the Government's declaration of it, there still remained much of the traditional tooth-and-nail bargaining to be done over individual measures.

Members passed immediately a measure approving whatever expenditure was necessary in enlisting man-power for the armed forces. But at three minutes to one, when it came to discussing the National Service Bill, there was tortuous and at times heated discussion on whether the minimum age for military service for Britons should be eighteen, as the Bill provided, or twenty.

An opposition amendment raising the age to twenty was pushed back and forth across the House for an hour before being withdrawn. Almost every speaker apologized in some way for taking up the House's time. Government and Opposition members prefaced general arguments and personal reminiscences of the First World War with such remarks as . . . 'Naturally, I do not wish to break the spirit of unity in any way' . . . 'I did not make a long speech because I was very anxious, if possible, that we should not have a long debate' . . . 'I interrupt the Right Hon. Gentleman because I am anxious to avoid controversy' . . .

As the debate dragged on, speakers introduced themselves with . . . 'It seems to me that we really are disputing on nothing at all' . . . 'I see no reason why we should be forced into the Division Lobby.' Finally, at 1.59 p.m., Mr. Hore-Belisha, Secretary of State for War, broke the deadlock by announcing that the previous two speakers, who had offered modified forms of the Opposition proposal, 'have made it quite easy for me.

'I understand that what Hon. Members require is an assurance from me that, if possible, before sending any man called up under the Bill out of the country when under the age of twenty, I should, if still in my present position, make a statement to the House . . . explaining the circumstances which have rendered that course necessary. That, I understand, is the sense of the request. I hope there has been no ill will in the discussion, and I cannot think there is any real difference between us, and therefore I can give an affirmative answer to the question.'

Before the amendment was withdrawn, there was a quick exchange of parting thrusts between Hore-Belisha and Mr. Alexander, the chief Labour spokesman for the amendment. Mr. Alexander: 'I hope that on any further Amendment we may get a quicker acceptance when we offer a reasonable compromise.' Hore-Belisha: 'The original request was different or there would not have been a difficulty.'

Hore-Belisha spoke as Big Ben chimed two o'clock. The House had been sitting for two hours and it was clear that all the great traditions of Parliamentary democracy at Westminster could not be swept aside by even the urgency of war. It was reassuring to detached observers, but rather irritating to Chamberlain and his fellow Ministers, anxious to set the machinery of war in full motion.

At 2 p.m. the House, still in Committee, was ready to move on to further clauses of the Bill. But Colonel Wedgwood, the member for Newcastle-under-Lyme, became embroiled in a lengthy dispute with the Chairman, Sir Dennis Herbert, on a point of order. The

Colonel wanted the Bill amended so that non-British subjects, such
as refugees from Austria or Czechoslovakia, could enlist as volunteers
for service under the British flag. In between interjected rulings by
Sir Dennis, Colonel Wedgwood was at least able to make his point,
if not to have it discussed.

'In the last War,' he said, with one eye warily on the Chair, 'directly
the Government got power to conscript Englishmen and Scotsmen the
people in the War Office immediately said: "Now we have all the
real, true Britons we need, and we can avoid calling upon the services
of black men, half-castes, Maltese and Cypriots."

'I want to know whether that silly business is going on in the War
Office again. Now that they have these powers of conscripting Englishmen, will they still think that only Englishmen are fit to be called up?
Will they not accept the voluntary offers of British subjects or of people who are refugees in this country?'

Colonel Wedgwood, repeatedly ruled out of order, gave up finally
after telling the Chairman, 'I deny your ruling.' (The 200,000-odd
aliens in Britain—many refugees from Nazi oppression—were destined
to wait a few more weeks before, after being vetted by special Alien
Courts, they could take up arms under the British flag against Hitler.)

III

News of the British and French actions against Germany reached Warsaw soon after noon and touched off the last hours of unrestrained
rejoicing and happiness that the Polish people have known. All the
tensions, suspicions and fears of the previous days were dissolved in a
few hours of radiant joy which remain one of life's most searing memories for all who were present in the Polish capital that day.

The first radio announcement of Britain's entry into the war, by all
accounts, was followed generally by an astonished silence which lasted
while several verses of the British National Anthem were played. For
a few minutes this was almost the only sound to be heard in all Warsaw. Then, spontaneously, pandemonium broke loose. People poured
into the warm, sunlit streets, cheering and laughing. Cars sounded
their horns continually. Weeping, shouting mobs milled everywhere,
appearing as though from nowhere. This poignant display of emotion
and relief that they were no longer alone reached an incredible climax
by one o'clock when France's intentions were also common knowledge.

Those fantastic scenes as Warsaw fired with fresh hope were burned
for ever into the minds of all who saw them. In later years they recalled with tears the irony of what then seemed the turn of the tide,
but was in fact the last time that a free Poland could have any occasion to rejoice. For three days the Poles had listened to the clipped,
unemotional war communiqués put out by their High Command. The
communiqués had not reflected the stark simplicity of the true picture
at the fronts—that Poland was on her knees. But Warsaw's man-in-the-
street knew instinctively that his country was in grave peril. He had
nothing on which to pin his hopes except the agonizingly delayed
promise of salvation by the western allies.

The Polish writer Rulka Langer recalled later that before the news that Poland's allies were with her, there was a 'strange apprehension in everybody's mind' and 'the whole atmosphere was sticky with suspicion'. When the announcement of the British and French declarations came, 'people went wild with joy, we yelled and whooped and almost kissed our neighbours. We sang "Jeszcze Polska" and "God Save the King". Of course no one knew how to sing it but we all tried our best.

'Now that Britain and France had joined the war, Hitler was sure to be beaten. Germany could never stand a war on two fronts. If we could only hold out for some time our western allies would launch a big offensive and then the pressure on our front would be relieved. Then our army, too, would start an offensive and we would chase the Germans as far as Berlin. Yes, Berlin. The big brutes needed a lesson. They would get it. Now that Britain and France had decided to fulfil their pledge to come to Poland's rescue whenever she was attacked by Germany we no longer had to worry about the outcome of this war. No matter what hardships and sacrifices lay ahead of us, the final victory was assured . . .'

Nothing could dampen the Poles' enthusiasm, not even an air-raid warning, although at that hour, as Warsaw pulsed with a new courage, a few German bombs could have decimated the city's population. Poles, who had hoped and prayed fervently for this moment, would not be denied any expression of their joy by the straining police cordon around the British Embassy. They surged up to the building, pinning and crushing the police, who cursed good-naturedly, against the railings. They climbed on to the running-boards of the diplomatic and military attachés' cars crawling out of the courtyard.

The British wife of a Warsaw citizen, caught up and carried along with the surging crowd, recalled later in her diary: 'I surged forward again to the same railings, fell back again before the same cordon, and shouted the same things over and over again until I was nearly voiceless and senseless.

'A thing called the crowd had taken my place. The wheel of an outgoing car did not crush my foot; only a foot belonging to the crowd. It was not I who had my ribs nearly broken by the pressure on both sides and was most uselessly exposing myself to massacre from the air if the raiders took their opportunity. Only the crowd felt, willed, changed or kept a direction . . .'

The happy demonstrators repeatedly shouted a Polish-coloured version of 'God save England'—which came out more like 'Gott safe England'. An old man, deeply moved by the scene and the reason for it, stood beside British Correspondent Cedric Salter outside the Embassy. Grasping the Englishman by the hand, with tears in his eyes, he murmured over and over again: 'Gott straf England.' Salter 'had not the heart to correct him'.

Among the official cars threading their way slowly through the exultant crowds as the clocks moved towards 1 p.m. was that of a deeply relieved and grateful Joseph Beck, on an errand of thanks for his people. Beck was relieved, but so was Sir Howard Kennard, the British Ambassador, that Britain had honoured her pledge. Kennard, though an undemonstrative man, had felt keenly his position in Warsaw in the long, anxious hours before Britain declared war. He had shared with the Government in London the agony and the embarrassment of Poland's entreaties for help. Now his faith in his own country had been vindicated, but he had an embarrassment of a different nature, as the insistent demands of the crowd drew him out reluctantly to the Embassy balcony.

The envoy made repeated shy, jerky appearances on the balcony, each time to a renewed, louder burst of acclaim before Beck joined him to add moral support. Indeed, on more than one occasion the Polish Foreign Minister, sensing and sharing the mood of his countrymen, tactfully blocked Kennard's way back into the Embassy and drew him forward again into view of the crowd.

The two men stood there amid tears and pelting of flowers until, urged on by Colonel Beck, Sir Howard made a brief speech to the frenzied Poles. Speaking in Polish—which drew a great roar of enthusiasm from the crowd—he declared: 'Long live Poland. We will fight side by side against aggression and injustice.' The throng yelled its approval. Even in the heat of the moment, every Pole knew what agonies the decision to enter the war had cost the men in Whitehall.

Each man and woman there realized that Britain, unlike Poland, had chosen this course. She was not threatened on her borders, her cities were not being ravaged by bombers. Enemy feet were not tramping across her island soil. Britain had elected to stand between Poland and Germany, to lay herself open to unimaginable sufferings and losses in the cause of friendship and freedom. So Sir Howard Kennard's words, albeit no great speech, were sufficient for the day.

Then Beck stepped forward and told the crowd: 'Britain and Poland have locked hands in a fight for freedom and justice. Britain will not be disappointed in Poland and Poland will not be disappointed in Britain.'

Warsaw was doomed to lie in ruins at the enemy's feet within twenty-four days when both men would have left the country. But at that moment, they appeared to be speaking for an alliance which would last for ever. Kennard at last left the balcony and the crowd began to pile it with flowers. The struggling police were co-opted into the task of passing up the flowers which soon filled the balcony to overflowing. Then British and French army officers appeared on the scene to add to the excitement, and to salute each burst of acclamation.

A company of young Polish soldiers marched by on their way to the front and the crowd made a path for them. As the Poles passed the Embassy, they chanted 'Long Live England and Poland! Long live King George! We'll soon be in Berlin now!' Each catch-cry was quickly taken up by the men, women and children crowding the avenue.

With the official departures, and the disappearance of Kennard from the balcony, the crowd's energy was spontaneously channelled by some universal impulse to the French Embassy. France was not yet officially at war with Germany, but the tide of enthusiasm accurately divined that it was only a matter of hours before she too would be fighting in Poland's defence. Warsaw now focused all its attention on the comings and goings of the diplomats and officers across the green lawns outside the reassuringly solid French Embassy.

Léon Noel, the French Ambassador, found himself, like Sir Howard Kennard, embarrassed, but for a different reason. He was at first unable to tell the crowd yelling 'La Marseillaise' below what they most ardently wished to know—that France too had officially thrown down the gauntlet to the hated men of Berlin.

Noel wrote afterwards that 'a little later', even before France's entry into the war had become official, the people of Warsaw came in large numbers to the front of our Embassy. The crowd was so big that traffic was brought to a standstill in the whole area. All classes of society and all ages were present; students, old men, *bourgeois*, intellectuals; women followed one another in their thousands under the windows of the Frascati Palace. Friends and unknown people brought flowers accompanied by letters, often very moving little notes, to the Embassy.

'They cheered France and sang snatches of the "Marseillaise". These scenes were indescribable. The crowd was so large that it was necessary to resort to closing the iron gates of the palace to prevent it being invaded.

'I thought of the day when, less than a year previously, the Polish authorities claimed it necessary to protect the Embassy of France, and of my comments to the Foreign Ministry on this matter. The demonstrators called for the Ambassador, and I appeared for a moment at a window to thank them with a wave and a word. I had not yet received the news of our entry into the war, and what I knew of the seriousness of the situation on the battle fronts in Poland did not allow me to present to this ardent crowd, still subject to all the illusions, the words which it without doubt wanted to hear.

'At last the information—at once so much awaited and dreaded—that the Franco-German war had begun. This brought relief to the conscience, but what anguish to the heart . . . The demonstration continued, but suddenly a car appeared, passing with difficulty through the ever more closely-pressed ranks of the demonstrators. It was Colonel Beck, coming officially to present the thanks of Poland to the Ambassador of France. He did so with tact, in suitable terms. I received him in one of the little salons on the ground floor. In the other rooms the hangings were being taken down in an attempt to save them from bombs and fire.

'I led the Minister to his car and witnessed a scene of a sort to inspire politicians to useful reflections: the man who, since his coming to power, and several weeks before this, had never gone out of doors into the streets of Warsaw without a strong guard and in a vehicle driving at a good speed, was now surrounded by a delirious crowd. The shouts of "Vive Beck" mingled for the first time—and also for the last time—with those of "Vive la France".'

Later, Noel drove across Warsaw to the Pilsudski Square where, in an elegant colonnade, stood the tomb of the Unknown Warrior and in front of it the imposing statue of Prince Joseph Poniatowski,

Marshal of France, who fell in the French ranks in the 1813 campaign; for France and for Poland.

Noel recalled: 'I paid homage to the unknown soldier of the other war with the flowers which had just been brought to me by his compatriots, and I left a wreath at the foot of the monument of Poniatowski. I seemed to say to him, to this legendary hero of the Napoleonic epoch: "We are here, Poniatowski." Passers-by stopped, touched, in the half-darkness to shout: "Vive la France." '

The crowds outside the two Embassies stayed until late in the day, clinging as long as possible to the illusion of carnival. They even paid cheering calls on neutral Embassies for obscure reasons, hundreds going to the U.S. Ambassador's residence to sing 'Long live the United States'. It was, perhaps, a way of forgetting reality for a few hours. But as the day wore on the screams of the sirens grew louder and the alerts on the wireless became more urgent. The warm sun passed and Warsaw could only contemplate another evening and night of bombing. Indeed, by 3 p.m., the German bombers were flying without interception again over the heart of Warsaw. But the raids would become easier to bear now that Britain and France were 'in'. And some Poles by late afternoon were scanning the skies confidently for the first of the British fighters and bombers that rumour said were on their way . . .

17. Hitler speaking at the Reichstag. CENTRAL PRESS, LTD.

18. German troops listening to a broadcast by Hitler, October 1939.
RADIO TIMES HULTON PICTURE LIBRARY.

19. Mussolini addressing a fascist meeting. PAUL POPPER, LTD.

20. A Polish farmer continues plowing while German tanks roll past.
RADIO TIMES HULTON PICTURE LIBRARY.

21. German troops advance across the Narew River, Poland, on temporary bridges built to replace those destroyed by the retreating Poles.
RADIO TIMES HULTON PICTURE LIBRARY.

22. A Polish train derailed after an air attack. RADIO TIMES HULTON PICTURE LIBRARY.

23. Abandoned Polish field guns. RADIO TIMES HULTON PICTURE LIBRARY.

IV

The announcement that Britain had entered the war at Poland's side passed like a black stormcloud over a sun-kissed Germany at 1.30 p.m. Berliners, talking over lunch of the advances in Poland, were shocked and subdued by the first official radio announcement, which came suddenly at that time. Berlin, ironically, became quiet and pensive at the very moment that Warsaw was at the peak of its new optimism and excitement.

The main national radio network was broadcasting a fiery rendition by the Hamburg Radio Orchestra of Liszt's First Hungarian Rhapsody. The music faded and a tense male voice said: 'Attention. In a few moments, we shall be making an important announcement.' The Rhapsody resumed. When it finished, Berliners paused in bars, restaurants and their homes. Conversation sank to murmurs and the air was heavy with expectancy.

The announcement was brief and factual. The British in a 'provocative note' had made the demand that the German troops which had advanced into Poland should be withdrawn to their original positions. It gave the gist of the British note and quoted the phrase that 'If a satisfactory answer is not received by eleven o'clock, England will consider herself at war with Germany . . .'

Few Germans had expected this. It was a shock of such stunning proportions that many Germans found difficulty in absorbing the news or in coming to terms with its implications. Wallace R. Duel, of the *Chicago Daily News*, was in Berlin when the news came over the radio. He wrote afterwards of the German reaction: 'It all seemed incredible, unreal. War? It was impossible.

'It was a dream, a nightmare. It had not happened; it was not happening; it had happened to somebody else, somewhere else, at some other time. And yet the voice went on. It really was war. There were the times, the places, the people, the papers. Everything was quite in accordance with protocol. All the proper formalities had been observed. All the proper honours had been rendered. All the proper courtesies had been exchanged.

'Only the people in the streets still did not seem to believe it. The sidewalk cafés along Kurfuerstendamm were well filled. There were no more uniforms than usual to be seen. A car with a diplomatic licence, piled high inside with clothes and rugs, stopped at an intersection and a man called out from the sidewalk: "You'd better get out of here." But nobody paid any attention to either the man or the car. A few feet away a fat, berouged and painfully corseted woman of fifty did not even take her greedy eyes off a new model evening gown in a shop window to see what was happening.

'In the Tiergarten, the people in their Sunday clothes walked slowly along the paths pushing their baby buggies and leading their dogs on leashes like any other Sunday crowd. The only gatherings of people in the park were those watching the spindly-tailed red squirrels begging for nuts.

'There was a crowd in the Wilhelmstrasse but it was a quiet, subdued and orderly crowd, moving as slowly as fish in a tank, and with as little sign of feeling. They looked with only blank interest at the big, canary-yellow, stone British Embassy with the lion and unicorn on the double doors, and standing silently across from the Chancellery down the street.'

A young ex-member of the Hitler Youth, who after joining the German Army at the age of eighteen was detailed to a 20-man Flak unit at Nuremberg, the day war broke out, drew later on his memories of 3rd September. He was A. Kellner, of Munich, who described the scene in Nuremberg thus: 'It was a glorious day, the sky cloudless. The church bells rang for services. There was a solemn atmosphere. We all felt there was something in the air. In Poland we were advancing victoriously. The reservists hoped for a quick end to the war . . . but we younger ones . . . wanted a long war. After lunch came the report that made our hearts beat faster . . . when the speaker of the Berlin Reich Radio gave the special report that England and France were at war with Germany from today onwards.'

Kellner remembered that he and his companions were all shocked.

None of them had expected England and France to take up arms for Poland. 'Then our Lieutenant explained the Führer's standpoint as follows: "Germany has been forced to war by England and France. Poland was England's first victim. The British were too cowardly to fight themselves, but we would get them to fight at last and that would be our great historic moment." '

The young Nazis listened to the Lieutenant 'almost convinced' by his arguments. 'We young soldiers were quite convinced that our war was just, whether against Poland or against the western powers. We did not listen to the objections of the older men.'

The German newspapers brought out rush special editions giving the news of the British declaration. The *Deutsche Allgemeine Zeitung* banner headline read: 'BRITISH ULTIMATUM TURNED DOWN—ENGLAND DECLARES A STATE OF WAR WITH GERMANY'; and lower down: 'BRITISH NOTE DEMANDS WITHDRAWAL OF OUR TROOPS IN THE EAST—THE FÜHRER LEAVING TODAY FOR THE FRONT'. Over the official German account of the happenings of that historic morning the D.A.Z. headline read: 'GERMAN MEMORANDUM PROVES ENGLAND'S GUILT.'

The American Correspondent William L. Shirer was standing in the Wilhelmplatz when the news that England was at war with Germany came over the loudspeaker. A crowd of about 250 people stood in the sun, listening attentively. Shirer recalled later, 'When it was finished there was not a murmur. They just stood there as they were before. Stunned. The people could not realize yet that Hitler had led them into a World War.' This strange inability of the German people to comprehend the seriousness of their position was in sharp contrast to their reaction to a similar situation twenty-five years earlier. On the first day of the 1914–18 war Berlin had been seized with a fit of patriotic fervour and the streets were filled with cheering, enthusiastic demonstrators.

There had been bitter demonstrations outside the British Embassy in 1914. But on that September Sunday in 1939 the pavements outside the British and French Embassies were empty. Even the recent vicious propaganda against the British and French coupled with the declaration of war had failed to strike a spark of true hate in the German people.

The city of Berlin carried on a normal, if subdued, existence. Murmuring groups clustered in the bars, restaurants and hotels. Berliners, many of them uniformed soldiers on leave from their units, carried on eating, drinking and talking, seemingly as usual. There was no hysteria—no thirst for war. One reporter of the *Deutsche Allgemeine Zeitung* recorded his impression that rather than being shocked, Germans were 'determined and ready' for the grave news on the radio and in the newspapers.

He wrote: 'The news that Britain regarded the rejection of her challenging ultimatum as the start of a state of war with Germany was, of course, being discussed everywhere. Wherever people were gathered together, they agreed. They have long been prepared for this moment.

'We drove through Berlin. Many were making their way to the Wilhelmplatz, which had not been empty since the Friday, when the Führer made his resolute speech to the Reichstag. The Berliner tries as far as possible to avoid the centre of his city on Sundays, but during that afternoon many were gathering near the man who held the leadership of the executive and the legislature at that critical time. They wanted to be there when he drove off to visit the troops in the east.'

But in most other ways Berlin carried on as if nothing had happened, or was going to happen. Hockey matches were in progress at the Berlin Sports Club stadium and at nearby Zehlendorf. Eight thousand spectators crowded into the Hertha football ground to watch Berlin East beat Berlin South 2–1. In the capital and Munich there were heavy racing programmes and over the rest of the country Germans indulged in or watched favourite Sunday sports and pastimes.

The announcement by mid-afternoon of a series of wartime decrees by the Nazis, however, did bring home to some the stark reality of war. The death penalty was decreed for espionage, aiding insurgents and other military crimes. Another vaguely-worded, sweeping decree provided the death penalty for soldiers or civilians who attempted to weaken the German Army or people in their 'defence determination', and for those trying to evade military service. Military penalties for desertion and unlawful absence from the country were sharply increased. A further decree created zones along certain border areas between Poland and Bohemia in which 'foreigners and questionable persons' were not permitted except in transit to some other destination. Such decrees were more effective in bringing home to the German people the reality of a World War than many more direct signs. The average German had no conception of what the British and French declarations might mean in terms of his own life; but the threat of the rope or the firing squad if he failed Germany brought home forcibly the change that had occurred in his national life.

While the bulk of the German people were left in the dark, or even discouraged from guessing at the real gravity of the situation, some of the politicians and economists close to the administrative core fully realized the dire, drastic peril in which the Reich had now placed itself by the Polish adventure.

Dr. Hjalmar Schacht, a former President of the Reichsbank, whose brilliant stabilization of the German currency after the First World War earned him a reputation as a financial wizard, was among those horrified by the radio announcement that afternoon. Schacht had had considerable influence on Hitler in the early years of the Nazi régime, but his prestige had declined steadily in the previous three years. Schacht believed that his professional downfall as an economist had been due to plain speaking with the Führer about economic problems and Jewish persecution. When the British ultimatum came, Schacht, who had just returned from a long visit to India and Burma, tried to exert his influence to avert the catastrophe of a general war. But he was no longer *persona grata* with Hitler and his efforts failed.

Schacht wrote later: 'In Hitler's challenge to the British and French ultimata which expired on 3rd September, I saw the downfall of my last hopes of stemming the tide of war. Not a German-Polish conflict, but the Second World War had begun. The attitude of the military leaders seemed to me incomprehensible. In all the conversations I had with Generals of my acquaintance, it transpired over and over again that Hitler had invariably reassured them on the subject of possible intervention by the western powers in the event of war with Poland.

'When the ultimata expired the leaders of the Army, Luftwaffe and the Navy were obliged to state frankly either that Hitler had been mistaken or that he had deliberately misled them. They should have made it clear to Hitler that Germany was not equipped for a Second World War, and would never come through such a war. Nothing of the sort happened. The evil ran its course.'

Other reactions among thinking Germans—for the bulk of the populace, either for lack of understanding or indifference, showed little feeling one way or the other—ranged from solid, Nazi support of Hitler to secret joy that his downfall now seemed at least a possibility. The outspoken Pastor Martin Niemoller, a U-boat commander in the First World War, had already been under arrest for more than two years when the war broke out and had spent eighteen months' solitary confinement in Sachsenhausen concentration camp. In a letter he wrote to the author subsequently he recalled that his sole personal reaction to the events of 3rd September was a feeling 'that from then on a gigantic catastrophe would descend not only on his own people but on the whole world'.

The other side of the coin showed such men as Fritz Muehleback, a stormtrooper of the Sturm Abteilung—the Nazi uniformed military—who was thirty-two when war broke out and working as a district A.R.P. officer. 'Now that we knew we were at war we saw clearly just how clever our leader has been,' he recalled afterwards. 'We only had to look at the map. We stood behind him like one man, shoulder to shoulder and ready for anything.

'I regarded England's and France's interference and declaration of war as nothing but a formality. There was no doubt that as soon as they realized the utter hopelessness of Polish resistance and the vast superiority of German arms they would begin to see that we had always been in the right and it was quite senseless to meddle in our private business.

'But of course we had to let these warmongers know that this was the last time that Germany would stand for any sort of foreign interference. It was only as a result of their guarantee of something that wasn't their business that the war had ever started. If Poland had been alone she would certainly have given in quietly. Otherwise, we had no quarrel with France or England. Our West Wall was perfectly secure and we never thought that we would have to invade these countries or fight them actively . . .'

Many Germans, for one reason or another, felt a sense of relief that the intolerable tensions which had wracked the Fatherland were now resolved into a clear-cut issue of men and arms. Among them was a 28-year-old freelance writer, Werner Harz, who hated Hitler, the Nazis, and everything they stood for. Harz was among the ranks who realized then that Hitler was blindly dragging most of the reluctant German nation into a catastrophic bloodbath not of their own choosing.

But, he wrote later, 'dreadful as it was the outbreak of hostilities

seemed to us almost like a relief. We had known for some time that
there was no possibility of opposition to the régime from inside. Now
at last the people outside seemed to be in earnest. We knew that
Hitler was now going surely to his doom, and I remembered I invited
about ten friends home and we celebrated, with the best of food and
a great deal of Schnapps, the end of the thousand-year Reich.'

A woman's side to the story of 3rd September comes from the pages
of a post-war book by Elizabeth Hoemberg, a Canadian girl married to
a German and living in Witten, in the Ruhr. When the German Army
invaded Poland, her husband told her, 'Courage girl, courage! The
sooner it starts the sooner it will be over.'

Mrs. Hoemberg later wrote: 'Despite my first flood of feelings, the
events of 3rd September were to arouse in me a similar sense of relief.
Overwhelmed as one was by the prospect of war in Western Europe,
the prospect of peace to be sought at such a price seemed even more
intolerable. It was as though the oppressive, overcharged atmosphere
of unreality in which we had been living had suddenly been pierced
by the cool wind of fact.'

From 1 p.m. onwards, Adolf Hitler began issuing a stream of
directives and exhortations to the German people and his officers. In a
masterfully brash but transparent statement he played upon the political ignorance of most Germans to arouse the requisite blood-thirst and
hate for Britain. His special early afternoon message to the German
nation said: 'Great Britain has for centuries pursued the aim of ren-
dering the peoples of Europe defenceless against the British policy of
world conquest by proclaiming a balance of power, in which Great
Britain claimed the right to attack on threadbare pretexts and destroy
that European state which at the moment seemed most dangerous.
Thus, at one time she fought the world power of Spain, later the
Dutch, then the French and, since the year 1871, the Germans.

'We ourselves have been witnesses of the policy of encirclement
which has been carried out by Great Britain against Germany since
before the War. Just as the German nation had begun, under its National Socialist leadership, to recover from the frightful consequences
of the Diktat of Versailles, and threatened to survive the crisis, British
encirclement immediately began once more.

'The British war inciters spread the lie before the War that the
battle was only against the House of Hohenzollern or German milita-

rism; that they had no designs on German colonies; that they had no intention of taking the German mercantile fleet. They then oppressed the German people under the Versailles Diktat, the faithful fulfilment of which would have sooner or later have exterminated twenty million Germans.

'I undertook to mobilize the resistance of the German nation against this, and to assure work and bread for them. But as the peaceful revision of the Versailles Diktat of force seemed to be succeeding, and the German people again began to live, the new British encirclement policy was resumed. The same lying inciters appeared as in 1914. I have many times offered Great Britain and the British people the understanding and friendship of the German people. My whole policy has been based on the idea of this understanding. I have always been repelled. I have for years been aware that the aim of these war inciters has for long been to take Germany by surprise at a favourable opportunity.

'I am more firmly determined than ever to beat back this attack. Germany shall not again capitulate. There is no sense in sacrificing one life after another and submitting to an even worse Versailles Diktat. We have never been a nation of slaves and we will not be one in the future. Whatever sacrifices Germans had to make in the past for the existence of our realm they shall not be greater than those which we are today prepared to make.

'This resolve is an inexorable one. It necessitates the most thorough measures, and imposes on us one law above all others. If the soldier is fighting at the front, no one shall profit by the war. If the soldier falls at the front, no one at home shall evade his duty.

'As long as the German people has been united it has never been conquered. It was the lack of unity in 1918 that led to collapse. Whoever offends against this unity need expect nothing else than annihilation as an enemy of the nation. If our people fulfils its highest duty in this sense, that God will help us who has always bestowed his mercy on him who was determined to help himself.'

Then the Führer published his second 'Directive for the Conduct of the War' to follow that of a few days earlier.

'1. After the declaration of a state of war by the British Government, the British Admiralty on 3rd September, 1939, at 11.17 a.m. gave orders for the opening of hostilities. France has declared that

from 5.00 p.m. on 3rd September, 1939, she will be in a state of war
with Germany.

'2. The German war objectives remain for the time being the speedy
and victorious conclusion of the operations against Poland. Any decision to transfer sizeable forces from the east to the west rests with
me.

'3. The principles for the conduct of the war in the west, in accordance with Directive No. 1, remain in force. After the opening of
hostilities by Britain, now announced, and the declaration of a state
of war by France, the following conclusions have been reached:

(a) Against Britain:

'Navy: Offensive operations are permitted. The warfare against merchant shipping is for the time being to be conducted according to the
prize regulations, also by submarines. Preparations are to be made
for intensification (of the war) pending the declaration of danger
zones.

'The approaches to the Baltic Sea are to be blocked by mines with-
out infringing on neutral territorial waters. Barrage measures in the
North Sea intended for our own defence and for the attack against
Britain are to be carried out.

'Luftwaffe: Offensive operations against British naval forces in naval
ports and on the open sea—including the Channel—as well as against
troop transports definitely identified as such are only to be permitted
if British attacks from the air on similar targets have taken place and
if prospects of success are particularly favourable. The same applies
to operations by naval air formations. The decision on attacks on the
British mainland and merchant shipping rests with me.

(b) Against France:

'Army: In the west, the opening of hostilities is to be left to the
enemy. The Commander-in-Chief of the Army will decide on reinforcements for the Western Army from the forces still available.

'Navy: Offensive operations against France are only to be permitted
if she opens hostilities. If she does so, then the orders given against
Britain apply also against France in the same way.

'Luftwaffe: Offensive operations against France are only to be permitted after French attacks have been made against German territory.
The principle to be followed is that the beginning of the war in the
air should not be caused by German measures. Generally, in the use

of the Luftwaffe in the west, it is to be borne in mind that its fighting power must be conserved for the decision against the western powers after the defeat of Poland.

'4. The "X" Order issued on 25th August, 1939 (concerning mobilization) will be extended to the whole of the Wehrmacht with effect from 3rd September, 1939. The conversion of the whole of industry to war economy is ordered. Further mobilization measures in the civil sphere will be taken, on application from the Supreme Reich authorities, by the High Command of the Wehrmacht.'

                                                    Adolf Hitler.

The Führer had eight copies made of the directive and distributed to the High Command of the Army (one copy), High Command of the Navy (one), Goering (one), the Wehrmacht Operations office (one) and the Defence Department (four).

Hitler then turned his mid-afternoon attention from the civilian population to issue a 'pep-talk' to the German Army on the western front: A statement to them from the Führer around 2 p.m. read: 'Soldiers of the Western Army; just as before the War, so after the War, Great Britain has pursued the policy of Germany's encirclement. In spite of the fact that Germany has no demands to make on any state to the west of the Reich; in spite of the fact that Germany claims no territorial revision in this area; and in spite of the fact that Germany has made, above all to Great Britain, just as to France, the offer of a cordial understanding, indeed of friendship, the British Government, driven on by those warmongers whom we knew in the last War, have resolved to let fall their mask and to proclaim war on a threadbare pretext.

'The German youth and your comrades in the east now expect from you, soldiers of the western front, that you shall protect the frontiers of the Reich, unshakeable as a wall of steel and iron, against every attack, in an array of fortifications which is a hundred times stronger than the western front of the Great War which was never conquered.

'If you do your duty, the battle in the east will have reached its successful conclusion in a few months, and then the power of the whole National Socialist state stands behind you. As an old soldier of the (First) World War, and as your Supreme Commander, I am going, with confidence in you, to the Army on the east. Our plutocratic enemies will realize that they are now dealing with a different Germany from that of the year 1914.

Adolf Hitler.'

Shortly after Hitler's exhortation to the troops, Heydrich, head of the security police, issued strict instructions on internal security for the duration of the war. The original document appears to have been destroyed, but a hint of its ruthless tone can be gleaned from a teleprinter message, dated seventeen days later, to all state police stations and offices:

'As was stated in the rules of 3rd September, 1939, every attempt to undermine the resolve and will to fight of the German people must be suppressed from the start with ruthless firmness and harshness . . . in cases under rule one, a distinction is to be made between those who can be dealt with in the normal way and those who must receive special treatment. The latter are those cases where the facts of the case are so objectionable, dangerous or of propaganda effect that they must be eradicated without regard to the person involved by ruthless action (execution).

'Such cases are, for example, sabotage attempts, incitement to rebellion or undermining of members of the armed forces or a large group of people; large-scale hoarding, Communist and Marxist activities, etc. . . . These crimes are to be regarded only as examples, and this list can by no means claim to be complete. It must be left to State police stations and offices to decide whether this or that case is suited for special treatment.'

The message ended with the significant warning: 'This decree is not of a kind to be passed on to local police authorities' (i.e. non-Gestapo police).

At 2 p.m. there was a quiet, anxious suspense in the German ranks on the western front itself. The troops were waiting for the holocaust to begin; waiting for the bombs, the grenades, shells and bullets. But nothing came, and nothing of any real military significance was to occur on the western front for months to come. But neither the French nor the Germans knew this and the tension was in time to become almost unbearable. No one knew when the front might erupt into an inferno of blood and fire.

So, on both sides of the Franco-German border that afternoon the authorities began moving out the civilian populations. On the German side, about 500,000 men, women and children were being evacuated from the front—the aged and infirm in special trains, the rest on foot. Healthy Germans between ten and sixty were given two hours to pack, lock up their homes, and get to their appointed assembly points. The evacuation began at 3 p.m. that Sunday. Many had to leave their most precious belongings behind and some protested vigorously. Where, they asked, were the enemy aircraft, the bombs, the invading troops?

But they were hustled from their homes—the first German civilians to taste first-hand the tragedy of a new World War—and herded through a blinding thunderstorm to the assembly points. Most had to walk ten miles or more that afternoon, bowed beneath their most valuable possessions, wet, weary and bewildered.

As the civilians were evacuated, the troops moved up to the front in tens of thousands in an orderly train operation. Army engineers laid mines at the bridges along the front. As the last of the half million refugees was carried away into the interior, a bolt of lightning struck one of the land mines and blew up a bridge over the Saar.

In Berlin only the last miserable formal moves remained to be played out before the state of war in Europe was complete; the embarrassing, uncomfortable business of diplomatic withdrawals. The French and British diplomatic complements in Berlin were tiny compared with the stout corps maintained by the Germans in most European capitals. While fewer than forty French Embassy staff took the train out of Berlin that Sunday, a German entourage numbering well over a hundred waited in Paris to return to Berlin.

The United States Government had agreed to British and French requests to conduct their diplomatic business in Berlin for the duration of hostilities, and Mr. Alexander Kirk took over the affairs of the two departing Ambassadors during the Sunday afternoon.

Fifty women and children attached to the American Embassy also left Berlin, bound for Denmark. Sir Nevile Henderson, the tall, slim, elegant British Ambassador in his final report to Lord Halifax from Berlin, noted that the telephone lines from his Embassy continued to function for several hours after Britain and Germany were officially at war. But by mid-afternoon on the 3rd all the Embassy lines were cut off, and both the Embassy and its staff, who assembled in the Adlon Hotel, were isolated from external contacts.

Henderson, who had little more than three years to live—he died on 30th December, 1942—felt a keen sense of regret and failure. A hint of his feelings were revealed in the title of his memoirs published later: *Failure of a Mission*. Since taking up his appointment in Berlin in 1937 he had done everything in his power to foster Anglo-German friendship and to maintain world peace.

In his memoirs, Henderson described his miserable hours in Berlin that afternoon: 'After returning from my interview with Ribbentrop at midday I did not leave the Embassy again until Mr. Alexander Kirk rendered me one final service by driving me in his own car to the station next morning.

'Up to those last twenty-four hours I had gone freely in the streets of Berlin, either on foot or in my motor with its British flag; and I am glad to take this opportunity to bear witness to the fact that throughout those anxious weeks, and up to the very end, when we crossed the German frontier, neither I nor any member of my staff was subjected at any time to any discourtesy or even a single gesture of hostility. It was a very different eve of war from that of August, 1914. Then, a howling mob had surged in front of the Embassy, had broken its windows and hurled abuse at its inmates and at Great Britain.

'My impression was that the bulk of the German people—that other Germany—were horror-struck at the whole idea of the war which was being thus thrust upon them. It is true that I could only judge of Berlin itself, and that I was not in a position to witness the reaction of German youth or of the soldiers in the troop-trains which were leaving for the Polish front.

'It is true also that the trial blackouts, the bread cards, and the strict system of rationing, which was already in force, were not exactly cheerful beginnings to a war. But what I can say is that the whole general atmosphere in Berlin itself was one of utter gloom and depression. Every country has the Government which it deserves, and the German people must share the responsibility for the present war with those to whose authority they so meekly and readily submitted.

'But they have a share also of the immense pity which I felt for all those who have got to suffer because the Nazi war party, which had been foiled in September, 1938, won the day in Germany in

August, 1939, and because one man was ready to sacrifice their united happiness to the satisfaction of his individual lust for military glory, which must be greater even than that of Frederick the Great.'

During the afternoon the British and French missions made arrangements, with the help of the Americans, for leaving Berlin. The French arranged finally to leave at 9 a.m. the next day, and the British diplomats two and a half hours later. And both groups of diplomats were destined to leave for home without any demonstrations of hostility at the Charlottenberg station.

V

While the House of Commons in London was debating whether aliens
in Britain should be allowed to enlist with the forces, the French
were welcoming men of every nationality to the colours. A special
recruiting office for all foreigners who wished to fight for France and
her cause had been opened in the Champs-Elysées by the Association
of the Friends of the French Republic. By 3 p.m. volunteers were
pouring in by the thousand.

M. Paul Boncour, Senator, and the Association's chief, gave a Gallic
salute 'with emotion and gratitude' to the droves of eager aliens
calling at the recruiting office. Various government departments were
already co-operating in the running of the recruitment office, which
was acting as a private information centre to encourage foreigners
wishing to enlist either in the French armed forces or in civil defence
operations. The French wanted particularly to encourage foreign
specialists—doctors, chemists, engineers and technicians—whose services
could be of great value. Eager women volunteers of non-French
nationality could partly meet the urgent need for nurses, typists and
social workers.

During Sunday afternoon, the Union of Polish Reserve Officers in
France called on all Poles in France and abroad to enlist with them.
But even before this appeal several thousand Polish-born citizens
had volunteered for service, underlining their fervour by putting gold
wedding rings, jewellery, cars and motor-cycles at the disposal of the
cause.

The Rumanian Friends of France, conscious of the strong links between the two countries, renewed on Sunday afternoon an appeal to
all compatriots in France to enrol in the Rumanian Legion, and asked
them to call on their Paris headquarters.

Italian People's Union and Franco-Italian Ex-servicemen's Association delegates to the Friends of the French Republic announced that
Italians had already come forward in great numbers to defend France.
Colonel Garibaldi, of Cauderan, near Bordeaux, was busily enlisting
volunteers from among his compatriots with a view to forming an
Italian Garibaldi Legion to be put at the disposal of the French
military authorities.

The Paris office of the Union of Chinese People in Europe appealed to Chinese in France to come forward and stand in the
French ranks. The Union announced: 'Considering that China fought
beside France in the 1914–18 war, and convinced that in the present
circumstances France would not have taken up arms except to defend
in Europe the same principles that China is defending in the Far
East, we ask the whole Chinese colony in France to put themselves
at the disposal of the French authorities.'

France devoted Sunday afternoon to an intense, but extremely
orderly effort to complete the mobilization of her armed forces. At
3 p.m., with two hours left before France was officially at war with
Germany, the authorities were using the last minutes of peace to put
the finishing touches to the nation's defences.

M. Bonnet, whose personal involvement in the events of the
previous hours brought the tragedy home to him so keenly, was still
holding the fort at the Foreign Ministry, though his role was virtually
finished. He had nothing to do but wait. The Ministry now seemed
dead; long, deserted corridors, empty salons, silent telephones; there
was not a trace or echo of the feverish excitement which had pervaded
the building so shortly before. There was nothing but an all-engulfing
silence and an oppressive sadness. One of the few interludes was the
arrival and swift departure of the German *Chargé d'Affaires*. All he
wanted were his passports.

Most of civilian Paris, like Bonnet, was waiting. On the surface
much of the life of the capital went on as normal. Anglers dotted the
banks of the Seine and the swimming baths were well patronized.
People on café terraces discussed the oncoming war, cursing the
Nazis . . . 'Les salauds, les salauds . . .' But there was another side
to the civilian scene—the stations, covered with gay posters, were
clogged with dense crowds carrying the meagre luggage of refugees who
did not know where they were going.

Long columns of troops poured out of barracks. Scores of men of forty and over, still in civilian clothes, had been called up from reserve with their haversacks, gas-masks and capes. The whole city resounded with the heavy tramp of boots of men called to arms. There was no gaiety, only a subdued camaraderie, among men who had suddenly left behind their work, wives and children. The future seemed almost as dark as it later turned out to be. A conscripted shopkeeper in the boulevards hung a sign in his window saying: 'The unhappiness of the individual is nothing compared with that of the nation.' Every Frenchman understood those words that afternoon.

A reporter in the offices of *Le Petit Parisien* was hammering out this story on his typewriter after a tour of the city: 'It has happened. The too famous war of nerves has ended and the war itself has begun . . . Under their outward appearance of calm resolution spirits have oscillated, until now, between hope and resignation. But when the radio gave the decisive news, Paris quickly acquired an atmosphere in which signs of the most moving gravity were added to the customary calm and discipline . . .

'The strangest thing was the mobilization of the underground railway. Many stations were closed. It was strange to see names like "St. Michel" or "St. Germain" classed as unimportant stations and closed. Few passers-by . . . many uniforms . . . women hurrying to get food . . . faces reflecting the seriousness and tragedy of a grave hour, but nowhere the slightest sign either of bravado or despair. Paris entered one of the most terrible and glorious periods in its history with the most admirable dignity.'

Another journalist, a columnist calling himself 'Le Masque de Fer' (The Iron Mask) was composing his daily story for *Le Figaro* of the following day. He wrote: 'What struck the traveller on the roads of France yesterday was the air of sweetness that bathed the countryside. Whether in the Macon district, the Loire Valley, the banks of the Yonne, the Landes or Normandy, everywhere the French countryside was a picture of grace and harmony.

'Military lorries dotted the roads, peasants went, leading their horses, to recruiting offices and somehow one would have said that nothing had changed. On roads which one expected to find choked, perfect order reigned. Exoduses of endangered populations organized themselves without the least confusion, the coolness and discipline of the leaders made this immense movement less costly in accidents than the Easter or 15th August holidays.

'At all points where military traffic had reached a certain intensity, soldiers controlled the movement of vehicles with the same authority as Paris policemen. It was a miracle to see how people reputed to be intolerant of authority adapted themselves to the necessities of mobilization.'

In a flurry of activity and paperwork, numerous official and semi-official organizations made mid-afternoon preparations for the fighting. The French Aero Club announced that it was registering pilots with licences for transport, training or tourist aircraft, as well as mechanics free of military obligations, to fill posts at the club's flying school. The Women's Civic and Social Union and the League of Mothers in the Home asked the Government to issue 'maternity cards' giving expectant mothers the right of priority and special facilities in public transport and elsewhere. Around 4 p.m., M. Jean Zay, Minister of National Education, and at thirty-five the youngest member of the French Government, asked to be relieved of his post so that he could join the Army. M. Zay told newspaper reporters: 'How could I decline to share the destiny of the young people for whom I have worked in the Government for more than three years?'

As in Britain and Germany, measures were being taken to protect France's national artistic heritage from the ravages of war. At Dunkirk, a hundred canvases from the museum were being packed into strong-boxes and moved to safety. The Fine Arts Commission, visiting the country's principal churches, had just decreed that several paintings —including 'The Martyr with four Crowns' by Jean de Reyn and 'The Lord's Supper' by Otto Vermis—should be removed from the churches of St. Eloi and John the Baptist.

The Ministry of Public Health said that because of the importance blood transfusions might assume in the coming months, the transfusion centre at St. Antoine's hospital in Paris had been put at the disposal of doctors wishing to familiarize themselves with techniques of ascertaining blood groups. Practical tests could be carried out daily by all doctors who applied to the hospital. The National Federation of French Newspapers announced that small advertisements would only be accepted under strict control, and would then be held back for forty-eight hours before publication. Abbreviations and the mention of cities and localities were banned. The Federation added that any small advertisement which appeared doubtful (from an espionage

point of view) would be suppressed. Another Federation edict was that
weather forecasts must no longer be published.

M. Emile Faure, President of the Paris Municipal Council, decided
to remain permanently at the City Hall. He was to be assisted by
non-mobilized members of his office and other councillors, ready
to pass any resolutions which circumstances might demand. The
Council expected an almost immediate bombing siege and beds and
emergency cooking equipment were installed in many offices. Fresh
arrangements to evacuate expectant mothers and women with very
young children were announced by M. Max Rucart, Minister of Public
Health, who gave details of centres being established in country areas
to receive them. A further 3,000 sick people were moved from Paris
hospitals during the afternoon. At Cabineres, near Pontpellier, M.
Pierre Altier, a wealthy property owner, decided to cancel the cele-
brations that afternoon of his 100th birthday 'because of the world
situation'.

Police toured Paris all afternoon warning people of hastily-made
preparations to ensure distribution of water supplies under enemy
attack. Householders were warned not to squander water and to keep
at least forty-eight hours of emergency supplies. Part of this supply,
the police suggested, should be kept in well-corked bottles in case
of gas attack.

Not all women in Paris, however, were preparing their homes for
an immediate siege. Some were present at a meeting of the National
Committee of Socialist Women which two hours before the conflict
was due to begin issued a last call for peace to the Government. These
women said in their appeal that they 'did not despair that peace can
still be saved, that the madness which is spreading through the world
can be stopped, that the final appeal made by the representatives of
the French people for "free negotiations" in place of violence will be
listened to . . .'

As the United States Ambassador in Paris, Mr. William Bullitt,
worked feverishly to evacuate his fellow countrymen, one dogged old
lady resolved to remain and see the war out in Paris. She was non-
agenarian Mrs. Dora Delano Forbes, the aunt of President Roosevelt.
She told the Ambassador: 'I have had a full life. How can I die better
than by a German bomb?'

Here and there traditional aspects of French life were bowing themselves out before the storm, many of them not to reappear again until the war was over. The Comedie Française cancelled its re-opening after the annual summer holiday although the cinemas carried on. On 3rd September, Parisians could see such films as 'Pygmalion', 'Confessions of a Nazi Spy', and 'Jamaica Inn'. The races at Longchamps were cancelled, but a big football match was played at the Saint Mande stadium in east Paris. There was also a well-attended 'pre-Olympic' athletics meeting at the Jean-Bouin stadium.

In the Brie plain, where the hunting season should have begun the next day, the butts for partridge-shooting had already been carefully lined up, each bearing a newly-painted number so that the hunters could quickly find their allotted places. The partridge flocks flew lazily from one spinney to another, as if sensing that the war was in their favour and that the fields were now theirs.

'Three dazzling weeks', announced the posters for the Cannes Festival at each bend of the road along the Côte d'Azur. But in a matter of hours the Riviera had lost its holiday mood. The hotels emptied, the cars vanished and troops began to take the place of the holidaymakers. Gun batteries had been set up on the point of Palm Beach and Senegalese soldiers began bivouacking on beaches where the day before scantily-clad limbs had broiled on the sand and children had paddled in the surf.

The Duke of Windsor was still waiting anxiously on the Riviera to fly home to Britain. A private aircraft he had summoned for the flight to his homeland had been grounded by bad weather at Farnborough, England. The Duchess of Windsor was expected to accompany him. She had not been in England since the Duke abdicated on 10th December, 1936.

VI

At 3 p.m., six armed men pounced upon a soldier of the 8th Belfast H.A.A. Regiment of the Territorial Army in Belfast's East Bridge Street. They swiftly stripped the soldier and burned his uniform. Forty-five minutes later, another member of the same unit was shot in the stomach and seriously injured. That man's blood was the first to spill from a British uniform in World War Two.

The two attacks threw into sharp relief a serious British home front weakness. They gave plain warning to the authorities that the outlawed Irish Republican Army intended to take full advantage of Britain's preoccupation with Hitler in order to argue their case on Irish partition with guns and bombs.

The Northern Ireland Government reacted swiftly to the outrage and set a pattern of firm retaliation which they followed faithfully and successfully until 1945. The Ministry of Home Affairs had already been authorized to mobilize the Special Constabulary if necessary. This was done immediately the I.R.A. began shooting that afternoon. Within the hour, orders were being drafted for the internment of forty-five men known to belong to the organization and the security forces were to be told: 'Seize all these men before the night is out.'

Simultaneously, neighbouring Eire was declaring its neutrality to the world. Mr. Eamon de Valera, the Prime Minister, made clear in a statement in the Dail that the country would not be following the other members of the British Empire and Commonwealth in declaring war on Germany, Mr. de Valera said it would be necessary at every stage to protect Irish interests and to avoid giving to any of the belligerents any doubt of Eire's neutrality or any cause of complaint in that regard. He added that he had told the German Minister that the Government of Eire wished to remain at peace with Germany and all other powers.

Eire's neutrality, while a tribute to the freedom cherished within the British Family of Nations was to be a thorn in the side of Britain during the war if only for geographical reasons. To begin with, it precluded allied use of harbours and potential bases in the south-west of Eire to intercept German U-boats lurking in the western approaches. It also meant the continued presence in Dublin of a German diplomatic mission to Eire which maintained an open frontier with Northern Ireland. During the war, the Northern Ireland Government was to repeatedly draw the British Government's attention to the dangers inherent in this situation. They were to stress the parallel dangers of the comparatively easy infiltration of enemy agents over the border into Northern Ireland, and the proximity of German diplomatic staff to England's western defences.

Eire's neutrality, though not exactly a shock to Whitehall, raised prickly and unforeseeable problems in the deployment of troops. It would henceforth be necessary to provide not only normal defence forces for vital military, naval and air centres such as shore bases and airfields but also to protect, against infiltrated saboteurs, such important civil installations as Belfast harbour.

To a limited extent, the local authorities had foreseen some of these problems, mobilizing on 1st September a special home defence force, the 200th Group, National Defence Battalion. This had been built up of First World War veterans and British Legionaires. By Sunday afternoon, these men were already being drafted to the defence of such vulnerable areas as the Aldergrove airfield, the ordnance depot at Carrickfergus, the gun sites at Kilroot and Grey Point and the B.B.C. station at Lisnagarvey. But the outbreak of war and the immediate I.R.A. action brought the extra defence problems forcefully home to the London and Belfast administrations, and immediate consultations were called that afternoon on the provision of additional forces to meet the contingency of Eire's neutrality. Few trained troops were available who had not been already assigned for prospective service elsewhere in Britain or abroad. The main hope was that a large force of Territorial Army reinforcements could be brought in from other parts of Britain, and this, in fact, was to happen in the next few

months. The four battalions in Northern Ireland on 3rd September
were to grow to full division strength by the following May.

The Northern Ireland Government pledged that it would do all
in its power to avoid wasteful use of military forces to cope with civil
disruption. But for the whole war, the British forces in the north
were to be overstretched by the double task of standing by to repel
air and seaborne onslaughts and at the same time protecting civil
and military targets from I.R.A. attacks or sabotage by enemy agents.
The latter were to prove less of a problem than seemed likely on 3rd
September, but that could not be foreseen at the outbreak of war.
There was evidence that two enemy agents had been active in Northern
Ireland during the summer of 1939 and there were in addition more
than 250 Germans over the age of sixteen in the six counties. Police
began rounding these aliens up on the first day of the war. Some
were destined to be taken to Britain for internment, but many were to
be freed to play a part in the war effort against the nation they had
rejected.

Despite the fact that the I.R.A. threat put Belfast closer to the
immediate firing line than the rest of the United Kingdom, the
Northern Ireland authorities decided not to close cinemas, other places
of entertainment or schools. So in some respects life continued on far
more normal lines in Belfast than in London—even though the threat
of a street shooting or bomb outrage was ever present. Even the frontier
with Eire remained virtually open—a fact which was to cause irritation
and anger among Ulstermen throughout the war. From the first
day it was more difficult to cross from Northern Ireland to other parts
of the U.K. than to enter neutral Eire with its German Embassy
and colony. A rigid system of checks was imposed on travel across
the Irish Sea from the north. Air services were suspended and businessmen could only travel through 'approved ports' like Belfast and
Larne.

This feeling of isolation from the rest of the U.K. began on that
first day with the announcement of the emergency regulations. It was
to grow in the minds of Ulstermen as a humiliation and a ridiculous
anomaly and was even to be noted in Northern Ireland's official *War
History*: 'Wartime activities in Northern Ireland were thus not properly isolated from the prying gaze of the enemy with his Legation
staff in Dublin and this was the cause of much heartburning in

Northern Ireland. More vigorous protests might have been made had it been generally known that a cable-line ran from Eire to the outside world which was independent of the British system of cable communications and that during the early stages of the conflict an unlocated private radio station was operating in Eire. It was the anomaly of an open frontier which so irritated men and women in Northern Ireland who had themselves to submit to the permit system . . .'

24. A Polish village burns furiously after a German bombing attack. RADIO TIMES HUL-TON PICTURE LIBRARY.

25. French troops guard the munitions store in the Maginot Line. RA-DIO TIMES HULTON PIC-TURE LIBRARY.

26. Parisians reading the announcement of general mobilization, September 1939. RADIO TIMES HULTON PICTURE LIBRARY.

27. French children being fitted with gas masks. RADIO TIMES HULTON
PICTURE LIBRARY.

28. Children being evacuated from London. RADIO TIMES HULTON
PICTURE LIBRARY.

29. London children on their way to evacuation. RADIO TIMES HULTON
PICTURE LIBRARY.

VII

Between 1 p.m. and 4 p.m., Neville Chamberlain made up his mind on the top priority issue of a War Cabinet and selected the key men to lead Britain through the coming struggle. During those hours, he worked quietly and shrewdly weighing the merits of colleagues, sifting the talent and experience at his disposal and trying without success to bring the Labour and Liberal opposition leaders into the wartime administration.

Chamberlain threw himself into the task of government-building immediately the House of Commons went into committee. His decision was to stop short of a complete Government reshuffle which would involve him in considerable personal troubles and complications. Basically, the Prime Minister decided, he would seek to carry on for as long as possible with the bulk of his pre-war team. He began his negotiations within the Houses of Parliament where he took aside his old friend, Sir Samuel Hoare (later Viscount Templewood), and invited him for a walk in St. James's Park.

Chamberlain knew that under any official roof in London he would have been besieged by anxious subordinates with questions and problems. So he chose the Park for one of the crucial interviews which studded that momentous day, aware that while it was a favourite Sunday haunt of Londoners it was not a place where Whitehall would hunt a Prime Minister in a crisis. He could hardly have chosen anywhere in London where war seemed further away. As he strolled with Hoare in the green, peaceful surroundings he outlined his plans for the War Cabinet.

It was to consist, Chamberlain told Hoare, of himself, the Foreign Secretary, the Chancellor of the Exchequer, a Minister for Co-ordination of Defence, three Service Ministers and a Minister Without Portfolio. Chamberlain then asked Hoare to join as Lord Privy Seal, a post with a very high political and social standing but with no specific departmental duties. He offered him the alternative of retaining his present post as Home Secretary without a Cabinet seat.

Hoare nobly offered to retire, suggesting that Chamberlain might feel it wise to have a completely new Government. But the Prime Minister had already decided against this and turned down both the idea and the proffered resignation. Hoare then agreed to enter the War Cabinet as Lord Privy Seal. As an indication of the pace Chamberlain was setting, Hoare recalled later that he was sworn in 'within a couple of hours'.

Having set the ball rolling, the Prime Minister then began the exhausting round of formal discussions which such a major reorganization entailed. He spoke to some of those involved on the telephone, others he saw at Westminster, still others he summoned to Number Ten. One of these was Winston Churchill, who left the Commons telling his personal detective and chauffeur, W. H. Thompson: 'Ten Downing Street.' Thompson later recalled: 'There was a gleam in his eye, but even he did not anticipate his exact appointment.'

When he emerged from Number Ten to join Mrs. Churchill in the back of the car, he said happily: 'It's the Admiralty,' and added with a chuckle: 'That's a lot better than I thought.' Churchill went home for a quick meal, then made straight for the Admiralty, where he was to stay until early the next morning.

Chamberlain had invited his colleagues in the Administration to place their resignations collectively in his hands so that he could put into effect his newly-made decisions. By 4 p.m., the War Cabinet had been settled, although it was to be a further two or three hours before the public would be told of the country's new leadership. The top wartime administration was to consist of: Prime Minister and First Lord of the Treasury: Mr. Chamberlain; Chancellor of the Exchequer: Sir John Simon; Foreign Secretary: Lord Halifax; Minister for Co-ordination of Defence: Admiral of the Fleet Lord Chatfield; First Lord of the Admiralty: Winston Churchill; Secretary of State for War: Leslie Hore-Belisha; Secretary of State for Air: Sir Kingsley Wood; Lord Privy Seal: Sir Samuel Hoare; Minister Without Portfolio: Lord Hankey.

Other Ministerial appointments outside the Cabinet were to include: Lord President of the Council: Lord Stanhope; Lord Chancellor: Sir Thomas Inskip; Home Secretary and Minister of Home Security: Sir John Anderson; Secretary of State for Dominion Affairs: Anthony Eden.

Churchill and Lord Hankey were new members of the Government and the latter had not held ministerial office before. But he had amassed valuable experience as Secretary of the War Cabinet set up by Lloyd George in 1916 and of the subsequent Imperial War Cabinet. Between the wars he had held jointly the positions of Secretary to the Cabinet, Secretary to the Committee of Imperial Defence and Clerk of the Privy Council. Anthony Eden's return to the Government was another notable feature of Chamberlain's re-shuffle, particularly as he was promised 'special access' to the War Cabinet itself, though he was not actually a member. It was more than a year since his resignation from the Foreign Secretaryship he had held for three years.

Other new posts which Chamberlain created included a Minister of Information. He gave this new Ministry, for which plans had been laid in the spring and summer of 1939, to Lord Macmillan, then one of the judicial members of the House of Lords and an authority on international law. Sir Samuel Hoare, as Home Secretary, had previously organised a skeleton staff for the new Ministry in four sections: Home, Neutral Countries, Enemy Countries and Censorship. Lord Macmillan's job was to handle all Government Press news, to apply the necessary censorship and to organise the dissemination of propaganda in Germany and the neutral countries.

Chamberlain also resurrected, with a new name, the Ministry of Blockade, initiated by Lloyd George in the First World War. The 1939 version was the Ministry of Economic Warfare. The job was given to Mr. Ronald Cross, whose task was the systematic disorganization by hook or by crook of the enemy's economy.

The Prime Minister, apart from disappointing a number of his closest Conservative supporters by the promotion of Churchill and Eden, was also drawn immediately into a sharp War Office battle over top Army appointments. The new Secretary of State for War, Hore-Belisha, was the youngest member of the War Cabinet by a dozen years and had all youth's traditional lack of regard for established position and precedents. When Hore-Belisha swung into action that afternoon to reorganize the higher echelons of the British Army, he encountered stiff resistance from entrenched First World War chiefs to proposed Command changes. Hore-Belisha was determined, however, to get his own way and turned to Chamberlain for support.

At issue were the appointments of a Commander-in-Chief of the British Expeditionary Force to France and the resultant re-shuffle at the top of the Army hierarchy. His diary for the day included this entry: 'I told the P.M. I would like to have a further word with him about the C.-in-C. and the proposed new appointments. Went across to No. 10.

'P.M. told me he left the new appointments to me, but suggested that I discuss the matter with Kingsley and Winston. Telephoned Kingsley, who came over from Air Ministry to see me. Left message at the Palace, where Winston had gone to receive the seals of office, asking him to come too.'

Hore-Belisha told his two ministerial colleagues that he intended to appoint General the Viscount Gort Commander-in-Chief of the British Expeditionary Force. Both Churchill and Sir Kingsley Wood agreed to this. Hore-Belisha then moved on to the proposed appointment of General Sir Edmund Ironside to succeed Gort as Chief of the Imperial General Staff. This appointment, which Churchill favoured, but which Wood opposed, was being made in the face of bitter criticism from influential Army chiefs. 'Ironside's appointment is not popular in the War Office,' Hore-Belisha's diary for the day noted. But he justified Ironside's selection by adding: 'If he had the disqualifications attributed to him—indiscreet, intriguer, not liked in the Army—he had that dynamic strength which was essential in the present crisis.'

Late that afternoon the Cabinet met and among other matters approved Ironside's appointment. Again, there was opposition to the posting, but Churchill came down heavily on the General's side and his intervention settled the matter. The Cabinet meeting further agreed to entrust command of the British Expeditionary Force to 53-year-old Lord Gort, whose outstanding First World War exploits had brought him four wounds, the V.C., D.S.O. and two bars, the Military Cross and nine mentions in dispatches. Among the positions he had held between the wars had been the post of Director of Military Training in India.

Chamberlain and his ministers ruled, too, that Gort should serve under General Georges, French Commander-in-Chief in the North-East Theatre, instructing the British leader to 'co-operate with our allies in the defeat of the common enemy', and to 'carry out loyally' Georges' instructions. But the Cabinet cautiously left a loophole empowering Gort to appeal to London if he felt that the French General's orders imperilled the British Field Force.

Gort was also instructed: 'It is the desire of His Majesty's Government to keep the British Forces under your command, as far as possible, together. If at any time the French Commander-in-Chief, "North-East Theatre of Operations", finds it essential for any reason to transfer any portion of the British troops to an area other than that in which your main force is operating, it should be distinctly understood that this is only a temporary arrangement and that as soon as practicable the troops thus detached should be re-united to the main body of the British Forces . . .

'Whilst the Royal Air Force Component of the Field Force is included under your command, the Advanced Air Striking Force, which will also operate from French territory, is an independent force under the direct control of the Air Officer Commander-in-Chief, Bomber Command, in the United Kingdom. The War Office has nevertheless undertaken the maintenance of this force from the common bases up to railhead, and for this you, as Commander-in-Chief of the Field Force, will be responsible.'

The Cabinet's final instruction was that Gort should keep in constant touch with the War Office and make regular reports. He was sent on his way backed by the 'full and unqualified support of the Government, of the Army Council and of the British people'. Gort's instructions were signed by Hore-Belisha, who after the meeting put the Cabinet recommendations before King George at an audience. He then returned to the War Office to confirm the appointments.

'I saw Gort on my return to the W.O. and told him of his selection as C.-in-C.,' Hore-Belisha noted in his diary. 'I saw Ironside and told him of his appointment as C.I.G.S. At first I thought he was a little disappointed, as he had expectations of being C.-in-C., but he warmed to it during our talk.

'I said I was going to be quite frank about what his critics had said. When he spoke up for himself, I told him he need not put up any defence. The decision had been made and I would stand by him. I urged him to be frank with me always and that if he had any criticism to make to say it to me and not outside.'

According to his own account, General Sir Edmund (later Lord) Ironside, regarded his own appointment as 'pretty devastating'. He told Hore-Belisha that the allegation he talked too much and was unreliable was a 'most scandalous, lying accusation'. The General warned the War Minister that if he (Hore-Belisha) thought the same, he had no intention of taking the job. Hore-Belisha replied that he had complete faith in Ironside, and finally appealed to the General to dismiss their conversation from his mind.

Ironside's recently published diaries reveal his impressions of the interview as follows: 'I am bitterly disappointed that I am not to command the Army in the field. My great ambition. I am not suited in temperament to such a job as C.I.G.S., nor have I prepared myself to be such. My whole life has been based upon doing what I was told, and there it is.

'The disgust I feel that I was considered unreliable and difficult to get on with makes me feel angry. I am not one to mince my words, but war does not require the same characteristics as peace. I'll do my job to the best of my ability and honestly, but I confess I have misgivings.'

Hore-Belisha's decisions that day, besides sparking immediate controversy in Whitehall and the Army, were to remain a matter of recurrent dispute for almost twenty years afterwards. As late as 1958, they were still fresh in the mind of Field Marshal Viscount Montgomery of Alamein. Writing his memoirs, the Field Marshal classed Gort, Major-General Henry Pownall (Director of Military Operations and Intelligence) and Major-General Douglas Brownrigg (Director-General of the Territorial Army), as 'three of the most important officers in the War Office at the outbreak of the war'.

Yet Montgomery, a divisional commander when war broke out, recalled: 'All of these three officers left the War Office on the day war was declared: Gort to become Commander-in-Chief of the B.E.F., Pownall to become Chief of the General Staff of the B.E.F., and Brownrigg to become Adjutant-General of the B.E.F. It is almost unbelievable that such a thing should have been allowed to happen. But it did. I understand that the War Office emptied in a similar way in 1914.'

Montgomery also wrote: 'I have always held the opinion that Gort's appointment to command the B.E.F., in September, 1939, was a mistake; the job was above his ceiling. One only has to read his instructions signed by Hore-Belisha, and dated 3rd September, 1939, to see what he was in for; that directive is a pretty fair commentary on the command set-up and it would have taxed a much better brain than Gort's to deal with such a complicated problem. Furthermore, he was asked to attempt the impossible: his Headquarters had to act as a G.H.Q., and at the same time had to exercise direct command over the fighting and administrative forces allotted to him.'

British servicemen were already established on French soil that evening, as the Royal Air Force had flown 18 officers and 31 other ranks across the Channel the previous day. The first Army advance party was due to leave from Portsmouth on the Monday, and the first convoy of troopships from Southampton and the Bristol Channel ports five days later. By the end of September, 152,000 British Army personnel, 9,000 R.A.F. men and almost 24,000 service vehicles were to be landed in France without loss. The British Army, in the throes of an expansion programme designed to increase it to thirty-two divisions, had promised four divisions within the first month of hostilities to stand beside seventy-two divisions of front line French troops and a further twelve divisions of fortress personnel.

At 4.23 p.m. after the House had been sitting for more than four hours, Captain Margesson, Parliamentary Secretary to the Treasury, moved the adjournment. In doing so, he said Parliament would be meeting again the following day at 2.45 p.m. to continue considering emergency legislation—six Bills presented in the Commons that day and four from the Lords.

Mr. Lloyd George, on the adjournment, asked the Parliamentary Secretary to the Treasury whether the House could give time to a discussion on 'certain essential services', in particular food production. He said the food producing community were 'in the dark as to what the Government expect them to do'. The First World War leader added that he understood there were certain things which might not be regarded as essential, but others which were. He instanced a restriction on farmers on the acreage they could have under potatoes and asked about pigmeat and cereal production. Calling for information on the Government's plan, Mr. Lloyd George said: 'Are we to assume that the war will be a short one? Everybody hopes for the best but I am not at all sure that a short war will be the best for us.

'That, however, is another matter. If it is to be a long war, then we are confronted with very great and new difficulties in regard to the carriage of food to this country—difficulties with which we were *not* faced in the last war. Therefore it is very important that we should not put off the problem of increased and intensified production for one moment longer than we can avoid. I would ask the Chief Whip whether he can give us any information as to whether we shall have a chance of having full conversation in the House, so that publicity may be given on the advice of the Government upon these subjects, and we may be able to call attention to things in regard to which we are entirely in the dark.'

Captain Margesson replied that he had not had notice of Mr. Lloyd George's question and it was difficult for him to answer. But he could say the Government would be ready to supply facilities for the discussion Mr. Lloyd George had outlined. In subsequent exchanges, Margesson said he understood some legislation would be necessary and undertook to convey the views of Lloyd George to the Prime Minister and other responsible ministers.

At 4.33 p.m. Mr. Gurney Braithwaite asked: 'Some of us who are officers in His Majesty's Forces have to take up important appointments tomorrow and there is one matter which I should like to bring before the notice of the Chief Whip. We have met today on the first day of a great and critical war. Can the Chief Whip give the House this assurance: that until such time as this House becomes completely untenable through enemy action, which I personally think unlikely, the House of Commons, the people's House, will continue to meet in the capital, in London, at a time when the morale of the people is so important.

'Some of us who have to go on war service will attend here when we can, but it would be a great encouragement to us if we could be given an assurance that the House will meet in the capital of the Empire.'

Captain Margesson: 'Yes, sir. With complete confidence I can give that assurance so far as it affects His Majesty's Government. The only reason for taking the precautions so far is in case this particular building should become untenable and we were compelled to meet somewhere else. If we could not meet here, we must obviously meet somewhere else. I can say that His Majesty's Government are determined that the seat of Government will remain in London as long as it is absolutely possible.'

Mr. Cluse: 'May I ask that if Hon. Members are brought here the Government will take the opportunity of using their services in some way?'

Captain Margesson: 'Yes, sir. The Government are fully aware how anxious all members of the House are to do whatever they can to aid the common cause which we all have at heart. I do not think it is possible for me at the moment to say any more, but when the moment comes and the Government can say something more, I can assure the Hon. Member that they will do so.'

Mr. McGovern: 'Can the right Hon. Gentleman assure us that he will be able to extend the military age to 70 for Hon. Members of this House?'

The House adjourned at 4.37 p.m.

VIII

France entered the war against Germany at 5 p.m. in a mood of quiet confidence. The bars and the cafés were full of people, but so were the churches. Only at the railway stations and bus terminals was there bustle and noise as huge batches of young evacuees and their mothers or aged relatives left for safe provincial havens. Occasionally a military convoy would rumble through the capital, but otherwise all was peace. 'Paris,' noted the great writer Colette, 'never seemed calmer.'

That shrewd observer of the Parisian scene wrote down her impression of that hour for posterity as follows: 'With an army leaving and a civil population going to the provinces, in silent, thoughtful crowds, Paris never seemed calmer. Everyone wondered at the helpfulness and coolness of his neighbour and did not pause to think that the neighbour was thinking the same of him. Extreme situations bring forth almost all our basic characteristics. Who would have thought that the Frenchman, in the gravest emergency, would be above all an angel of moderation? He is though.

'The admirable organization which is directing the military movements of an entire nation, has not the only right to our praise. In France the smallest cog in the machinery knows how to make himself intelligent when he wants. He wants to now with all his strength. He supports the action of the great powerful hand which is leading him away from his own business . . .

'The best of Paris has gone from a Paris suddenly enlarged and echoing. A new, uncertain life is beginning for those who remain . . .'

Soon after the declaration of war, Cardinal Verdier, the Archbishop of Paris, delivered a moving and encouraging address to his devout Catholic followers and the nation as a whole. He declared: 'The departure of your children, your husbands and your brothers has brought

sadness, anguish and tears into all our homes. But I dare to tell you
not to weep as people who have no hope. The struggle which is now
beginning appears, thanks to God, to be very different to that which
made so many graves in our beloved country twenty-five years ago.

'Our preparations leave nothing to be desired. Our collaboration
with Great Britain, who is so powerful, is immediate and total. I feel
that other countries will soon be at our sides to obtain a swift victory.
The civilized world bows before the noble action of our leaders and
the truly magnificent behavior of our soldiers. A breath of superhuman greatness arouses our dear France once more.

'I was struck, as you all were, by powerful emotions at the time of
separation. But pride and hope dried my tears. I know that the Holy
Father, whose work for peace has been admirable, and other nations
who love us and support our cause, still have hopes of limiting and
even stopping the conflict . . .

'In your name and mine, I salute the courageous people of
Poland, who are fighting so heroically for their liberty, for ours, and
for the freedom of the world.'

Another distinguished Frenchman whose thoughts went back to the
similar situation of 1914 was M. Jerome Tharaud, a member of the
Academie Francaise, who wrote on Sunday evening: 'During the last
few hours I have been overcome with memories, as have many of the
men of my generation who lived through similar hours twenty-five
years ago.

'I see before me the same faces. I hear the same voices. I find the
same calm and resolution. How the people of Paris rise naturally and
effortlessly to the level of these great tragedies in which their destiny
is in the balance!

'I could have said "the people of France". The day before yesterday
I was in Marseilles. The whole population, with a unanimous intui-
tion, knew that this thing was inevitable, and that shortly they would
know what had doubtless been in Hitler's mind for weeks. But in the
huge crowds which wandered all night through the dimly-lit streets,
from Canebiere and the old port to the alleys of Meillan, it was the
same as in Paris; the same silent emotion and the same dignity before
an ordained destiny.

'Yes, that was something fine. From the south to the north of
France, from the east to the west, there was this calm and resolution

which are the hereditary virtues of our people, and which come, I believe, from the deep feeling that they have never in their history done other than honour commanded.'

Tharaud added: 'The Paris I see today is the same as I saw in 1914. Nothing seems changed, except perhaps that there is less fever, as if our people feel more sure of themselves this time; feel that they have taken up arms not simply for the most just cause, but for their very existence.'

A reporter for *l'Intransigeant* recorded the moments which brought France into the war: 'Five o'clock came and nothing changed. We were in the Montholon Square. The terraces of the cafés were still filled with people—subdued certainly, but keeping personal anxieties under control.

'In the gardens outside the open underground shelters, children who had not yet been evacuated played with a zest which showed that their families had managed to keep them calm. On the beaches women were quietly sewing those charming pieces of embroidery in which improbable multicoloured vegetation flourishes. Indifference? Certainly not. But the need to affirm in the simplest and humblest manner that life goes on.'

The late editions of the evening newspapers brought out their biggest and blackest type for the headlines. LA GUERRE, declared *l'Intransigeant* in letters six inches deep. But the editorial comment inside was generally restrained, in the national mood of sober determination, mingled with chauvinism. Thus *Paris Soir*: 'All French people are ready to do their duty, to give their lives if need be. What would life be worth in a subjugated France in any case? The hour has struck for the liberation of Europe by the free nations. For Hitler and his men the purging of their sins is about to begin. Long live immortal France: Long live France.'

A reporter on the same newspaper noted at Montparnasse the following scene as an example of the way that social barriers were forgotten as the nation went to war: 'There were very few porters and we saw a Lieutenant Colonel together with a private, pushing a luggage cart at the Montparnasse station. The colonel had put his family's luggage on the car and the private had sat his little daughter on the luggage. Everywhere there was the same calm, coolness and determination to be finished once and for all with the obsession of

Hitler. (But it could have been that readers of the newspaper were more interested that evening in the serialization of Agatha Christie's *Ten Little Nigger Boys*, then enjoying a great vogue in France.)

Firemen and civil defence workers were still working on air-raid precautions as the evening shadows lengthened. *Paris-Midi* readers were assured: 'The most highly-trained staffs and the most modern equipment are ready and all that could be foreseen has been prepared for to ensure the efficiency of rescue work . . .' An evening announcement from the State Railway said nothing had changed so far as they were concerned, except that arrival and departure times and the normal delivery of registered parcels could no longer be guaranteed. It added: 'Luggage will still be accepted and registered, however, and dogs will still be allowed to travel on trains.'

But patriotic fever had not gripped every Frenchman that evening. One Louis B. . . ., of Annemasse in eastern France, a professional thief, was arrested as the war began for car thefts. He had cashed in on the situation by dressing up as a naval officer and had spent the week-end working the Haute Savoie region.

The first day of the war had also found many of the nation's shop-keepers only too willing to seek to profit from the crisis. A 6 p.m. statement from the National Committee for Price Control said that most trades and industries had dutifully responded to an appeal to impose a rigorous stabilization of prices in preparation for the war. 'Nevertheless, certain abuses, although rare, have been recorded,' the Committee added grimly. 'Consequently the Committee reminds all concerned that such lapses will not be tolerated at the present time. All abnormal increases will be immediately suppressed in accordance with this policy, a number of potato traders in the Nord and Haute-Garonne departments have been summoned to appear before a court.' Police were also reported to have swooped on traders who 'raised their prices considerably' in the Paris suburb of St. Germain en Laye, and issued 'the most serious warnings'.

Police not engaged in tracking down the first of the war profiteers were likely to be involved in raids on branches of the Communist Party and the homes of leading members. Several hundred arrests were reported by *Le Temps* to have been carried out during the week-end in Paris alone. Numerous code documents had been seized and were being examined by the military authorities on Sunday evening.

A court in Paris's 16th district had handed out sentences of three months in prison, topped by fines of fifty francs, to twelve communists who had been found distributing leaflets in favour of the German-Soviet Pact. Every radio news bulletin and each fresh edition of the evening newspapers during the day had brought fresh reports of communist leaders and members being arrested all over France. Major swoops had taken place on communist branches in St. Foy and Nancy.

All afternoon and evening, French trade unions had been issuing statements expressing the bitterness and the puzzlement of the workers at the agreement with Nazi Germany. The Confédération Général du Travail (the French Trades Union Congress) declared that the Pact had struck the 'heaviest blow at the Peace Front policy'. The Aircraft Workers Union approved a resolution on Sunday evening that it could not understand or approve the change in foreign policy of the U.S.S.R., cause of the extreme tension in international relations. The National Federation of Underground Workers condemned the German-Soviet Pact in equally strong terms.

With the beginning of the war, officialdom eased into top gear with a flow of directives to French civilians. First edict to the non-military population from the Defence Ministry after 5 p.m. was that the distribution of gas-masks to civilians would be interrupted to 'permit the renewal of stocks by the military authorities'. The public would be informed later of the resumption of distribution.

The Ministry of Home Defence issued a statement advising civilians 'what to do and what not to do to ensure one's safety': During the day 'you must be ready for any eventuality and have your gas-mask ready for instant use. You must not leave home without your mask, as carrying them is obligatory day and night.' At night 'you must always have an electric torch on hand. You must not light matches, candles or torches at a time of alert.'

In the car, 'you must travel with white sidelights or blue masked headlights. Stop in an alert and seek a shelter. You must not travel with ordinary headlights or leave the lights on or the car engine running in an alert.' At home or in the street, 'you must go as fast as possible to the nearest shelter. By being prudent, you will save other's lives. You must not go to the window or stay on the pavement to see what happens.'

During air attacks, the Ministry told the French civilian, 'you must call the rescue service as soon as possible, lie injured persons down and wait for help in moving them, and have food available in an hermetically sealed box. You must not move an injured person or remove his gas-mask, run away when someone is injured, or eat food or drink water contaminated by a near explosion of a gas bomb.'

Another statement reminded the public of the signals for air attacks—by sirens and police klaxons—and the 'warning for gas' which Parisians had been taught to dread most of all. This would be given at contaminated points by special detector vans and would consist of a continual klaxon alarm.

So France prepared for the struggle . . . The bankers could take confidence from Press accounts that day of the strength of the nation's economy. Gold had continued to flow into France even until Saturday morning and there was every prospect of it continuing the following day. Bank deposits had remained higher than withdrawals and generally there was every hope that this display of public confidence would continue. From the following day, the Bank of France would be authorised to issue notes of five, ten and twenty francs following the week-end announcement of the withdrawal from circulation of nickel five-franc and silver ten- and twenty-franc pieces. At the other end of the social scale, the Ministry of Labour announced that allowances for dependents would still be paid to unemployed men whose families had been evacuated, provided they did not accept financial help or obtain jobs in the provinces. Airlines would continue operations on a limited scale and a leading woman aviator signed on to become an airline pilot to free a man for active duty. She was Maryse Hilsz, famed for her flights to Madagascar and Saigon.

But there was one Frenchman whose confidence in his country was marred by nagging doubts about French military strength that evening. His name was Colonel Charles de Gaulle, the officer commanding the tanks of the French Fifth Army at Wangenburg, Alsace. De Gaulle, then 48, had been a professional soldier of revolutionary ideas for thirty years. Even before the First World War he had become convinced that cavalry was on the way out and that machine-guns and cannon would be the decisive factor in future wars. As a Lieutenant aged 24, in August, 1914, he had undergone the sickening experience of seeing his riflemen mown down by German machine-guns. After the 1914–18 war, four wounds and capture by the Germans, he had fought against the Russians in Poland in 1919–20. Then, from 1920 onwards, he had formulated theories of armoured warfare, first as a lecturer at a Polish military school, then as Professor of Military History at St. Cyr, and next as a member of the French General Staff.

Throughout the nineteen-twenties and the 'thirties, de Gaulle had written and lectured on his recurrent theme that the days of static warfare were over. He had advocated a modern army for France, with mobility, strong firepower and the ability to launch surprise attacks. He had organized 'paper armies' of highly-mechanized units which closely resembled the later German Panzer divisions. But his writings had been read mainly in Germany and ignored at home. His friend and First World War commander, Marshal Petain, had supported him for a time, but had then become a backer of the Maginot Line concept of defence. As Secretary-General of the Council for National Defence, de Gaulle had tried in 1935 to get the French Army reorganized on modern lines with six armoured divisions, but the Army chiefs and the National Assembly had both opposed the idea.

In that same year, Germany's first Panzer unit had begun to take shape, while France's military leaders continued to maintain that tanks and aircraft had not altered the basic rules of warfare and that secure fortifications remained France's greatest need. De Gaulle, his views ignored, had left the Defence Council and 'marked time' as a Lieutenant Colonel. But he continued to campaign for armoured divisions and in December, 1938, the decision was taken to equip France's first two. By 1939, however, Germany had twelve Panzer divisions and France was too far behind to catch up within the foreseeable future.

Now, the German armoured divisions were over-running Poland and a bitter de Gaulle was seeing all his theories of a war of movement vindicated to a terrifying degree. That week-end he decided to begin the drafting of a secret memorandum urging a rapid build-up of France's armoured units. With the encouragement of his friend, Reynaud, it was destined to go to eighty leading politicians and Generals, with Daladier at the head of the list. As France entered the war, de Gaulle was at work drafting the memorandum in his careful, scholarly language. Within a short time, its outspoken, prophetic statements about the nation's unpreparedness were due to cause a major rumpus in the ruling political and military circles . . .

Here is an extract from the remarkable document that Colonel de Gaulle was working on that Sunday evening in his quarters at Wangen-

burg: 'As for us, attached as we are even more solidly than most to
ancient ideas, we have begun the war with five million soldiers, but
an Air Force only in embryo and an armoured force completely insufficient in numbers and in power. There was, therefore, never any
possibility that we could lend our allies in the east that direct or indirect aid which was essential . . .

'To break an attack by a mechanized force only mechanized force
has any certain efficiency. The massive counter-attack of aerial and
land squadrons directed against an adversary with freedom of movement demands the use of modern defensive methods. When we have
limited the advance of our own military forces to the frontier of our
territory the creation of a shock instrument, an instrument of manœuvre and of speed, is an absolute necessity.

'If the enemy has not already built up a mechanized force sufficient
to break through our lines he soon will. The startling success of his
motorized divisions in Poland will encourage him to try again in the
new way. Now it is necessary that we should realize that the Maginot
Line, for all the reinforcements that it has received and will receive,
whatever the quantities of infantry and artillery which occupy it or
support it, is capable of being overcome. Tanks employed *en masse*
are capable of over-running our defences, active and passive. For these
engines of war it is only a matter of armour, of armament, freedom of
movement—all attributes it is easy to give to them . . .

'It is essential to create new armoured and mechanized divisions.
On land, fast divisions and divisions of the line, each provided with
tanks in sufficient number and powerful enough, armoured infantry,
enough artillery to sustain themselves in battle, equipped with all the
means of break-through and movement necessary to overcome the ob-
stacles which the enemy and the terrain would place against them,
and provided with special vehicles which would clear the roads for
the transports and supplies. In the air, assault divisions capable in the
course of battle of maintaining a position and of swooping down on
the enemy to attack on land or water, and of long-range squadrons
capable of attacking the industrial vitals of the enemy.

'The combination of these land and air forces will permit large
ruptures of the enemy lines, widespread manœuvres, and the ability
to exploit the gains. By these means a new strategy will be born, on
the land, on the sea, and in the air . . .'

IX

Shortly before 6 p.m. the Admiralty in London received word that its new chief was on his way. Within minutes a signal flashed across the seas to every ship of the British fleet: 'Winston is back.' The words brought a flood of memories to the Navy's First World War commanders who had served under Churchill, and young officers who knew him only as a man of legend felt the surge of confidence a tried leader gives those he leads.

Promptly at six, Churchill arrived at the Admiralty and went straight to the desk he had last occupied nearly a quarter of a century before, with the familiar maps and ornaments around him. He summoned the First Sea Lord, Admiral of the Fleet Sir Dudley Pound, and other Naval leaders, and the group went into immediate conference. Churchill was eager and excited, but his confident, businesslike approach as he called for the map on which he had plotted the British fleet's wartime movements in 1914 and 1915 quickly won him the respect of his new colleagues. Most were to remain there with him at work until early the following morning.

When Churchill took over at the Admiralty, the fleet was already well and truly at war, having begun the blockade of Germany six hours before. After satisfying himself with the arrangements for this, Churchill turned his attention to a hunt for what was potentially the first big prize which Britain might take on the high seas: the 51,731-ton *Bremen*, pride of the German merchant fleet, then on her way home from New York.

Here was a golden opportunity for the British fleet, as the *Bremen* had left only thirty-six hours before Germany invaded Poland. She had been delayed in New York for thirty-six hours by a forty-man squad of American Customs and Marine Bureau inspectors who combed her from top to bottom in search of war contraband. For almost two days the inspectors had peered and poked into every corner of the great ship, the monotony being relieved only when one of them fell overboard, causing a shortlived burst of merriment among the impatient German officers.

Finally, the inspectors, working under orders approved by President Roosevelt, had given the 'all clear' to furious German officials, who claimed that the delay had cost them thousands of dollars. President Roosevelt was later to deny that there had been any discrimination against Germany in the operation of the contraband regulations, and other ships searched during the period included Britain's *Aquitania*, France's *Normandie*, the Italian *Roma* and many others. But the delay to the *Bremen* had, in fact, given the British cruiser *Berwick* time to slip out of Bar Harbour, Maine, and position herself for a chase of the German luxury liner.

The *Bremen*, however, had already evaded the *Berwick*, another British cruiser, and a British merchantman, the *California*, which she passed with all lights blazing before completely 'disappearing'. That evening she was being hunted by a large part of the Royal Navy. Submarines from flotillas based on Dundee and Blyth were lying in wait for her at the entrances to Germany's home ports. The six-inch gun cruisers *Southampton* and *Glasgow*, which together with eight destroyers made up the Humber Force, were cruising off the Norwegian coast. And the main bulk of the Home Fleet, positioned about 400 miles to the west of the Hebrides, had been ordered by Admiral Sir Charles Forbes, its Commander-in-Chief, to make a wide sweep of the North Atlantic.

But the British warships were dealing with a worthy foe. The *Bremen's* Captain, Commodore Adolf Ahrens, was an experienced sailor, tough and resourceful and a wily tactician. He was aware that half the world was asking: 'Where is the *Bremen?*' As the hunt intensified that evening he called his crew of nearly 1,000 together and told them: 'Men, war in Europe has started. It doesn't look very good for us, for I have sworn that the British won't seize me and my ship while I'm alive. I would rather sink the *Bremen*.' At these determined words everyone gave the Nazi salute except the Dutch cook, Eddie Post, who later commented: 'Quite frankly, as a Hollander, the prospect of disappearing below the surface for good didn't attract me very much.'

To impress his determination on the crew, Ahrens ordered them to place barrels of petrol around the deck so that the *Bremen* could be set on fire rather than fall into enemy hands. He had the crew cabins in the forepart of the ship evacuated that evening so that if a collision occurred the men would be safer. The ship had now been painted a drab grey all over, but Ahrens wanted the job of camouflage extended and told everyone on board to take a brush and a pot of grey paint whenever he had nothing to do and add to the good work. Sailors, ship's butchers, stewards and cooks had all been conscripted to this work and one of them recalled afterwards that when they had finished the *Bremen* was invisible in mist at a distance of only a few hundred feet. Ahrens also reiterated that evening his standing order that all radio calls must be ignored. *Bremen* therefore sailed on in complete silence, refusing to give away her position in answer to every ruse tried by the British.

Only a few senior officers knew the roundabout route that their captain was taking to avoid capture. The only clue for the crew was the continual drop in temperature, indicating that they were sailing all the time into waters farther north, well off all the normal shipping lanes. Emergency drills were obligatory several times a day and every man available was on lookout duty. There was little sleep for anyone and the crew were becoming colder by the hour. But the hardship was already paying dividends: when night closed in on the first day of the war the *Bremen* was already sailing into waters where her pursuers would not expect to find her. Ahren's modest comment later was that 'we were able, in the dark and in favourable weather conditions, to defy all attempts to follow us'. The *Bremen* was to sail all through the night and for three more days before reaching Murmansk on 6th September. Later, the plucky Commodore was to sail the liner home safely to Bremerhaven with a skeleton crew of 150, passing within firing range of a British submarine on the way. His courage and seamanship, however, preserved the great liner only until March, 1941, when she was set ablaze and destroyed, probably by an act of sabotage.

While the *Bremen* was being hunted, the world's largest liner, Britain's 81,000-ton *Queen Mary*, was nearing New York with her ports and windows blackened, her radio silent and her crew watching anxiously for German U-boats. *Queen Mary*, nearing safe waters as Churchill took over the Admiralty had been convoyed by British ships part of the way. Aboard was a forty-four million-dollar shipment of gold and more than 2,300 people, including banker John Pierpont Morgan, cinema magnate Harry M. Warner, author Erich Maria Remarque and many other celebrities. Some of them slept on the floor, others in cots in the liner's public rooms. Morgan, who normally took a whole suite, occupied a small room with only one bed. He was anxious to put everyone at ease and remarked during the crossing: 'it's the size I always sleep in at home. Really, I don't need a bed half an acre large.'

Author Remarque, whose *All Quiet on the Western Front* had been the most famous novel of the First World War, would not comment on the Second. He had lost his German citizenship and was travelling on a Swiss identity card. But he had only sympathy for his native country, commenting: 'Poor Germany, I cannot fight against her.'

A British liner travelling in the opposite direction that evening was carrying Britain's much publicized 'first prisoner of war'—a beautiful blonde German woman. She was Fraulein Helen Mutterer, a 27-year-old interpreting stewardess in the Cunard White Star liner *Georgic*. Taken off the *Georgic* in New York a few hours earlier, she was now being shipped back to Britain in the brig of the Cunard liner *Carinthia*. To some American newspapers, her 'capture' was front page news and the occasion for quips about British inability to seize the *Bremen*.

'She is technically a prisoner,' Captain W. C. Battle of the *Carinthia* told delighted newspapermen as his ship slipped out to sea, wearing a new camouflage of mud-grey and carrying a heavy cargo but only seventy-three passengers. The *Carinthia's* officers described the blonde fraulein as 'one of the most beautiful stewardesses ever to sail' and said she was intelligent and charming. Chief Steward Thomas Brennan declared: 'She is just unlucky enough to be a German.' He added that the girl had told him: 'I would rather be going to an English prison camp than returning to Germany.'

Parallel with the hunt for the *Bremen* came news of bigger prey for Churchill and his Admirals: units of the German fleet had left Wilhelmshaven and were entering the Schillig Roads. This report, however, had been delayed by an unfortunate set of circumstances. The R.A.F. Blenheim which had left Wyton that morning soon after the declaration of war, had arrived over the German warships just two hours later and had begun taking photographs of them immediately. But, flying at 24,000 feet, their radio had suddenly iced up and they had been unable to transmit the vital information back to base. The Blenheim came home with 75 photographs of German warships and the squadron's logbook was able to record proudly: 'Duty successful . . . The first R.A.F. aircraft to cross the German frontier.'

A striking force of British bombers took off at dusk to attack the enemy fleet but was forced to turn back by bad weather and poor visibility. Units of the Home Fleet, also armed with the Blenheim's reconnaissance report, were steaming towards the German coast that evening in the hope of intercepting the warships in the Schillig Roads. Another reconnaissance flight was to be made by the same Blenheim the next day, which was again to be handicapped by radio trouble; but the 4th September mission was to result in a raid which caused damage to two German warships with the loss of seven out of twenty-nine R.A.F. bombers.

Britain's prompt aggression in the war at sea made a strong impression on Germany's naval chiefs, already very conscious of their weaknesses in both ships and men. No one that evening in the German Navy was contemplating the future with more despondency than Grand Admiral Erich Raeder, Supreme Commander of the Führer's young fleet. Raeder had been fighting a running battle for years with Hitler, who favoured land battles, and Goering, whose heart was always in the Luftwaffe. Until 3rd September, he had lost no opportunity to point out that Germany was only at the beginning of her naval building programme and that 'even if we kept all our shipyards fully employed we could not contemplate a naval war with Britain before 1945 or 1946'. All his plans had been based on the assumption that he would have many years more to prepare for action.

Early in 1939, Raeder had suggested to Hitler plans for building an effective German fleet. The Grand Admiral had told his leader 'if we concentrated primarily on submarines and capital ships, then in a short time we should be able to build up a fleet capable of representing a real threat to Britain's overseas communications in the event of war. However, such a fleet would not be well balanced and would not be in a position to engage British naval forces on any large scale. A fleet able not only to attack Britain's overseas communications but also to engage powerful British naval forces would take much longer to build . . .'

Hitler had then stressed that he would not need the fleet as an instrument for his purposes until 1946 and had declared that he antic- ipated a long period of peaceful development in which the Navy would have an opportunity of building up its strength unhindered. He was therefore in favour of a stronger fleet to be completed at a later date; the Navy should draw up its building plans on that assumption. So Raeder had gone away to draw up his famous 'Z-Plan', which he had presented to Hitler a few months before war broke out. Raeder's idea was that the plan could be completed in 1948, but Hitler had impatiently cut the time limit to 1945.

Now it was war, and the 'Z-Plan' still in the embryo stage. Raeder was so pessimistic about the situation on the evening of 3rd Septem- ber that he drafted a note for the naval files summarizing his views: 'Today, the war against England and France began—the war which, according to the Führer's previous assertions, we had no reason to ex- pect before about 1944. The Führer believed up to the last minute that it could be avoided, even if this meant postponing a final settle- ment of the Polish question. (The Führer made a statement to this effect to the Commanders-in-Chief of the armed forces at the Ober- salzburg on 22nd August.) At the turn of the year 1944–45, by which time, according to the Führer's instructions, the Navy's Z-Plan would have been completed, Germany could have begun a war against Great Britain with the Navy at the following strength: For merchant warfare on the high seas: 3 fast battleships; 3 converted pocket battleships; 5 heavy cruisers; several minelayers and reconnaissance cruisers; 2 air- craft carriers; about 190 submarines, including about 6 gun sub- marines; 6 fleet submarines and 6 mine-laying submarines.

'Two groups, each consisting of 3 of the heaviest type Diesel-pow- ered battleships equipped with 40 cm. guns, would have had the task of intercepting and destroying the heavy British forces which, more or less dispersed, would pursue the German forces engaged in merchant warfare.

'Two ships of the *Scharnhorst* and two of the *Tirpitz* class would have remained available in home waters to hold down some of the heavy British ships.

'In this way, especially with the co-operation of Japan and Italy, we would have held down a section of the British Fleet and the pros- pect of defeating the British Fleet and cutting off supplies, in other words of settling the British question conclusively, would have been good. On 3rd September, 1939, Germany entered into a war with Great Britain, as the latter—contrary to the Führer's assumption that "England did not need to fight on account of the Polish question"—thought it expedient to fight now with the Polish question as a pretext. Sooner or later, as he saw it, she would have to fight Germany, and then probably under unfavourable military conditions, i.e. against an expanded German Fleet.

'As far as the Navy is concerned, obviously it is in no way adequately equipped for the great struggle with Great Britain by the autumn of 1939. It is true that in the short period since 1935, the date of the Fleet Treaty, it has built up a well-trained, suitably organized submarine arm, of which at the moment about twenty-six boats are capable of operations in the Atlantic; the submarine arm is still much too weak, however, to have any decisive effect on the war. The surface forces, moreover, are so inferior in number and strength to those of the British Fleet that, even at full strength, they can do no more than show that they know how to die gallantly and thus are willing to create the foundations for later reconstruction.

'The pocket battleships—with the outbreak of war only the *Deutschland* and the *Graf Spee* are ready for operations in the Atlantic—if skilfully used should be able to carry out cruiser warfare on the high seas for some time. The *Scharnhorst* and *Gneisenau*, which are still by no means ready for action or reliable in operation, will have to attempt to hold down enemy battle cruisers in home waters and keep them away from the pocket battleships. The pocket battleships, however, cannot be decisive for the outcome of the war, either.'

With war on his hands Raeder had the new battleships *Scharnhorst* and *Gneisenau*; the *Schlesien* and *Schleswig-Holstein*—2 ancient and sluggish coal-burning battleships; 3 pocket battleships; 2 heavy cruisers, 6 light cruisers, 34 destroyers and a total of 57 submarines. Of the submarines, which were commanded by Admiral Karl Donitz, only about 40 were fully operational, and of these only 26 were judged fit for operation in Atlantic conditions.

That evening, two of the pocket battleships, *Deutschland* and *Graf Spee*, were cruising along British trade routes and seventeen of Donitz's 740-ton U-boats were lurking at patrol points stretching from Ireland to Gibraltar. Six of the smaller 250-tonners had taken up positions in the northern part of the North Sea. Six more were in the central North Sea and a further four waited in the Channel ready to attack British and French harbours. Six 500-ton U-boats were deployed between the Orkneys and Iceland.

Two signals during the afternoon had alerted these German warships. The first read: 'To Commanders-in-Chief and Commanders afloat: Great Britain and France have declared war on Germany. Battle stations immediate in accordance with battle instructions for the Navy already promulgated.' Next came Donitz's instructions to his U-boats: 'Battle instructions for the U-boat arm of the Navy are now in force. Troop ships and merchants ships carrying military equipment to be attacked in accordance with Prize Regulations of the Hague Convention. Enemy convoys to be attacked without warning only on condition that all passenger liners carrying passengers are allowed to proceed in safety. These vessels are immune from attack even in convoy.'

Later that evening, among the welter of official orders and instructions flashed to the German Navy, came one which gave a hint of the Führer's desire to contain the conflict in its early stages, particularly in relation to France. This order said: 'Since 1700 hours, France has been in a state of war with Germany. Hostilities from our side, including action against merchant ships, are for the time being only allowed in self-defence.' (According to Donitz, Hitler wanted to leave the opening of hostilities to the western powers as he still hoped to avoid an extension of the Polish conflict, despite the allied declarations of war.)

Adherence to the Hague Convention was a restraining and even dangerous course to impose on the U-boat men and angered some commanders when they heard the orders. As Vice Admiral Friedrich Ruge, German naval historian, explained later: 'This meant that attacks without warning could only be made on armed merchant ships or on those escorted by warships. All other ships had to be stopped and, after examination of their documents and cargoes, only those carrying contraband goods could be sunk. These restrictions robbed the U-boats of their best weapon—invisibility—for they were compelled to surface and expose themselves to the risk of being attacked by ships carrying concealed weapons. The 250-ton U-boats whose principle weapon was one automatic gun, could hardly be considered an impressive instrument of war, however much Donitz valued them. Their value at sea was made even more problematical by Hitler's strict order to avoid any incidents with France and not to molest any French merchant ships. Thus the French ships were better treated than the neutrals, which could be searched in accordance with international usage.'

Germany's reluctance to commence an all-out war at sea until the Führer had discovered whether he could still get what he wanted without a major war, was understandable. For Raeder and his men were faced from 5 p.m. onwards with a massive Anglo-French display of sea power which included 22 battleships, 7 aircraft carriers, 83 cruisers, 255 destroyers and 135 submarines. Against this, Germany had an ill-balanced force which Raeder was to blame twenty years later on 'Hitler's self-deception'. This policy had 'deplorable results' for the Navy as the pre-war construction programme had been completely at variance with the actual political situation'.

The first twenty-four hours of the war were also to provide chastening lessons for the Royal Air Force, particularly concerning the bombers in which the nation had placed so much faith. The failure of the reconnaissance Blenheim's radio over the German fleet, the half-successful 4th September raid on the German warships—when most of the bombs went astray and seven bombers were shot down—were swift and bitter pointers to the limitations of air action against naval targets.

Coastal Command's aircraft at the outbreak of war were only sufficient to maintain an effective look-out for German air and surface attack—no more. The Command had ten Anson squadrons, slow and with limited range but good enough for reconnaissance; four squadrons of London and Stranraer flying boats; two squadrons of the superior Sunderland flying boats, heavily armed and with an 800-mile range and one Hudson reconnaissance squadron. Coastal Command could also field as strike planes the obsolescent Vildebeest torpedo bomber with a top speed of 150 miles an hour and a range of less than 200 miles, which meant that Bomber Command had to undertake any major attack on the German fleet.

Britain and France together could field 3,400 front-line aircraft of all types on 3rd September, with nearly 4,000 in reserve, against Germany's modern, well-equipped force of over 1,000 long-range bombers and 400 short-range bombers for ground attack. Germany's fighters numbered about 1,200, with 3,000 training planes in reserve, of which about 1,000 were capable of front-line service.

Britain's air chiefs had calculated that the country needed about fifty fighter squadrons to provide comprehensive protection against German bomber raids. They could only field thirty-nine when the war started. But Sir Hugh Dowding, Air Officer Commanding Fighter Command, was already involved in a determined campaign to have the fighter forces built up to forty-seven squadrons, largely of Hurricanes and Spitfires, at the expense of bomber production. This was a calculated move, to be justified later in the Battle of Britain. Bomber Command, which had fifty-five squadrons ready when war broke out, trimmed this down to a front-line force of thirty-three squadrons during September. By 3rd September as the Air Force leaders hunted the German fleet, ten of these bomber squadrons, armed with the obsolescent Fairey Battle, were settling into France as the Advanced Air Striking Force. Of the bomber squadrons left at home, most were armed with Wellingtons, Whitleys and Hampdens. Six had Blenheim bombers like the one which brought back the first photographs of the German fleet.

X

King George VI, like many other British fathers, spent the afternoon persuading an aged relative to withdraw from London to the country during the war. The King needed all his patience and persuasive powers to convince his 72-year-old mother, the widowed Queen Mary, that by continuing to live at Marlborough House, St. James's, she would cause her relatives and friends much needless anxiety. But Queen Mary did not approve of the plan, made some time previously, for her to leave for the West Country.

The Queen's interests were essentially metropolitan, and she felt it would be a 'dereliction of duty' for her to leave London at such a time. According to her biographer, she declared that it was 'not at all the thing'. Finally, however, the King's view prevailed and Queen Mary agreed to accept the wartime hospitality of the Duke of Beaufort, her niece's husband, at Badminton House in Gloucestershire.

It was arranged over the telephone that she should abandon plans to return to London from Sandringham and should instead travel the next morning from the Royal Norfolk residence in a huge car convoy carrying the bulk of her 63-strong Marlborough House staff and their dependents. The convoy was to travel across country through Peterborough, Oundle, and Northampton to Althorp, where Queen Mary would lunch with Lord and Lady Spencer before resuming her journey through Oxford, Swindon and Chippenham to arrive at Badminton House on Monday evening.

There she would face a completely new and unfamiliar routine— life in the country. Had she known she was to spend the better part of six years at Badminton Queen Mary would undoubtedly have offered her son even more resistance to the project, despite the fact that the Beaufort seat, of handsome yellow Cotswold stone, with a park nine miles in circumference, was one of England's finest country homes.

During the afternoon King George, knowing how unfavourably Queen Mary would react if she felt cut off from events in London, wisely arranged to have Foreign Office news summaries sent to his mother 'for the duration' in an official red leather dispatch box. Then, having disposed of this family problem, he turned his attention to affairs of state and the speech to the nation which he was to broadcast from his study at Buckingham Palace at 6 p.m. that evening.

As Queen Elizabeth listened in another room of the Palace, the King, in the undress uniform of an Admiral of the Fleet, told the nation and the world: 'In this grave hour, perhaps the most fateful in our history, I send to every household of my peoples, both at home and overseas, this message spoken with the same depth of feeling for each one of you as if I were able to cross your threshold and speak to you myself.

'For the second time in the lives of most of us we are at war. Over and over again we have tried to find a peaceful way out of the differences between ourselves and those who are now our enemies. But it has been in vain. We have been forced into a conflict. For we are called, with our allies, to meet the challenge of a principle which, if it were to prevail, would be fatal to any civilized order in the world.

'It is the principle which permits a State, in the selfish pursuit of power, to disregard its treaties and its solemn pledges; which sanctions the use of force, or threat of force, against the sovereignty and independence of other states.

'Such a principle, stripped of all disguise, is surely the mere primitive doctrine, that "might is right"; and if this principle were established throughout the world the freedom of our own country and of the whole British Commonwealth of Nations would be in danger. But far more than this—the peoples of the world would be kept in the bondage of fear; and all hopes of settled peace and of the security of justice and liberty among nations would be ended.

'This is the ultimate issue which confronts us. For the sake of all that we ourselves hold dear, and of the world's order and peace, it is unthinkable that we should refuse to meet the challenge. It is to this high purpose that I now call my people at home and my peoples across the seas, who will make our cause their own. I ask them to stand calm, firm and united in this time of trial. The task will be hard. There may be dark days ahead and war can no longer be confined to the battlefield. But we can only do the right as we see the right, and reverently commit our cause to God. If one and all we keep resolutely faithful to it, ready for whatever service or sacrifice it may demand, then with God's help, we shall prevail.

'May He bless and keep us all.'

At almost the same time, General Francisco Franco, Spain's Head of State, was broadcasting an appeal to the belligerents to localize the conflict. Franco's address gave the first hope to the allies that his fascist régime might preserve neutrality during the war rather than join Nazi Germany, which had backed his cause so strongly in the Spanish Civil War. Franco declared in his dramatic evening radio appeal that he was speaking with the authority of one who had suffered during three years the burden of a war fought for the liberation of his country.

The General added: 'I address myself to the Governments in whose hands lies the responsibility for releasing a catastrophe without precedent in history, in order that they may avoid for their peoples the sufferings and tragedies which befell the Spanish people, notwithstanding the voluntary limitations upon the use of methods of destruction—horrors which would be multiplied a hundredfold in a new war.

'It is a great responsibility to extend the conflict to seas and places distant from the actual scene of the war without an imperious reason to justify it. Its extension, without benefit to the belligerents, would produce intense and insuperable disturbance of the economy of the world, incalculable losses in its riches, paralysation of its commerce, with grave repercussions in the standard of life of the humbler classes. The more the conflict is extended the more the germ of future wars is sown. In these circumstances, I appeal to the common sense and the responsibility of the rulers of the nations in order to direct the efforts of all toward the localization of the present conflict.'

As Franco, in Fascist Spain, made this earnest and obviously heartfelt appeal, Ciano was busy in Rome trying to convince the British and French Ambassadors that his country sincerely desired to steer clear of war with either of them. Daylong activity by Pope Pius XII and his Secretary of State, Cardinal Maglione, may have been one of the reasons for the Italian régime's anxiety to proclaim her neutrality. The Pope, shocked and saddened by the German agreement with communist Russia, had already made several appeals for peace and had spent the week-end conferring anxiously with Ambassadors of the great powers accredited to the Holy See. His greatest anguish was the thought of the blood already being shed among Catholics on both sides: 38 million German, Austrian and Czech members of his flock were locked in combat with 23 million Polish Catholics. Now millions more of his followers in the British and French Empires were entering the war.

Italy's Sunday afternoon assurances of neutrality were summarized at 6 p.m. in a cable sent to Secretary of State Cordell Hull in Washington by the U.S. Ambassador in Rome, Mr. William Phillips. Phillips, who had close contacts with all the other envoys in the Italian capital, reported that Ciano, anxious to avoid a Franco-Italian conflict, had begged the French Ambassador to keep the French Press from attacks on Italy 'and from saying anything which might annoy the authorities' in Rome.

The British Ambassador in Rome, Sir Percy Loraine, felt that Ciano had undergone a change in his former pro-German attitude in the previous few days, and that the recent developments had shocked and disturbed the Italian. Phillips himself had the impression 'that Italian public opinion, so hostile to war, is having a deciding influence on the Government's present and future attitude, perhaps for the first time in years'.

Washington's man in Rome also reported to his chief: 'It is too early to guess from this angle the steps which the British and French may take to preserve Italian neutrality. The question of blockade is uppermost in Loraine's thoughts and he has confessed to me that in his opinion any move of the Allied Powers, such as a blockade in the Mediterranean which would result in the stopping and examination of Italian vessels, might swing Italian sentiment in the wrong direction.

'He argues that Italy and other Mediterranean countries have few supplies to give Germany and that few countries outside would be willing to do so, except on a cash basis, impossible for Italy. Nothing should be done, says Loraine to antagonize Italy, but on the contrary everything should be done to take advantage of the present attitude of the public and of Ciano's apparent revulsion of feeling against Germany, in the hope that gradually Italy may be drawn into closer relations with the Allied Governments.'

PART FOUR

6 p.m. to midnight

I

Germany formally invited Russia to invade Poland from the east at 6.50 p.m. Von Ribbentrop urged the Soviet leaders to share the spoils of conquest as quickly as possible in one of the most brazen communications ever dispatched by a Foreign Minister. His invitation was contained in a top-secret telegram sent to the Kremlin via Count von der Friedrich Werner Schulenburg, the German Ambassador in Moscow.

The telegram read: 'Very urgent! Exclusively for Ambassador! Strictly secret! For Chief of Mission or his representative personally. Top secret. To be decoded by himself. Strictest secrecy!

'We definitely expect to have beaten the Polish Army decisively in a few weeks. We would then keep the area that was established as German sphere of interest at Moscow under military occupation. We would naturally, however, for military reasons, also have to proceed further against such Polish military forces as are at that time located in the Polish area belonging to the Russian sphere of interest.

'Please discuss this at once with Molotov and see if the Soviet Union does not consider it desirable for Russian forces to move at the proper time against Polish forces in the Russian sphere of interest, and, for their part, to occupy this territory. In our estimation, this would be not only a relief for us, but also, in the sense of the Moscow agreements, in the Soviet interest as well.

'In this connection, please determine whether we may discuss this matter with the officers who have just arrived here and what the Soviet Government intends their position to be.

'Ribbentrop.'

This was to be the first of several German exhortations to Russia to enter Poland with the aim of speeding the end of resistance, of sharing with a partner the world-wide opprobrium for the action, and of freeing troops to reinforce the Western Front. But the Russians were to turn a deaf ear to the 3rd September appeal and to all its successors until Stalin considered the time ripe for his intervention on the safest and most favourable terms. Still, the Russians were already aiding the Germans in a variety of ways. Radio messages from within Soviet territory had guided numerous German bombers to their targets in Poland and there had been radio exchanges of information between military chiefs on both sides.

The Polish writer, Dominik Wegierski, describes in his account of September, 1939, meeting an old man who had served in the Austrian Army as an officer before the First World War. It was the evening of the 3rd and the veteran, a keen radio amateur, had his ears glued to a wireless receiver in beleaguered Cracow. The old soldier was trying to piece together information from all the messages that were coming over the set. He claimed to have mastered the German military codes thanks to his own experience and to have heard before the German attack of the Nazi plan to invade Poland. Now, his greatest worry, he told Wegierski, was that the 'German and Soviet stations are maintaining contact with each other'. He could not understand the Russian code and was still trying to decipher messages sent from Moscow on the first day of the German attack, but the contact between the two great powers all seemed 'very suspicious'. As Wegierski left, the man frowned fiercely and commented: 'Events will soon bring a solution to my puzzle.'

Only a few very senior Russian diplomats and service chiefs were aware of what was afoot. There was, in fact, that week-end, according to many reports, a widespread feeling in the Soviet Union that the country was about to attack Germany. Despite the Pact with the men in Berlin and the change in the tone of the official Press, the average Russian could still not conceive his country standing by and allowing the Germans to sweep through Poland unchecked. Troop movements within the Soviet Union sparked rumours of an impending attack on the Nazis which began that week-end and were to snowball during the following week. These rumours were to create an atmosphere of emergency, the feverish hoarding of foodstuffs and a minor run on the savings banks.

Even Communist Party organizers in positions of strong authority in the provinces had no inkling of the large-scale military and diplomatic co-operation that had been agreed between Berlin and Moscow. There was considerable confusion within the party ranks and this was to be worsened within the next few days by the launching of an official campaign against people who let themselves, in Molotov's words, be 'taken prisoner by mere anti-Fascist propaganda'. A fortnight of furious brain-washing lay ahead of the Russian people that evening. It would be aimed at convincing them of Russia's need to consider the implications of Germany's advance into Poland, especially the fate of their 'blood brothers', the White Russians and the Ukrainians inhabiting East Poland. Parallel with this brain-washing of the civil population, military mobilization was to be carried out in earnest.

One of the top Russians privy to Stalin's plans that evening was a man destined to step into his shoes and to wield even vaster personal power within two decades: Nikita Khrushchev. On 3rd September, Khrushchev knew he would be playing a major part in the incorporation of large parts of Eastern Poland into the Ukraine. Sent to the Ukraine in 1937 to carry out a purge of local leaders considered by Moscow to be 'enemies of the people', Khrushchev had remained in the province to play a notable part in its administration. In January of 1938 he had been elected First Secretary of the Central Committee of the Communist Party of the Ukraine. Then, in 1939, he had been elevated to the dignity of being a full member of the Politbureau, following the 18th Party Congress. As a member of the Politbureau, he knew by then the secret codicils of the Russo-German agreement of 23rd August.

Khrushchev's role in the Ukraine was the drastic reorganization of a country in which industrial and agricultural production was lagging, the transport system was in a chaotic state and where the supply of raw materials had for years been in a muddle through inefficient, bureaucratic rule. By the outbreak of the Second World War he had achieved a great deal through highly efficient, if ruthless, organization. Khrushchev had also reversed the policy of 'Ukrainianization' which the Communists had approved in the 1920s and the early 1930s to calm down the rebellious peasants and workers in the non-Russian provinces. In his two years in the Ukraine he had launched a programme of Russification to support Moscow's policy of making the border territories safe for the Soviet Union.

The incorporation and Sovietization of the part of Ukraine ceded to Poland after the First World War was to be Khrushchev's biggest political assignment. This programme—already well prepared by 3rd September—was to involve the deportation of nearly 1,500,000 Polish nationals to the Siberian and North Russian forced labour camps. Leaders of all political parties, Jews, government officials, industrialists, merchants, landowners, judges, lawyers, teachers and senior white-collar workers were also destined to be swept by Khrushchev and his lieutenants out of the area of Poland to be known henceforth as the 'Western Ukraine'.

Ironically, the message sent to Moscow at 6.50 p.m. by von Ribbentrop coincided almost exactly with the issue of a statement to the Press by one man Stalin wished to wipe off the face of the world: his one-time bitter rival for supreme power in the Kremlin, Leon Trotsky. Since the signing of the Pact with Nazi Germany reporters had been pressing Trotsky for a comment on the new Moscow-Berlin alliance. For days he had maintained silence in his place of exile, Mexico City. Then, on the evening of 3rd September, he released the following brief statement, which was to be published all over the world and broadcast to Russia:

'The Pact is a capitulation of Stalin before Fascist imperialism with the end of preserving the Soviet oligarchy. The only merit of the Pact is that in unveiling the truth it broke the backbone of the Comintern. The world proletariat will step over the treason of the Kremlin and also the cadaver of the Comintern.'

II

Dusk found Paris still without the sense of urgency and foreboding which pervaded London and Berlin. The Parisian blackout was full of gaps, and the city was surrounded with a belt of light provided by the blazing headlamps of cars on the outer boulevards. The people of Paris were showing a reluctance to face the realities of war—a mute resistance to change their way of life. It was to be many nights before the brilliant Paris plumage of flashing lights and glittering façades was to be completely dimmed by Hitler; the Seine lights would continue to twinkle here and there long after the Thames had been cloaked each evening in an inky shroud.

Officialdom was anxious about the population's laxity in effecting a proper blackout. Police toured the city and suburbs as night fell, reprimanding house and flat-dwellers whose lights were not sufficiently hidden. Bicycle patrols took a strong line with offenders, warning them that people contravening the blackout regulations were liable to face proceedings for 'giving information to the enemy'. But the independent Parisian resented official interference in his affairs and many lights were turned on again after the police patrols had passed on.

Owners of cafés, nightclubs and bistrots were threatened with closure of their establishments if they contravened the blackout regulations. Another order affecting them came from the Prefect of Police, and became effective that night. It decreed that all establishments which served alcoholic drinks in Paris must close by 11 p.m. from 3rd September onwards. This revolutionary restriction had already been in force for two days in other parts of the Seine Department. Normally, Paris cafés were at liberty to serve drinks round the clock. Two more changes affecting the public broke on Paris during the evenings.

The Post Office announced that a third of Paris's post offices—40 out of 120—were to be closed, as many of the staff had been mobilized. Also, private telephone calls to foreign countries were suspended 'until further notice from military headquarters'.

As the clocks in the Foreign Ministry ticked towards 8 p.m., a tired and disillusioned M. Bonnet dozed fitfully in an armchair. A telephone ring shattered the heavy silence of the office, startling him out of his half-sleep, and a friendly voice on the other end offered him hospitality for the evening and the night. It was a M. Ribardière, a property-owning friend of the Foreign Minister's. Bonnet accepted his offer gladly and prepared to leave for his friend's home. 'Where could I find a better place for a few hours of rest and forgetfulness?' he wrote in his diary.

As Bonnet's day's work finished, Daladier was still preparing his executive for war. After evening discussions at the Chamber of Deputies, he made plain his intention to make no ministerial changes in the French Government but to continue with his administration under President Albert Lebrun. The Government comprised: President of the Council and Minister of War: Edouard Daladier; Vice-President of the Council: Camille Chautemps; Foreign Minister: Georges Bonnet; Minister for the Interior: Albert Sarraut; Minister of Finance: Paul Reynard; Military Marine: Cesar Campinchi; Air: Guy La Chambre; Commander of National Defence: Marshal Maurice Gustave Gamelin; Commander of the Navy: Admiral Francois Darlan; Commander of the Air Force: General Joseph Vuillemin.

Daladier's next task, one which could be postponed no longer, was to tell his people of the situation, convince them of the necessity for war and fire them with the patriotism necessary to carry them through the dark days ahead. The few brief, unspectacular formalities necessary to declare war had clearly been insufficient to impress the import of the day's happening on the population. So the French leader hurried back to the Ministry of National Defence, where he broadcast a brief speech which all the French radio networks carried. At 8.30, a programme of music from Strasbourg came to an end. After a brief announcement Daladier spoke: 'Since daybreak on 1st September, Poland has been the victim of the most brutal and most cynical of aggressions. Her frontiers have been violated. Her cities are being bombed. Her army is heroically resisting the invader. The responsibility for the blood that is being shed falls entirely upon Hitler's Government. The fate of peace was in Hitler's hands. He chose war. France and England have made countless efforts to safeguard peace. This very morning they made a further urgent intervention in Berlin in order to address to the German Government a last appeal to reason and a request to stop hostilities and open peaceful negotiations.

'Germany met us with a refusal. She had already refused to reply to all the men of goodwill who recently raised their voices in favour of the peace of the world. She therefore desires the destruction of Poland so as to be able to dominate Europe quickly and to enslave France. In rising against the most frightful of tyrannies, in honouring our word, we fight to defend our soil, our homes, our liberties. I am conscious of having worked unremittingly against the war until the last minute. I greet with emotion and affection our young soldiers, who now go forth to perform the sacred task which we ourselves performed before them. They can have full confidence in their chiefs, who are worthy of those who have previously led France to victory.

'The cause of France is identical with that of righteousness. It is the cause of all peaceful and free nations. It will be victorious. Men and women of France! We are waging war because it has been thrust upon us. Every one of us is at his post, on the soil of France, that land of liberty where respect for human dignity finds one of its last refuges. You will all co-operate, with a profound feeling of union and brotherhood, for the salvation of the country. Vive la France!'

After Daladier had spoken, M. Roger Langeron, Prefect of Police, echoed his leader in an appeal issued to the Paris police force. He told his gendarmes: 'A grave hour has struck. The most cynical aggression has been the brutal reply to all France's efforts to avoid war. And now, as the great voice of the head of the Government said, we have to defend our land, our homes, our liberty. Your chief knows your courage and high sense of duty. He has seen you, in the dramatic hours we have lived through, spend your energies without counting the cost, following the directives of the Minister of the Interior, to help the Paris population who are collaborating with the mobilization services. He knows he can count entirely, totally on you. And he does count on you. My dear and brave defenders of order during peacetime, our work goes on. Together we must give body and soul to the security of Paris. I place in you my deepest confidence. And in the same spirit I cry with you: "Vive la France".'

Some of the men to whom Langeron addressed his appeal were at that moment forming a strong police guard outside the German Embassy in the Rue de Lille. There, the 130-strong staff were preparing to leave for the Invalides station to board a special train for Switzerland. Police would not allow cars or pedestrians into the street while the Germans made ready for their departure. Finally, several railway lorries drew into the courtyard, where the departing diplomats loaded them with carefully packed records and private possessions. Then, a small force of police motorcycle outriders and cars escorted the Embassy staff, their families and a few newspaper correspondents in a motor convoy to the station.

There, a group of French officials, led by M. Loze, Director of Protocol, and M. Langeron, waited to say farewell to the German *Chargé d'Affaires*. Herr Brauer was first out of the car and took a courteous leave of Loze and the others as his staff embarked in nine first-class coaches on the special train. Shortly before 11 p.m. French security police boarded the train and took up posts which they were not to leave until the Germans reached the frontier. The train pulled out of the station just after 11 p.m., and was only held up once, at the frontier. There it waited briefly to allow a train to pass carrying the French diplomatic staff from Berlin home to Paris.

As the German diplomats left Paris the French Ministry of War issued its first war communiqué. The one-sentence statement simply said: 'Operations have begun, involving the entire land, naval and air forces.' It was in good time for the later editions of Monday morning's newspapers. The early editions then on the streets were still sermonizing on the week-end events. *Le Petit Parisien*, for instance, lamented: 'Hitler has remained deaf to the last warnings of the British and French governments as he has to suggestions from Rome. Perhaps he imagined that once more his audacity could drive back justice and reason. Already, millions and millions of human beings pronounce the name of Hitler with a holy horror. If he wanted that honour he has it and will continue to have it.

'Mr. Chamberlain was right to say that today was a sad day for him. As he said, with a sort of heroism, all that he had believed in and everything for which he has worked has fallen into ruins. Today is also sad for all of us who, with him and our own leaders, have made superhuman efforts to spare mankind from the terrible struggle which is beginning. Mr. Chamberlain has nothing to reproach himself with, and neither have we.'

III

'Surface ship sighted!' The urgent message flashed down from the bridge of German submarine U-30 cruising about 200 miles north-west of the Irish coast. It was shortly before 9 p.m. B.S.T. and Ober-leutnant Fritz Lemp, U-30's stocky young skipper, had just finished his evening meal. Lemp, excited by the news of Britain's war declaration which had reached him only a few hours earlier, was eager for action. Moving slowly after his heavy meal, he left the officer's ward-room and climbed topside to the bridge. Through his powerful binoculars he made out the dim shape of a large single-stacked ship about two miles away.

No one will ever know what went through the young skipper's mind as he watched the big ship move closer through the Atlantic dusk. The sky was clear and the heavy swells were lit by the faint rays of a rising moon. Lemp gave the order for the U-30 to submerge to peri-scope level, and told his First Officer: 'Crew to battle stations.' Though Lemp did not know it, the dim shape across the water was the 13,581-ton twin-screw liner S.S. *Athenia*, built sixteen years earlier and owned by the Donaldson Atlantic Line. But at the time the Cunard White Star Line was operating the ship between Glasgow, Liverpool and Montreal.

Two days earlier the *Athenia* had left Glasgow for Liverpool, and had then headed west along the North Atlantic steamer route with 1,432 passengers and crew on board cutting through the water at a steady fifteen knots. Many were Americans and Canadians returning to their homelands from crisis-racked Europe. They were relieved that night to be on their way out of the danger area. But the *Athenia*'s commander, Captain James Cook, did not share the general opti-mism, as weighed down with responsibility, he sat alone at dinner in his cabin. The *Athenia* was a big ship—526 feet long, with a 66-foot beam and a draft of 38 feet—and would make a clear silhouette on the horizon from many miles away. Before dining, Cook had alerted the watch to look out for submarines and ordered the ship to be blacked out by nightfall. Cook's thoughts were interrupted by the entry of Chief Officer Barnet Copeland. Copeland reported that he had inspected the ship thoroughly and she was safe. Canvas screens had been placed around some of the doors on the main deck and the rest had been closed. All portholes had been covered. After making his report, Copeland left to dine with the passengers.

During the dinner hour, Third Officer Colin Porteus kept the watch on the *Athenia's* bridge. Around him the extra look-outs scanned the ocean on all sides. None of them saw anything unusual. They did not observe the ominous little tube poking up above the waves in the half darkness more than a mile away.

Aboard *U-30*, Lemp watched fascinated through the periscope as the big ship drew nearer. Gradually, he made out her white superstructure and big black stack. There were no lights showing. Lemp remained poised in uncertainty for a few seconds, then made a decision which was to rock the world. As he tracked the ship in his periscope he barked out the figures giving her distance, estimated course and speed, to be fed into the submarine's torpedo target computer. When the computer's humming and clicking died, Lemp ordered the preparation for firing of a complete batch of torpedoes. With the range at less than a mile he ordered: 'Fire.' Three high-speed torpedoes shot from their tubes and streaked through the water towards the *Athenia*. At least one appeared to be on a course which would carry it past the liner's stern, but another headed straight for the rear of the *Athenia's* port side.

Lemp ordered the *U-30* to dive deep at once and head away from the target. As the submarine plunged downwards, the hydrophone operator heard the unmistakable clang of a torpedo striking the liner's hull. Tearing his headphones off to save himself from the earsplitting roar of the explosion, he cried out: 'A hit, Captain! One hit!' Even as he shouted in triumph the roar of the explosion, muffled by the water, reached Lemp's ears, and the submarine shivered violently as the shock-waves from the blast pummelled her hull.

Porteus, on the *Athenia's* bridge, was raising his glasses to scan the sea around once more when he heard a tremendous explosion deep in the ship's holds. Shaken, he turned to see a huge jet of smoke, water and debris blasted skywards through the deck above one of the holds. The torpedo had torn a great hole in the *Athenia*'s port side and a flood of churning water was pouring into the engine room. The blast shot upwards, devastating the dining-room where some of the passengers were still dining. All the lights went out. The huge liner faltered and reared up in the water, then settled again with an immense splash, listing to port. A stunned Porteus galvanized himself into action. He immediately signalled the engine room to stop, then ran into the wheel-house and spun the automatic controls which shut the watertight doors below decks.

Then he tugged wildly on the handle of the 'action stations' alarm and the whistle shrilled out its message. Meanwhile, Chief Officer Copeland ran aft to the sight of the explosion to assess the damage and report to Cook. As he began to climb down the ladder below decks he caught a brief glimpse of the surfacing U-30 only a few thousand yards away on the port side. Swearing bitterly, Copeland clambered swiftly below and made his way towards the shattered cargo hold, which was almost filled with water. The watertight bulkhead between the hold and the engine room had split and the sea was rising above the deck grating. Copeland could feel the *Athenia* listing and settling deeper in the water, and there was a noise of cargo breaking loose from its lashings inside the hold.

Dispirited, the Chief Officer called up to Cook, who had by this time reached the bridge, and told him the grim position. Cook snapped: 'Prepare to abandon ship,' and then ordered Chief Radio Operator Don to send out the SOS. Don punched out the Morse message that was to save more than 1,000 lives: '*Athenia* torpedoed, 56 degrees 42 minutes north, 14 degrees 5 minutes west.'

One by one, Don got through to an Irish shore station, the Norwegian tanker *Knute Nelson*, the Swedish yacht *Southern Cross* and the British destroyers *Electra* and *Escort*. He stayed at his keyboard hammering out the distress call until the last possible moment, then tore up on deck to find scenes of panic. Screaming women and crying children milled around as the officers and deck hands tried to launch the lifeboats. But the list was so heavy that the davits on the starboard side could not be swung out. Some of the lifeboats on the port side had been shattered by the explosion and dangled in useless shreds over the turbulent water beneath. Those that could be launched were swiftly packed with passengers and lowered jerkily into the Atlantic. Most of the boats shipped water, which swirled ominously round the legs of the frightened occupants. One boat drifted under the ship's heaving stern and was shattered by the huge propellers.

Finally, at about 10 p.m., Copeland was able to report that all the passengers were off the liner and the Captain recalled one of the lowered lifeboats. There were tears in Cook's eyes as, with the last score of his crew, he clambered over the ship's side and the lifeboat pulled away.

Oberleutnant Lemp had noted with satisfaction through his periscope that the target ship was down by the stern. Smoke billowing all around her prevented him from noting his victim's identity. So he ordered the submarine to surface again, and move nearer to the *Athenia*. According to his own version of the incident later, he was horrified to see the milling mass of men, women and children being herded on to the deck by the ship's officers. The *Athenia* had been floodlit and he could discern all the details of the tragic scene. Silently, he turned away and went below to think about the consequences of his action against an unarmed vessel.

Captain Cook, gripping the gunwale of a bobbing lifeboat, looked back at his stricken ship. She was now listing heavily and her stern was beginning to disappear below the water. Then a sudden rain squall darkened the sky and hid the *Athenia* from him. He turned his attention to supervising the marshalling of the lifeboats, already scattered over a fairly wide area. When the squall had passed and he looked again at the liner, she was deeper in the water and only just afloat. Don's SOS message had reached the *Knute Nelson* when the Norwegian ship was less than fifty miles away and the merchantman had hauled around and immediately steamed towards the *Athenia*'s radioed position.

Just before midnight, one of the crew members in an outlying lifeboat sent a red distress flare soaring into the sky. Almost at once an answering flare was seen some miles away and in the closing minutes of 3rd September the *Knute Nelson* steamed into sight. Later, the *Southern Cross* and the two British destroyers were to arrive and between them to rescue more than 1,300 people by daybreak. Another British destroyer, H.M.S. *Frame* and the merchantman *City of Flint* also arrived and joined the search.

But the U-boat's torpedo had taken a heavy toll. The first western maritime deaths of the war were all civilians—112 of them, including more than eighty women and children. Fifty Britons, some Poles and Germans, nineteen crew members and twenty-eight Canadians and Americans had died in the explosion or the water afterwards. Only the three British destroyers were to remain through the night to see the final chapter in the tragedy played out the next morning, when the *Athenia* slipped beneath the waves stern first and sank to the sea bed.

Through that night, the words which burned themselves into the mind of Oberleutnant Lemp were his firm instructions, based on Article Two of the London Naval Treaty, to which Germany had acceded in 1936: 'In their action with regard to merchant ships, submarines must conform to the rules of International Law to which surface vessels are subject. In particular, except in the case of persistent refusal to stop on being duly summoned, or of active resistance to visit or search, a warship, whether surface vessel or submarine, may not sink or render incapable of navigation a merchant vessel without first having placed passengers, crew and ship's papers in a place of safety, unless the safety of the passengers and crew is assured, in the existing sea and weather conditions, by the proximity of land or the presence of another vessel which is in a position to take them on board.'

Long before midnight, news of the attack on the *Athenia* had swept the world. Lemp, maintaining the strict radio silence imposed on German submarines to avoid giving away their positions, did not report his action or its consequences to his chiefs. As a result, Donitz knew nothing of it that night and immediate denials of German guilt were issued, to be followed up by allegations that Britain had sunk the ship in order to gain American support and sympathy. Dr. Josef Goebbels, Nazi Propaganda Minister, was even to accuse Churchill of personal responsibility for sinking the liner.

The sinking sent a chill of horror down the spines of the thousands of civilians then afloat in other liners scattered across the Atlantic between Europe and North America. Its implied threat that total war at sea was now imminent caused the captains of other liners to tighten up their precautions immediately. Lord Reith, the Chairman of Imperial Airways and former Director-General of the British Broadcasting Corporation, recalls in his diary the effect the *Athenia* sinking had aboard the *Aquitania* in which he was then travelling from New York to Cherbourg.

Lord Reith had already been told by the Captain of the liner that the ship had been darkened and was preserving radio silence because of the threat of a surface raider which might disembark the passengers and crew and then sink the vessel. Interference from aircraft or submarines was not expected without an announcement of ruthless warfare by the Germans. But, a few hours after the *Athenia* sinking, the second steward came to Reith's cabin and said he had been instructed to fit him with a gas-mask. The peer's diary adds: 'I said I had been warned about this, but surely it was unnecessary to fit gas-masks to people in the ship because gas-masks were irrelevant to torpedoes or submarines or even raiders. Anyhow, I added, I was sure there would not be any interference.'

The steward then told him quietly of the *Athenia* sinking and the diary reference adds: 'Now I was glad I had left behind me in New York my wife and children of eleven and seven and a nursery governess; *Aquitania* would be a considerable prize and, with her three funnels, she would be recognizable over a great area of ocean.'

In Britain and France, the *Athenia* sinking aroused immediate popular anger and was regarded as clear evidence that Donitz and his U-boat fleet had no intention of abiding by the London Treaty. Before the waters closed over the *Athenia* Mr. Kennedy, the American Ambassador to Britain, was awakened at the country house to which he had just moved from London with his family. Told that the *Athenia* was sinking, he immediately woke his undergraduate son Jack. The future President was later to travel to Glasgow to take care of the American survivors and to investigate the incident on his father's behalf. It was to be young Kennedy's first major official assignment. Joseph Kennedy's first dispatch to the State Department said: 'Report Steamship *Athenia* Donaldson Line torpedoed 200 miles off Maylin Head with 1,400 passengers aboard. SOS received. Ship sinking fast.'

Cordell Hull, U.S. Secretary of State, later recalled receiving this cable just before President Roosevelt's address to the nation. Hull described it as 'an ominous portent of the destruction on the high seas that was to follow for nearly six years'. A few minutes later in a statement to reporters, White House Secretary Steve Early said: 'I'd like to point out . . . that there was no possibility . . . that the ship was carrying any ammunition or anything of that kind.'

But if there was anger in Washington, Paris, London and other western capitals, there was also anger at the German Admiralty. For though they had no indication beyond the western allegations, the German naval chiefs had a sneaking fear the reports of the U-boat attack might be true, and that Hitler's policy of postponing aggressive action against the west for as long as possible would have received a heavy blow. But for the time being they agreed to make the strongest possible denials. Grand Admiral Raeder reported the incident to Hitler that night and told him he was convinced that a U-boat had not been responsible.

When the news reached the German Foreign Office, Ernst von Weizsacker was 'greatly alarmed' (according to his evidence at the Nuremberg Trials seven years later). But Raeder assured him it could not have been a German warship as a check had shown the nearest U-boat at the time was 75 miles from the scene. Weizsacker was later to swear that he had repeatedly stressed to Raeder that nothing should be done to bring America into the war, and had cited the case of the sinking of the British liner *Lusitania* in 1915, with the loss of 1,198 lives, which inflamed U.S. opinion against Germany.

Germany was not to admit that U-30 sank the *Athenia* until after the war, and indeed the German naval chiefs themselves were not to learn the truth until the end of September, when Oberleutnant Lemp brought his boat into Wilhelmshaven. Lemp saluted Donitz on the dock and then said gravely: 'Sir, I have something to report: it was I who sank the *Athenia*.'

'What?' roared the startled Admiral.

Lemp went on: 'I mistook her for an auxiliary cruiser and realized my mistake only when it was too late.'

Hitler himself then took the decision not to issue a retraction of the earlier denials.

Germany's Admiral Eberhard Goth declared later that the Naval War Staff ordered the incident to be erased from the U-boat's log-book. Goth said this was one of only two occasions in the whole war when a U-boat's log was changed—the other being when a U-boat sank a German ship returning from Japan.

Lemp's action was to be excused on the grounds of 'his excitement in the first hours of war', and his only punishment a few days under nominal arrest so that he could give his full attention to the study of ship silhouettes. He and his crew were ordered to maintain strict secrecy about this incident.

Whether he spoke the truth in pleading a genuine mistake will never be known. The next year his ship was to be paid off, and Lemp, his officers and crew transferred to the new *U-110*, which was to carry them to the bottom of the Atlantic with their secret when it was sunk on 9th May, 1941.

IV

As the first torpedo ripped into the *Athenia*, Hitler was making ready to leave for the Eastern Front to take command of the German forces in Poland as the Reich's 'first soldier'. One of his last tasks before quitting the Chancellery was to draft a belated reply to Mussolini's eleventh hour peace bid. Eager to leave for the front as quickly as possible, Hitler wrote a hurried but diplomatically-phrased letter to his nervous partner. The Führer's object was to make clear, without hurting Mussolini's feelings too much, that Italy would sooner or later be in the war up to the neck alongside Germany, whether the Fascist leader wanted it or not.

Hitler dispatched the message at 8.51 via von Ribbentrop and the German Embassy in Rome. It read:

'Duce: I must first thank you for your last attempt at mediation. I would have been ready to accept, but only on condition that some possibility could have been found to give me certain guarantees that the conference would be successful. For the German troops have been engaged for two days in an, in parts, extraordinarily rapid advance into Poland. It would have been impossible to allow blood which was there sacrificed to be squandered through diplomatic intrigue. Nevertheless, I believe that a way could have been found if England had not been determined from the outset to let it come to war in any case. I did not yield to England's threats because, Duce, I no longer believe that peace could have been maintained for more than six months or, shall we say, a year. In these circumstances I considered that the present moment was, in spite of everything, more suitable for making a stand.

'At present, the German Wehrmacht in Poland is so vastly superior in all fields that the Polish Army will collapse in a very short time.

Whether it would have been possible to achieve this success in another year or two is, I must say, very doubtful in my opinion. England and France would have gone on arming their allies to such an extent that the decisive technical superiority of the German Wehrmacht could not have been in evidence in the same way.

'I am aware, Duce, that the struggle in which I am engaging is a struggle of life and death. In it, my own fate is of absolutely no importance. But I am also aware that such a struggle cannot in the end be avoided, and that the moment for resistance must be chosen with icy deliberation so that the likelihood of success is assured; and in this success, Duce, my faith is as firm as a rock.

'You kindly assured me recently that you believe you can help in some fields. I accept this in advance with sincere thanks. But I also believe that, even if we now march down separate paths, destiny will yet bind us one to the other. If National Socialist Germany were to be destroyed by the Western Democracies, Fascist Italy also would face a hard future. I personally was always aware that the futures of our two régimes were bound up, and I know that you, Duce, are of exactly the same opinion.

'Concerning the situation in Poland, I would only briefly remark that naturally we are leaving aside everything which is not important and are not wasting a single man on inessential tasks, but that all our actions are being directed by considerations of grand strategy. The Polish Northern Army, which is in the Corridor, has already been completely surrounded by this action of ours. Either it will be wiped out or it will surrender. For the rest, all operations are proceeding according to plan. The daily achievements of our troops have greatly exceeded all expectations. The mastery of our Luftwaffe is complete, although scarcely a third of it is in Poland.

'In the West, I shall remain on the defensive. France can shed her blood there first. The moment will then come when we can pit ourselves there also against the enemy with the whole strength of the nation.

'Please accept once more my thanks, Duce, for all the support you have given me in the past, and which I ask you not to refuse me in future either.

'Adolf Hitler.'

Mussolini was not to receive the message until the following morning.

To emphasize his friendly feelings towards Italy, Hitler summoned the Italian Ambassador in Berlin, Bernardo Attolico, before leaving for the front. In an interview at the Chancellery, Hitler entrusted Attolico with his warmest 'greetings to the Duce'. Attolico found Hitler calm and optimistic and reported immediately to his chief, Count Ciano, that the Führer was confident Poland would be at his feet in four weeks.

In Rome that night Ciano set down in his diary Attolico's report, adding that the Duce, 'who still prizes German friendship, was happy to know of Hitler's gesture'. Ciano also wrote down his estimate—different from the Duce's—as to what the future held: 'In what way can France and England bring help to Poland? And when Poland is liquidated will they want to continue a conflict for which there is no longer any reason? The Duce believes not. He believes, rather, that after a short struggle peace will be restored before the clash which in any case he considers impossible from a military point of view. I am not a military man. I do not know how the war will develop, but I know one thing—it will develop, and it will be long, uncertain and relentless. The participation of Great Britain makes this certain. England has made this declaration to Hitler; the war can end only with Hitler's elimination or the defeat of Britain.'

As Ciano sat writing his diary in Rome, Vatican sources were being quoted by news agency journalists as saying that Pope Pius, having finally abandoned hope of preventing war had turned his attention to the question of reducing the war's horrors as far as possible. The Pope was reported, in fact, to be preparing at that hour a message to the warring nations seeking to restrict air attacks on open cities and asking for a ban on poison gas.

Nine o'clock passed in Berlin. Now Hitler had one more chore before leaving for the east. This was to approve instructions to be sent by the State Secretary of the Foreign Office to all German diplomatic missions abroad giving them the official line on the past three days' events 'for their information and to regulate language'. The note said: 'After efforts to hold direct German-Polish talks had remained unsuccessful because the Polish plenipotentiary did not turn up—although the German Government had waited two days—and we were forced to reply to Polish military attacks by ourselves taking military action, England and France demanded from us on 1st September that German troops must be withdrawn from Polish territory. It still seemed possible to avert the danger of war through the intervention of Mussolini who proposed a cease-fire and a conference to solve the German-Polish conflict.

'This proposal was answered positively by us and by the French Government, but today the British Government repeated with a two-hour time limit its demand for German troops to be withdrawn and declared itself as being in a state of war with Germany after this time had elapsed. France then followed with the announcement that she saw herself forced to stand by Poland. It would certainly have been possible to reach a reasonable German-Polish settlement but for England's intervention and her anti-German policy of encirclement. But instead of warning Poland to agree, England gave her *carte blanche* against Germany, made herself dependent upon Poland's decisions and finally, at the last moment on top of all this, condemned Mussolini's proposal to failure through her attitude. In this way the seed, sown by those men in England who for years have been preaching the destruction of Germany, has grown up.' This note was signed by State Secretary von Weizsacker.

Now at last Hitler could tear himself away from Wilhelmstrasse and its paperwork and turn to matters nearer his heart's desire. Five heavy cars with hooded headlights swept into the courtyard of the Chancellery. Hitler, dressed in field grey and army boots, with a gas-mask and a steel helmet slung over his shoulder and a revolver strapped to his belt, stepped swiftly into one of the vehicles. As the cavalcade swept out of the Chancellery gates a great roar rose from a crowd, several thousands strong, which had gathered in the street after a late afternoon statement that he was going to the front that evening. The crowd, assembled in the darkness of the blackest night Europe had seen for many years, gave the former Corporal cheer upon cheer, heil upon heil.

The Berlin that Hitler drove through that night on his way to board his special train for the front was blacked out with ruthless efficiency. A reporter for the *Deutsche Allgemeine Zeitung* wrote of that night: 'Berlin did not flare into a blaze of light as evening sank, it remained shrouded in darkness. But behind the doors of pubs, cinemas and

theatres the light shone as usual. Inside, the people sat as usual, many
of them in uniform on short leave from their units. They didn't say
much about what the special editions had told them. It was clear
and needed no explanation. And although the pubs and restaurants
were full of people eating, drinking, listening to music, talking, there
was no loud noise . . .'

Berlin's streets were dismal and dreary. Buses ran with only ghoulish
blue lights. Trams, with all inside lights shrouded by blackout cloth,
had only their route numbers faintly illuminated. Automobile headlamps were masked except for narrow slits. Here and there a faint
square of pallor glowed through a blacked-out window. The normally
brilliantly-lit street arc lamps now only shed a sickly greenish glow
over deserted streets. The only flashes of light which relieved the
blackness were the fiery red tail-lights of cars and the blinding blue
sparks from an occasional passing trolley.

Beneath the surface of the blackout German and Austrian principal
cities continued almost normally the round of urban entertainment.
At the Berlin State Opera *La Bohème* was being performed, while
the *Master Singers of Nuremberg* was played at the Volksoper
(People's Opera). The theatres, cinemas and cabarets were also well
attended.

Films shown in Munich included 'Katia, the Uncrowned Queen'
starring French actress Danielle Darrieux, and 'Sea Cadets', with
Lionel Barrymore, James Stewart, Florence Rice and Robert Young.
At Munich's National Theatre, the opera 'Der Rosenkavalier', by
Richard Strauss, was performed and 'The Merry Widow' was ap-
plauded by large audiences at the theatre on the Gartner Platz.

Women attending theatres and other shows were well dressed and
wore, predominantly, the medium-length hair style then fashionable;
not quite down to the shoulders, parted on one side, slightly waved
and swept back from face. The autumn fashions for women's evening wear featured white or light-coloured evening blouses, some with
frilly collars, some without, and some with low V-necklines. Long,
narrowish skirts in black or dark shades reaching almost to the
floor were much in favour.

In Vienna, the formerly gay capital of Austria which since the
Anschluss had become an almost provincial town, theatrical activities
were also pursued despite the grave hour. Schiller's 'Don Carlos' at

the Burgtheater, and 'Ingeborg', by Curt Goetz, at the Academy, were
on the programme for 3rd September. At the Volksoper, 'Martha',
by the composer Flotow, was performed. The world première of 'The
Girl from the Bohemian Forest', an operetta by Fritz Lehner, took
place at the Volksbuhne where a large audience enjoyed the new
work telling the story of the youthful amorous adventures of composer Carl Maria von Weber, who wrote 'Oberon' and 'Der Freischutz'.

Hitler's cavalcade of big, black juggernauts—heavily armoured Mer-
cedes cars with bullet-proof windows—swept through the Berlin darkness to the station where his train awaited him. Two other special
trains were also leaving Berlin that evening for the Polish front, one
carrying Goering and his staff and the other taking Himmler, von
Ribbentrop and Dr. Lammers, Secretary of the Reich Chancellery.

The Führer boarded his train—also heavily armoured, with anti-
aircraft guns mounted—and left to take command of the troops who
were crushing the life out of a tottering Poland. With Hitler's departure, high-level activity in Berlin came to a halt and all attention
switched to the Eastern Front, where it was to remain for some days.

At the French Embassy, Coulondre neared the end of his sojourn
in Germany with a detached feeling of relief. All there was left for
the Ambassador to do was to arrange for his departure and the departure of the Embassy staff. Coulondre's request to be allowed to
return to Paris via Belgium had been turned down by the Germans for
'military reasons'. They had offered to repatriate the French party
through Denmark instead, which did not suit the Ambassador. Finally,
they had agreed on Holland. A French train would take German diplomatic staff there and the exchange of diplomatic missions would take
place in neutral territory.

Since early afternoon, the French Embassy had been isolated, the
telephones cut off and the building surrounded by a fairly unobtrusive
police cordon to 'ensure its protection', as von Weizsacker had told
the Ambassador.

Coulondre wrote later: 'During the evening each of us busied himself choosing his most valuable possessions to pack into the two suitcases which was all we were allowed.' The French Embassy staff were
to leave early the next morning, without incident, for Paris—severing
Franco-German diplomatic links in bitter circumstances for the second
time in a quarter of a century.

Soon after Hitler left the Chancellery, *Chicago Tribune* correspondent Sigrid Schultz cabled this reaction home from Berlin: 'Germany is trying to break through Poland as rapidly as possible to establish contact with Russia and be able to draw on the vast economic resources of the Nazis' new partner in a non-aggression pact. Officials asserted that they were confident that the German Army would be able to open an outlet into Russia proper within four weeks at the most . . .

'Nazis clung to the hope that England and France would be satisfied with a 'passive' war and not go into armed conflict. Germans, with Russia as their hinterland, feel fully equal to a blockade. The fact that no battles had taken place on the Western Front up to 9.30 p.m. gave them new hope . . .'

V

By mid-afternoon in Washington (9 p.m. in London) President Roosevelt had drafted a clear statement of American neutrality to deliver to
the nation that night in one of his famous radio 'fireside chats'. He
had based his speech on drafts prepared for him during the week-end
by Mr. Cordell Hull and his principal associates in the State Department. Hull and his assistants had been busy all day assessing the impact that war in Europe was likely to make on the United States.

Hull recalled later in his memoirs: 'We agreed that the neutrality
proclamations and regulations prepared during the preceding weeks
should not be issued that day, but probably the next day. We sought
to determine whether the British declaration of war would automatically include the Dominions and decided to wait until the official
text of the declaration. We decided that new regulations should be
issued preventing Americans from going to Europe, with some legiti-
mate exceptions. I wanted to know whether many current shipments
of arms to Europe—France and Britain had placed large orders in the
United States—would be affected by immediate application of the
Neutrality Act, but was told that comparatively few shipments would
be involved. We debated the question of armed merchantmen and
agreed that we should treat merchant vessels armed for defence as
regular merchant vessels and not bar our ports to them. We discussed
ways to avoid difficulties with the British over the detention or deviation of American ships.'

About 3 p.m. (American time) Roosevelt called Hull to see him at
the White House, and asked for his opinion on the draft for the later
broadcast. Hull felt the speech was 'forceful and direct'. The Secretary
of State commented later: 'He had taken our draft, as he frequently
did, and rewritten it. He had great skill in taking a draft prepared by

others and heightening it by the change of certain phrases or the addition of new paragraphs.'

Hull advised Roosevelt of the need for great caution and for impressing on the American people that the Administration was taking a strictly neutral stand. He opposed one sentence in which Roosevelt virtually admitted that he did not expect Americans to remain neutral in thought as well as action. Hull, though himself emphatically in favour of the Allies, questioned the wisdom of proclaiming anything but a neutral attitude. He could visualize the fight that would face them in Congress to get the Neutrality Act revised. Hull declared that, in his opinion, any hint of a gap in American neutrality would strengthen the hands of political opponents who would argue that Roosevelt might lead the United States into war under the terms of a new Neutrality Act.

Roosevelt accepted several of Hull's suggested amendments to the speech, but over-ruled his assertion that American sympathy for Britain and France was already evident and did not need restatement. When the two had finished poring over the vital script, inserting phrases here, striking them out elsewhere, Hull picked up the draft to give it a final scanning. This is what he read:

'Tonight my single duty is to speak to the whole of America. Until 4.30 this morning I had hoped against hope that some miracle would prevent a devastating war in Europe and bring to an end the invasion of Poland by Germany. For four long years a succession of actual wars and constant crises have shaken the entire world and have threatened in each case to bring on the gigantic conflict which is today unhappily a fact.

'It is right that I should recall to your minds the consistent and at times successful efforts of your government in these crises to throw the full weight of the United States into the cause of peace. In spite of spreading wars I think that we have every right and every reason to maintain as a national policy the fundamental moralities, the teachings of religion, and the continuation of efforts to restore peace—for some day, though the time may be distant, we can be of even greater help to a crippled humanity. It is right too, to point out that the unfortunate events of these recent years have been based on the use of force or the threat of force. And it seems to me clear, even at the outbreak of this great war, that the influence of America should be consistent in seeking for humanity a final peace which will eliminate, as far as it is possible to do so, the continued use of force between nations.

'It is, of course, impossible to predict the future. I have my constant stream of information from American representatives and other sources throughout the world. You, the people of this country, are receiving news through your radios and your newspapers at every hour of the day. You are, I believe, the most enlightened and the best informed people in all the world at this moment. You are subjected to no censorship of news; and I want to add that your Government has no information which it has any thought of withholding from you. At the same time, as I told my Press conference on Friday, it is of the highest importance that the Press and the radio use the utmost caution to discriminate between actual verified fact on the one hand and mere rumour on the other.

'I can add to that by saying that I hope the people of this country will also discriminate most carefully between news and rumour. Do not believe of necessity everything you hear or read. Check up on it first. You must master at the outset a simple but unalterable fact in modern foreign relations. When peace has been broken anywhere peace of all countries everywhere is in danger. It is easy for you and me to shrug our shoulders and say that conflicts taking place thousands of miles from the continental United States, and indeed, the whole American hemisphere, do not seriously affect the Americans—and that all the United States has to do is to ignore them and go about our own business. Passionately though we may desire detachment, we are forced to realize that every word that comes through the air, every ship that sails the sea, every battle that is fought, does affect the American future.

'Let no man or woman thoughtlessly or falsely talk of America sending its armies to European fields. At this moment there is being prepared a proclamation of American neutrality. This would have been done even if there had been no neutrality statute on the books, for this proclamation is in accordance with international law and with American policy. This will be followed by a proclamation required by the existing Neutrality Act. I trust that in the days to come, our neutrality can be made a true neutrality.

'It is of the utmost importance that the people of this country, with the best information in the world, think things through. The most dangerous enemies of American peace are those who, without well-rounded information on the whole broad subject of the past, the present and the future, undertake to speak with authority, to talk in terms of glittering generalities, to give to the nation assurances or prophecies which are of little present or future value.

'I myself cannot and do not prophesy the course of events abroad— and the reason is that because I have of necessity such a complete picture of what is going on in every part of the world, I do not dare to do so. And the other reason is that I think it is honest for me to be honest with the people of the United States. I cannot prophesy the immediate economic effect of this new war on our nation, but I do say that no American has the moral right to profiteer at the expense of his fellow citizens or of the men, women and children who are living and dying in the midst of war in Europe.

'Some things we do know. Most of us in the United States believe in spiritual values. Most of us, regardless of what church we belong to, believe in the spirit of the New Testament—a great teaching which opposes itself to the use of force, of armed force, of marching armies and falling bombs. The overwhelming masses of our people seek peace —peace at home, and the kind of peace in other lands which will not jeopardize peace at home. We have certain ideas and ideals of national safety, and we must act to preserve that safety today and to preserve the safety of our children in future years.

'That safety is and will be bound up with the safety of the Western Hemisphere and of the seas adjacent thereto. We seek to keep war from our firesides by keeping war from coming to the Americas. For that we have historic precedent that goes back to the days of the administration of President George Washington. It is serious enough and tragic enough to every American family in every state in the Union to live in a world that is torn by wars on other continents. Today they affect every American home. It is our national duty to use every effort to keep them out of the Americas.

'And at this time let me make the simple plea that partisanship and selfishness be adjourned, and that national unity be the thought that underlies all others. This nation will remain a neutral nation, but I cannot ask that every American remain neutral in thought as well.

Even a neutral has a right to take account of facts. Even a neutral cannot be asked to close his mind or his conscience.

'I have said not once but many times that I have seen war and that I hate war. I say that again and again. I hope the United States will keep out of this war. I believe that it will. And I give you assurances that every effort of your government will be directed towards that end. As long as it remains within my power to prevent it, there will be no blackout of peace in the United States.'

This, then, was the speech Roosevelt was to deliver at 9 p.m. (American time) from Washington, as Europe moved into the second day of her cataclysm. His expressions of sympathy with France, Britain and Poland against the Nazi aggression were to be widely contrasted with the rigidly-neutral appeal of President Woodrow Wilson on 18th August, 1914. Wilson asked Americans to be completely impartial in thought as well as action when Europe took up arms at the beginning of the First World War. He told them to curb sentiment and avoid any transaction which might be construed as a preference for one party or another in the struggle. Two years later, Wilson was re-elected to the Presidency on the slogan that he kept the United States out of the war, but within six months he led her into it.

Roosevelt's views, though echoing those of perhaps a majority of Americans, were at variance with those of many leaders of public opinion. Former Senator William G. McAdoo, for instance, the First World War Secretary of the Treasury, said flatly that evening that he believed the United States would shortly be drawn into the European conflict. McAdoo declared: 'We will be forced to choose whether we will use force to maintain our rights or whether, because there is a war, we shall abandon the high seas and paralyse our world commerce. I do not believe this nation can or will withdraw from the seas and attempt to isolate itself from the world.'

Any American who felt strongly enough to take up arms privately over the issues at stake in Europe was officially reminded that day through statements to the Press, of a 1917 statute which made it illegal for United States citizens to enlist in any European Army for hostilities abroad. The penalty provided was a fine of not more than 1,000 dollars and imprisonment for not more than three years. Also, an American who enlisted in a Foreign Army and took an oath of allegiance to the government he was serving, automatically lost his

American citizenship. But those who looked back to the days when buccaneering Americans enlisted in the Spanish Civil War could find no evidence in the records of any convictions under the 1917 statute.

Though President Roosevelt was to speak a few hours later of a conflict 'thousands of miles' away from the American hemisphere, the war was already close, in some ways, to the American continent. Sharp evidence of this came that evening in a report from a Dutch coastal steamer in the canal zone at Cristobal that four German submarines were re-fuelling at Curacao in the Dutch West Indies.

The news was passed on to Washington where officials were preparing a Presidential proclamation concerning the use of the Panama canal by belligerent warships. The proclamation was to contain a detailed list of rules governing the conduct of warships in the Canal Zone, the length of their stay and restrictions that might be placed on them. The dual purpose of the regulations was to preserve American neutrality to as high a degree as possible and to prevent naval clashes from occurring close to the canal and making it unsafe for merchant vessels.

At Halifax, Novia Scotia—by no means 'thousands of miles from the United States'—four Canadian militia units received an alarm call that evening to man the harbour defences and to guard vulnerable port facilities from sabotage. Alerts were also in force aboard American naval ships, which had received earlier from Charles Edison, Acting Secretary of the Navy, a message declaring: 'France and England are now at war with Germany. You will govern yourselves accordingly.'

Notwithstanding Roosevelt's firm intentions to maintain strict American neutrality, the country was better prepared if war should come than she had been in 1914. Some Washington officials let it be known to Pressmen that afternoon that America had already reached the same stage in mobilizing her war industry as she had by the third year of the First World War. Armed with this and other official guidance, the same Press correspondents sailed forth to probe and test American public reaction to the upheaval taking place 3,000 miles away.

Some of the 'man-in-the-street' comments they reported included those of an insurance agent: 'The British will fight Germany to maintain British domination in Europe. British supremacy at sea will eventually be the deciding factor in the war'; and a bank clerk: 'It will be a

repetition of 1914—except that there will be no German empire to
divide. The French will win battles but the British will win the war
through control of the sea.'

From Ossining, New York, it was reported that the news of the
Anglo-French declaration of war on Germany had reached Sing Sing
prisoners over the radio and created intense interest and discussion,
especially in the death house, where one native of Germany and one
of Poland were awaiting execution. They were Gus Schweinberger, 32,
who had killed another German with a hammer at Yonkers, and Theo-
dore Maselkiewicz, a 53-year-old Pole who had murdered his wife at
Buffalo, N.Y. The war cast long shadows over New York's Polish community. Old John Traczyka, in his tiny Brooklyn second-floor flat,
counted his money that afternoon, turned his life savings of 1,000
dollars over to the Polish War Chest—and then jumped to his death
on the sidewalk.

Early in the evening, New York City with its large, foreign-born
and intensely volatile population went on an emergency footing, with
Federal authorities and local police taking precautions to prevent hostilities between radical partisans of the European warring nations.
Police by land and Coastguards by sea threw a protective net around
foreign ships lying in New York Harbour and special measures were
taken to ensure that only persons with 'official business' were permitted
to enter the Brooklyn Navy Yard, where a large part of the building
programme of the U.S. Navy was under way, including the 35,000-ton
battleship *North Carolina*. The usual host of week-end sightseers were
strictly excluded.

Czechs and Slovaks in Chicago during the evening hours were urged
to give moral support to Poland. Pleas were made by speakers at
Labour Day rally in Pilsen Park, Chicago, which was attended by
nearly 5,000 Czechoslovakians. One of the speakers mentioned reports
that Czechs in U.S.A. would go to Canada to form a legion to defend
Poland. On the other hand, news of the Anglo-French entry into the
war was received quietly in Riverview Park at the 28th annual folk
festival of United German-Austro-Hungarian societies. There was no
mention of war on the part of the speakers. Only American flags were
displayed. More than seventy-two organizations were represented, and
one spokesman declared that few of the picnickers approved Hitler's
methods.

Vladimir S. Hurban, Czech minister, asserted that his country partitioned by Germany was entirely on the side of Britain, France and Poland. They would organize forces in France and Poland to fight Germany. The Czech diplomat made the announcement from his Washington Legation which he had refused to hand over to the Germans when his nation was dismembered. 'Every Czechoslovak,' he declared 'according to his ability, will help Britain, France and Poland to eliminate this common danger. Unable to organize a military action in our own land, Czechoslovakian army units will be organized in France and Poland.'

In Los Angeles, the Douglas, Lockheed and North American aircraft factories were rushing through the last 25 million dollars' worth of a 61-million-dollar series of orders from Britain and France. The allied governments had guaranteed the American companies against losses in the event of Washington placing an embargo on the products. Nevertheless, the three producers had geared themselves to meet the immense British and French demands, and were anxious to complete and deliver the goods satisfactorily. Lockheed decided that day to speed delivery of the last 10 million dollars' worth of a 27-million-dollar British order for 250 twin-engined bombers by flying them through Canada. The French freighter *Wyoming* was sailing from Los Angeles with 23 bombers aboard, destined for the French Air Ministry at Le Havre.

In Cleveland, Ohio, the German-American League for Culture, holding its national convention, sounded a call for the German people to rise up and crush Adolf Hitler. The League said attempts would be made to broadcast the message through Germany over three shortwave radio networks—one in England, one in the United States and a secret station in Germany. Delegates representing more than 100,000 German-Americans passed a resolution at the conference blaming a 'barbarous' Hitler for 'destroying the good name of Germans throughout the world'.

But not all German-Americans supported the League's sentiments and the news agency wires hummed with the loud arrogant boast of Fritz Kuhn, leader of the American Nazis, who predicted that Hitler would get what he wanted and then announce 'that he is willing to negotiate'. As soon as Germany's invasion of Poland had begun, Kuhn had changed the map in his New York office to show all Poland as

part of Germany. 'It will be all over in a few days,' he told every
visitor.

Kuhn, who had emigrated to America in 1923 from Germany, where
he had worked as a chemist for Henry Ford, ruled thousands of German-Americans through the Amerika-Deutscher Volksbund. He had
made himself 'Führer' of the Bund and installed himself in a suite of
untidy, crowded offices on the corner of 85th Street and Third Avenue,
wearing a uniform decorated with the Iron Cross. In Kuhn's office
hung a large portrait of Hitler, but the beefy Bundster denied any
direct liaison with the Führer. Kuhn's thick accent barred him from
much public speaking, but his agents worked ceaselessly among the
eight million Americans of German descent, and by 3rd September
the Bund had sixty-five posts in New York and was publishing newspapers and newsheets in New York, Philadelphia, Chicago and Los
Angeles. Kuhn's followers were involved in many street riots and within
three months of the war's beginning he was to change his Nazi uniform for a prison convict's suit to begin serving a two-and-a-half year
jail sentence for embezzling Bund funds.

In Hollywood that evening members of the British film colony ear-
nestly discussed plans for returning home to help with the war effort.
Laurence Olivier, David Niven, Sir Cedric Hardwicke, Brian Ahern,
Cary Grant, Charles Laughton, Errol Flynn and Alfred Hitchcock
were among those preparing to leave the bright lights of the world's
film capital for blacked-out London.

History, repeating itself in the cockpit of Europe that day, also
looked as though it could repeat itself in one of the world's major
sporting contests. On the tennis courts of the Merion Cricket Club,
Haverford, Philadelphia, the Australian stars Adrian Quist and John
Bromwich were battling to keep their country in the running for the
Davis Cup in the Challenge Round against the United States. Twenty-
five years earlier, as the 1914–18 war began, the Australians (playing
with the New Zealanders as Australasia) had last won the Cup. They
had never recaptured it since the 1914 victory, but had travelled to
the U.S.A. in 1939 full of optimism.

When the news of Australia's declaration came, however, the country's sporting fans were gloomily reading reports of the Saturday's play,
in which Quist and Bromwich had both lost their singles matches.
Their only chance of staying in the fight, therefore, was to win the

doubles together on Monday afternoon. The team were practising when they heard the news that their country had become the first British Dominion to declare war on Germany. That day there was some doubt as to whether the series would be completed. This speculation, however, was ended when Sir Norman Brookes, leader of the Australian team, and a veteran of the 1914 series, announced that the Davis Cup matches would be finished, but that his team would hasten home immediately afterwards without waiting for national singles.

Postscript: Next day Quist and Bromwich made a weak start, and their opponents Joe Hunt and Jack Kramer wrenched the first set from them seven games to five. The 7,000 spectators took the sympathetic view that the Australians had been upset by the crisis, and sat back to watch the Americans romp through the remainder of the rubber. But the American crowd was to be disappointed when the Australians rallied magnificently, and swept home to victory in a brilliant, powerful display of tennis. Quist and Bromwich took the next three sets 6–2, 7–5, 6–2.

The following day Quist and Bromwich again took the field for singles matches, this time against America's R. L. Riggs and F. A. Parker respectively—a change-over of Saturday's line-up. Once more the Australians found their form, and soundly defeated their opponents to clinch the Cup.

Thus the Davis Cup which Australians captured ten days after Britain entered the war in 1914 was regained only two days after the opening of hostilities in another world war a quarter of a century later.

VI

King George received a weary, disillusioned Chamberlain in audience at Buckingham Palace that evening. The Prime Minister, an exhausting day's work behind him, had come to report on the events of the previous few epochal hours. The King wrote in his diary of the meeting: 'The P.M. came to see me in the evening. He was very upset—but very calm—that all his work of the past months had been of no avail to keep the peace of the world. He knew that the Munich Agreement had prevented a European War last year, and that he had been severely criticized after that for his foreign policy. He had at that time met Hitler face to face and he hoped that he had made an impression on Hitler, that a repetition of his behaviour then would be the end of our patience.'

During the audience, Chamberlain and the King were believed to have discussed a scheme to distribute the King's message, broadcast earlier that evening, to every household in the British Isles. Whitehall was excited by the idea at that moment, but the King was later to direct that the scheme be scrapped because of the cost which would be involved—£35,000—and the amount of paper that would be needed —250 tons. Distribution of the leaflets would also have placed a terrible strain on the Post Office.

Chamberlain was to describe his state of mind towards the end of that hectic day a week later, in the letter, already partly quoted, to his sister Ida. He described his feelings in these terms: 'And so the war began, after a short and troubled night, and only the fact that one's mind works at three times its ordinary pace on such occasions enabled me to get through my broadcast, the formation of the War Cabinet, the meeting of the House of Commons and the preliminary orders on that awful Sunday . . .

'One thing comforts me. While war was still averted, I felt I was indispensable, for no one else could carry out my policy. Today, the position has changed. Half a dozen people could take my place while war is in progress and I do not see that I have any particular part to play until it comes to discussing peace terms—and that may be a long way off. It may be, but I have a feeling that it won't be so very long. There is such a wide and spread desire to avoid war and it is so deeply rooted that it surely must find expression somehow. Of course, the difficulty is with Hitler himself. Until he disappears and his system collapses there can be no peace. But what I hope for is not a military victory—I very much doubt the feasibility of that—but a collapse of the German home front; for that it is necessary to convince the Germans that they cannot win.

'And U.S.A. might at the right moment help there. On this theory, one must weigh every action in the light of its probable effect on German mentality. I hope myself we shall not start to bomb their munitions centres and objectives in towns unless they begin it. If it must come it would be worth a lot to us to be able to blame them for it . . .

'It was, of course, a grievous disappointment that peace could not be saved, but I know that my persistent efforts have convinced the world that no part of the blame can lie here. That consciousness of moral right, which it is impossible for the Germans to feel, must be a tremendous force on our side.'

One of Chamberlain's last tasks of the day, after he had seen King George, was to approve a statement to be broadcast to the German people in his name—an attempt to present directly the British case. Confident that thousands of Germans would be willing to risk imprisonment or even death to listen to the prohibited British broadcasts, Chamberlain declared: 'German people: your country and mine are now at war. Your Government has bombed and invaded the free and independent state of Poland which this country is in honour bound to defend. Because your troops were not withdrawn in response to the Note which the British Government addressed to the German Government, war has followed.

'With the horrors of war we are familiar. God knows this country has done everything possible to prevent this calamity. But now that the invasion of Poland by Germany has taken place, it has become inevitable.

'You are told by your Government that you are fighting because Poland rejected your Leader's offer and resorted to force. What are the facts? The so-called "offer" was made to the Polish Ambassador in Berlin on Thursday evening, two hours before the announcement by your Government that it had been 'rejected'. So far from having been rejected, there had been no time even to consider it. Your Government had previously demanded that a Polish representative should be sent to Berlin within twenty-four hours to conclude an agreement. At that time the sixteen points subsequently put forward had not even been communicated to the Polish Government. The Polish representative was expected to arrive within a fixed time to sign an agreement which he had not even seen. This is not negotiation. This is a dictate. To such methods no self-respecting and powerful State should assent. Negotiations on a free and equal basis might well have settled the matter in dispute.

'You may ask why Great Britain is concerned. We are concerned because we gave our word of honour to defend Poland against aggression. Why did we feel it necessary to pledge ourselves to defend this Eastern Power when our interests lie in the west, and when your Leader has said he has no interest in the west?

'The answer is—and I regret to have to say it—that nobody in this country any longer places any trust in your Leader's word. He gave his word that he would respect the Locarno Treaty; he broke it. He gave his word that he neither wished nor intended to annex Austria; he broke it. He declared that he would not incorporate the Czechs in the Reich; he did so. He gave his word after Munich that he had no further territorial demands in Europe; he broke it. He gave his word that he wanted no Polish Provinces; he broke it. He has sworn to you for years that he was the mortal enemy of Bolshevism; he is now its ally. Can you wonder his word is for us not worth the paper it is written on?

'The German-Soviet Pact was a cynical *volte face* designed to shatter the Peace Front against aggression. This gamble failed. The Peace Front stands firm. Your Leader is now sacrificing you, the German people, to the still more monstrous gamble of a war, to extricate himself from the impossible position into which he has lead himself and you. In this war we are not fighting against you, the German people, for whom we have no bitter feelings, but against a tyrannous and forsworn régime, which has betrayed not only its own people but the whole of western civilization and all that you and we hold dear.

'May God defend the right!'

Shortly after Chamberlain's statement was broadcast to the Germans, Arthur Greenwood, acting leader of the Labour Party, went on the air to make the first broadcast to the British people outlining the Opposition's attitude on the outbreak of war. At 9.15 p.m. Greenwood declared: 'We are at war because the British people are united and steadfast in their conviction that there are cherished possessions of mankind which are worth defending, for without them, life is empty. We believe in liberty, through which alone the mind and soul of the peoples of the world can find free expression. All peoples, whether they be great powers or small nations, have a right to live in security and independence, without threats or menaces, or the use of force. If we do not overthrow the forces of Dictatorship now our turn will come sooner or later.

'We deny the right of any power to commit acts of brigandage or to seek to attain its ends by means of force or the threat of force. We believe that there is no kind of dispute between nations which cannot be settled by peaceful methods, if the will is present . . .

'This is a bitter hour for us all. It is a bitter hour for the Labour Party, which has always regarded peace with freedom as the greatest blessing of mankind. Those for whom I can especially speak are fighting for a world in which henceforth law shall rule instead of force. We do not want increased power for Britain in the world. We want no new lands. We do not want to destroy the German people, whose scholars, writers, musicians, democratic leaders and others have made such noble contributions to that European civilization which Hitler seeks to destroy.

'We want—having paid an incalculable price—when the air-raid sirens have been silenced and war is ended, to make a new start to build a world where peace will be eternal, and where the arts of peace may flourish for the enjoyment of the whole of mankind . . .'

Greenwood added: 'In view of the high sentiments expressed by the

President of the United States of America we are assured of the moral support of the people of that great Republic. The whole of the British Commonwealth of Nations will rally round us. The conscience of the vast majority of the human race will sustain us . . .'

While the statesman talked and exhorted, the fighting forces and the Civil Defence teams continued their preparations throughout the night. But in London, at any rate, the last gaps had not been closed— perhaps because officialdom had been thoughtless enough to start hostilities on a Sunday. Late that night the Air Ministry heard of a serious sin of omission which, in retrospect, makes ironically amusing reading, but might that evening have led to countless deaths if a mass air-raid had taken place.

Squadron Leader Basil (later Air Chief Marshal Sir Basil) Embry was duty Air Staff Officer at the Air Ministry that evening and was unable to get away for his dinner until late at night. He recalled later: 'I walked across the Green Park to the R.A.F. Club in Piccadilly to get something to eat, but when I tried to return by the same route I found that all the gates into the Park had been locked.

'This was, of course, before they removed the old railings. At that time, most of the air-raid shelters for the West End of London had been built in the parks, and in the event of a raid they would have been inaccessible. On my return to the Air Ministry I at once telephoned the Duty Officer at the Home Office and told him of my discovery. He confirmed that no instructions to the contrary had been given to those whose job it was to close all the gates at a given hour, and he was most grateful for my warning.'

Another impression of London during that first night of war was recorded later by American correspondent Oswald Garrison Villard of *The Nation*, who wandered through London watching the change that was taking place to a great 700-bed hospital from which every patient who could be moved had been moved. All its scientific work had stopped; its whole life had been made over; and here it stood empty but in such complete readiness that it gave him a sinking feeling at the pit of his stomach.

'Two kindly surgeons took me up on the roof. There was London in the dark, incredibly more majestic, more thrilling than by day or with its usual lights; more mysterious, more questioning of the why and the wherefore. A hundred feet above the street we could see only a few light spots and the faint will-o-the-wisp of buses and motors. "I wonder," I said to myself, "whether London has been as dark as this since Will Shakespeare walked the Strand."

'My astonishment never ended that I walked the streets of London with a shaded flashlight to find my way, as if I were on a Berkshire hill. I wondered if I, too, should be able to pilot a car through the dark with only parking lights—and those well wrapped—while the 'stop' and 'go' greens and reds and ambers had shrunk to little faded crosses.

'Every night not London alone but all England down to the smallest village was as quiet as a hamlet in Kent. And in these black and murky streets everybody was eager to help everyone else, to put the stranger in the right bus, on the right road.

' "We shall win", said my doctor friends on that hospital roof. To the west, tremendous flashes of lightning, the rumbling of thunder gave just the atmosphere the moment called for. "We shall win", said the doctors, "because every man and woman in this hospital is at his or her post in the dark-quiet, determined, efficient, prepared for the worst, uncomplaining, certain that we shall win in the end. And as they are, so is England." '

The blackout in London and other cities and towns claimed a heavy toll of life and limbs all that night. This carnage on the darkened roads was to continue for months until people had learned to accustom themselves to being without lights outside their homes. Despite the white lines on the roads and pavements and white splashes on car wings and bumpers, road accidents were to result in thousands of casualties long before German bombs killed any British civilians. September alone was to claim 1,130 lives on British roads, compared with only 554 in September of 1938.

Beyond the blackout, a subdued London night-life continued as near normally as possible. A R.A.F. observer who scanned the city from the air for gaps in the blackout reported one phenomenon which showed how the city clung to old habits. He noted that, at a late hour, the whole city suddenly began to twinkle like a sky full of stars. A little research showed that the short-lived sparkle coincided with closing time and the swinging open of countless pub doors to release the flood of late drinkers.

Writer Hector Bolitho, who began the war as an Air Ministry Intelligence officer, evokes a memory of the West End that night. He was on his way to dine with friends at the Ritz and writes: 'London was already dark. There was a menacing beauty in the canyons between the high buildings: the crawling, subdued lights of the cars, the secret rustling of people, sucked from the outer darkness of the streets into the deeper shadows of doorways. We ate well. "It might be our last good meal! Let's go the whole hog and have a partridge and a bottle of red wine." Afterwards we encouraged Noel Coward on to the platform in the restaurant, to play and sing to us. He strayed through old war songs, waltzes and tunes. Then we made him sing songs from "Bitter Sweet". When I asked him what he was doing, he said "Intelligence", in a voice that reeked of sealing-wax and invisible ink.' (In fact, Coward had spent the whole day at a 'hush-hush' headquarters in Bedfordshire, receiving a final briefing for his secret posting as head of a projected Bureau of Propaganda in Paris.)

While life continued little changed at the Ritz and London's other luxurious night-spots, women in countless thousands of humble homes were putting the finishing touches to blackout curtains, altering and repairing clothes in preparation for the days of scarcity and wondering what war would do to fashion. One of the newspapers had provided for them a lengthy article on female underwear for the guidance of 'women who during the past few days have found themselves in uniform for the first time'. The writer recommended fine wool or a mixture of artificial silk and wool as a practical outfit under uniform, adding: 'Knickers should be in Directoire style, with elastic at waist and knees, preferably in dark shades.'

Other big changes in the nation's way of life became known as the night progressed, and the B.B.C. injected hourly news bulletins into programmes which consisted otherwise of incessant electric organ medleys. Congregations at many Churches throughout the land heard with sadness at evening services that stained glass windows were to be removed 'for the duration'. Some churchgoers rolled up their sleeves immediately after services to help in removing windows and other precious objects to vaults or crypts. Fleet Street learned at 11 p.m., with the arrival of the first editions, that the war had provoked a newspaper revolution: the *Daily Mail* announced that henceforth its front page would be dominated by news instead of being devoted solely to a single mammoth advertisement.

Late that night, a hopeful and greatly relieved Count Raczynski saw British newspapermen and told them he was 'deeply moved and touched' by the manner in which their Government had implemented the Anglo-Polish Agreement for Mutual Assistance so soon after it had been concluded. Recalling the great demonstrations outside the British and French Embassies in Warsaw, the Ambassador said that never before had relations between Britain and Poland been as close as they were that day. Never, during the unsuccessful negotiations, were 'we given the slightest reason to doubt British determination to stand by Poland'. He wished to pay a warm tribute of admiration and personal devotion to Lord Halifax who throughout all difficulties and dangers had never ceased to be a tower of strength.

Count Raczynski then referred to the misery caused in Poland by the ceaseless air-raids which had been delivered. German statements had declared that Poland had already become German's *luftraum* and the Ambassador expressed the hope that aerial activity on the part of Poland's allies in the west would help to redress the balance and put a stop to such wanton attacks.

VII

At 10.45 p.m., Warsaw officials released to foreign correspondents a statement that was to send a thrill through the Western World for a few short hours. Units of Polish cavalry, they claimed, had smashed their way through the German armour and had carried the war into German territory in East Prussia. It was the sole item of news out of the Polish capital that night which could be regarded as even faintly cheering to her new western allies. The German war communique just before midnight acknowledged the attack, but said the cavalry, which tried to enter German territory north of Treuburg had been pushed back. There is no record of how long the Poles were able to keep up their attack, but it clearly lasted most of the evening and it was to be more than five years before German territory was invaded again.

Polish cavalry also that night carried out a remarkably successful raid in the vicinity of Kamiensk. Under cover of darkness, a Cavalry Regiment dismounted and stormed into the town on foot. The Germans—members of a motorized Regiment of the First Armoured Division—were taken completely by surprise. The Poles blew up petrol and ammunition dumps in the town and inflicted heavy casualties on the Germans before re-mounting and riding away.

Cavalry raids like these were operations in which the Polish Army had probably no superiors in Europe. It was the way they had expected any war with the Germans to be fought. It was the way in which they had defeated the numerically stronger Russians in 1920. Until 1st September, 1939, every war fought on Polish soil had been decided by the cavalry. Horsemen had always triumphed, whether in the vast Polish forest lands or the central plains. But since Friday morning the tanks and armoured cars had been masters of the plains:

blind mechanical monsters which rode over men and horses indifferently.

If there had been rain the Cavalry might even have played a big part in the September, 1939, fighting; but since Friday the Poles had been learning bitterly that courage alone no longer won battles. Poland's Cavalry, though superbly trained and magnificent in appearance, was utterly unsuited to warfare in which Panzer units comprised the enemy's spearhead. Charge after charge had broken against the German fire and iron on the hard ground and it was only the extreme valour of the Polish cavalrymen which had enabled them to inflict as much damage as they had with their outworn manœuvres and light weapons. British correspondent Cedric Salter recalled later that if the German attack had resembled the campaign against Russia in 1920 –21, 'I have no doubt that the story would have been a very different one—a tale of heroism, of charges over icy plains, of daring night raids upon the German lines, instead of a bewildered if gallant flight in face of reality for which they were not only practically but, even more so, emotionally unprepared.'

Similar isolated reports of Polish gallantry and occasional successes reached Warsaw in the last two or three hours of the day. The garrison at Westerplatte reported at 11 p.m. that it was still intact, despite the dropping of fifty or sixty bombs by some thirty Luftwaffe aircraft during the afternoon and evening. Machine-gun fire had driven off the low-flying bombers, the plucky little garrison claimed from within their small, red-walled fort overlooking Danzig Harbour. The Polish Navy was also hitting back as well as it could that night. Most of the trawler minesweepers still afloat chugged into Danzig Harbour late that night. They had been hastily-equipped to carry mines, which they dropped all around the harbour in the hope of damaging or immobilizing the two German battleships, twelve destroyers and smaller craft anchored there. It was one of the last thrusts possible for the small surface craft of the fleet which had been ordered to stay behind in the Baltic.

Despite minor setbacks, Hitler and his Generals that night could look back on another day of remarkable progress in their offensive. There was no need to exaggerate any of the signals sent to the Führer's train as it sped east across Germany to the front during the night. Within twenty-four hours, Hitler would be studying the triumphs at

first hand and hearing the opinion of his Army chiefs that the Poles
were 'practically beaten'.

Two official communiques issued in Berlin summarized the day's
progress. The first said that during the night of 2nd-3rd September,
German troops had captured Gestochowa and crossed the river Warta
east of Wielum. German troops east of Pless had reached the river
Weichsel. The Luftwaffe had shot down seven Polish aircraft over
Warsaw and a balloon without loss to themselves.

The second communique—at midnight—reported German troops
from Silesia as being in pursuit of their opponents who were retreating
on Cracow. The Germans were advancing north of the High Tatra
and south of the industrial area. German forces were chasing the retreating enemy over a line from Koniepol-Kamiensk and over the
river Warta. At the end of the day they were twenty kilometres from
Sierarz. The Pomeranian Army Group had reached the Vistula near
Kulm, cutting off Polish troops in the Danzig Corridor. German troops
in East Prussia had taken Przasnysz. Polish cavalry had tried to enter
German territory north of Treuburg but had been pushed back.

The German Air Force, the communique added, had attacked
important military communication centres and troop transports and
supported the Army by shelling and dive-bombing. Railway communications between Kutnau-Warsaw, Cracow-Lvov, Kielte-Warsaw and
Thorn-Deutsch Eylau had been destroyed. Several trains had been
derailed, burnt and blown up and an aircraft factory at Okecie near
Warsaw had been badly damaged.

German naval action had resulted in effective fire on Polish shipping in Hel Harbour. Off Danzig, a Polish submarine had been sunk.
Air attacks against Hel and Gdynia had succeeded in sinking the Polish destroyer *Wicher* and damaging a Polish minelayer.

The communique concluded by saying 'that there were no hostilities
on the Western Front'.

How long would the Western Front remain peaceful? The Poles
were pinning all their hopes of prolonging resistance on an immediate
offensive by the French. In fact, at midnight on the 3rd, a fresh invitation to France to do so was issued by Lukasiewicz, the Polish
Ambassador in Paris. Received by the President, Albert Lebrun, at
the Elysée Palace, the Ambassador expressed his satisfaction at
France's entry into the war at the side of Poland, and declared anew

the need for an attack in the west. Lebrun replied that he hoped the enemy pressure on Poland would soon be relieved.

Churchill, in a late night telephone call to Count Raczynski, admitted that Britain was pressing France for a genuinely powerful attack on the poorly-defended Siegfried Line, but unfortunately there was not a single division in the field which would enable her to take firm action. Britain would meet any aggressive action on land with all her air strength, but independent action by R.A.F. bombers was opposed by British military chiefs on the grounds that it would not produce strategic results and would be costly in human and material losses.

Apart from a few light thrusts against the Siegfried Line by French infantry, however, there were to be none of the colossal blows in the west that the Poles so confidently expected. France was not to exploit her great numerical advantage on the Western Front, despite the fact that the thirty-three divisions of German troops stationed there during the Polish campaign were less than half the total of divisions available to General Gamelin. And the British were not to unleash their bombing squadrons against Germany's industrial might to paralyse the Nazi war machine from the rear. Instead, Britain was to begin a series of leaflet raids—to the undisguised anger and disgust of many Poles.

Leaflet raids had been advocated by the British Air Ministry as a potent propaganda weapon a year earlier. The idea had appealed immediately to Government ministers who believed that a large part of the German population could be induced to disown Hitler. Chamberlain and his cabinet, in discussions immediately before the German invasion of Poland, had confirmed this view. They believed that a succession of leaflet raids would strike hard at German morale, both because of the message they contained and the defiance of German air defences that their dropping entailed. So millions of sheets of paper bearing messages to the German people had been printed hurriedly that week-end in preparation for war. They were not to shake German confidence in their leaders to any noticeable extent and were to offend some neutral opinion—but the leaflet raids were at least to provide some much needed practice for the Royal Air Force.

The first leaflet raid, begun just before midnight on 3rd September, was a successful training exercise and was followed by a similar operation every night for a week. British air crews were soon to become familiar with the whereabouts of German cities, airfields, power stations, roads and railways. These raids, too, were to provide valuable lessons in night flying in all weathers and, because they lasted between six and twelve hours, were to have no equal as tests of navigation and endurance. In some ways, they were to prove even greater tests of navigational skill than normal bombing, as the altitude, strength and direction of wind had to be discovered in greater details for leaflets than for bombs.

Six million leaflets were dropped by R.A.F. units over a wide area of Germany on that first night of war. These leaflets, written in German, told anyone willing to risk severe punishment by picking them up the reasons why the British and French Empires had gone to war. They said: 'Never before has any Government thrown a population to death for less sincere excuses. This war is unnecessary. The German Reich is not threatened from any side . . .

'President Roosevelt promised you peace with honour as well as future material welfare. Instead, your government convicted you to mass murder because of the scarcity of food, in a war in which you can never be victorious. Not we, but they, have cheated you . . .

'You are on the verge of bankruptcy. We have unlimited reserves of men and provisions. You German people have the right to live in peace now and for ever. We also desire peace and are willing to conclude it with any trustworthy, peace-loving German Government . . .'

That first leaflet raid was to create a minor diplomatic incident as some R.A.F. aircraft overflew Holland in their penetration of German territory. Within a few hours of the return of the aircraft to their bases in Britain the Dutch Government protested and drew the attention of all the belligerents to the 'infringement of Dutch neutrality' which they had guaranteed. The Dutch asked both sides to investigate the matter and told whoever was responsible to take steps to avoid such incidents in future. Germany was quick to declare her innocence and to point out that Britain had broken Holland's neutrality only a few hours after guaranteeing it.

Leaflet bombing was an appropriately gentle way of bringing to a close the first day of a new war and the last day of a world that was to disappear for ever. The scattering of six million earnestly-written propaganda sheets over German cities and towns was in the same spirit and tradition as the courteous notes and memoranda which had marked the formal declarations of war and diplomatic exchanges earlier in the day. That first leaflet exercise produced a story which swiftly went the rounds of the Royal Air Force messes. It may have been apocryphal, although some R.A.F. men still swear it really happened:

One of the pilots returned to his base far earlier than scheduled and was immediately asked for an explanation by his commanding officer. The young pilot replied: 'I reached my objective, sir, and threw the parcels overboard.' The C.O. asked: 'Didn't you untie the parcels?' The pilot answered: 'No sir, should I have done?' His superior looked at him in horror for a few moments, then exclaimed: 'Good God, man. Don't you realize you might have killed someone?' Hiroshima that night was exactly 2,163 days away.

ACKNOWLEDGMENTS AND
BIBLIOGRAPHY

The narrative in this book was based upon personal interviews and the study of nearly 1,000 books, official reports, newspapers, magazines, news agency despatches, and private letters.

The author's thanks are due to several hundred people who answered his appeal for personal reminiscences. Letters to British and German newspapers produced a flood of valuable recollections from men and women in all walks of life. Only a handful could be quoted, but all contributed something to the work.

Among the men who played key parts in the events of 3rd September, the author would like to record in particular the assistance of Count Raczynski, the former Polish Ambassador in London, who gave him access to unpublished diaries and the benefit of much wise advice. The reminiscences of Lord Reith and Mr. Robert Dunbar, formerly of the British Foreign Office, were also very helpful.

Organizations which contributed to the research included the Polish Library in London, the United States Information Service, the press offices at Buckingham Palace and the British Broadcasting Corporation, and the Reuter, Press Association, Associated Press and Daily Telegraph news libraries.

Various publishers gave permission to reproduce passages quoted in the book. These included The Hutchinson Publishing Group *Why England Slept* by John F. Kennedy; William Heinemann Ltd. *Ciano's Diary* and *Prelude to Dunkirk* by Major General Sir Edward Spears; William Hodge & Co. Ltd. *I Saw the Siege of Warsaw* by Alexander Polonius, and Hodder & Stoughton Ltd. *Failure of a Mission* by Sir Nevile Henderson. Messrs. Collins kindly gave permission for quotations to be made from *The Private Papers of Hore-Belisha* by R. J. Minney and from *The Memoirs of Field Marshal Montgomery*.

Faber & Faber permitted the quotation from the poignant "My Name Is Million" and Macmillan (New York) sanctioned the use of remarks by Cordell Hull in his memoirs.

The list of books below is not a complete bibliography, but it does record the publications which the author found most useful, and consulted frequently. He would like to express his deep gratitude to the authors and publishers of all the following:

Amery, L. S.: *My Political Life* (Hutchinson).

Anon: *My Name is Million* (Faber).

Australian Government: *Official War History.*

Beloff, Max: *The Foreign Policy of Soviet Russia, 1929–41* (O.U.P.).

Bolitho, Hector: *A Penguin In The Eyrie* (Hutchinson).

Bonnet, Georges: *Defense De La Paix.*

Broad, Lewis: *Sir Anthony Eden—The Chronicles of a Career; The War That Churchill Waged* (Hutchinson).

Carr, E. H.: *German-Soviet Relations* (O.U.P.).

Churchill, Sir Winston: *The Second World War*, Vol. 2 (Cassell).

Christiansen, Arthur: *Headlines All My Life* (Heinemann).

Ciano, Count: *Ciano's Diary* (Heinemann).

Collier, Basil: *The Defences of the U.K.* (H.M.S.O.); *Leader of the Few* (Jarrolds).

Coulondre, Robert: *De Staline a Hitler.*

Clark, Brigadier Stanley: *The Man Who Is France* (Harrap).

Coward, Noel: *Future Indefinite* (Heinemann).

Dahlerus, Birger: *The Last Attempt* (Hutchinson).

Dallin, David: *Soviet Russia's Foreign Policy* (New Haven Yale Univ. Press).

Dalton, Hugh: *The Fateful Years* (Muller).

Divine, A. D.: *Navies in Exile* (John Murray).

Donitz, Karl: *Zehn Jahre Und Zwanzig Tage* (Athenaum Verlag, Bonn).

Ellis, Major L. F.: *The War in France and Flanders, 1939–45* (H.M.S.O.).

Embry, Air Chief Marshal Sir Basil: *Mission Completed* (Methuen).

Falls, Cyril: *The Second World War* (Methuen).

Feiling, Keith: *Life of N. Chamberlain* (Macmillan).

Francois-Poncet, A.: *The Fateful Years* (Gollancz).

French Government: *French Yellow Book*.

Frischauer, W.: *Goering* (Odhams).

German Academic Exchange Service: *Dokumente Und Berichte Zur Deutschen Zeitgeschichte* (Herbert Stubenrauch Publishing Bookshop).

Gilbert, Felix: *Hitler Directs His War* (O.U.P., N.Y.).

Guderian, General Heinz: *Panzer Leader* (Michael Joseph).

Gunther, John: *The High Cost of Hitler* (Hamish Hamilton).

Hagen, Louis: *Follow My Leader* (Allan Wingate).

Hailstone, Alfred G.: *100 Years of Law Enforcement in Buckinghamshire* (Dimbleby).

Halifax, Earl: *Fulness of Days* (Collins).

Halder, General Franz: *Hitler as Warlord* (Putnam).

H.M.S.O.: *The British Blue Book; Bomber Command; Northern Ireland in the Second World War*.

Harsch, Joseph C. *Pattern of Conquest* (Heinemann).

Hasluck, Paul: *Australia in the War of 1939–45—Civil Section* (Australian War Memorial).

Hassell, Ulrich von: *The Von Hassell Diaries* (Hamish Hamilton).

Henderson, Sir Nevile: *Failure of a Mission* (Readers' Union and Hodder & Stoughton).

Hesse, Fritz: *Hitler and the English* (Wingate).

Hibberd, Stuart: *This is London* (MacDonald and Evans).

Hull, Cordell: *Cordell Hull's Memoirs* (Macmillan).

Kai-Shek, Chiang: *Summing Up At Seventy* (Harrap).

Kaufmann, William: *A Chapter In The Diplomats* (Princeton Univ. Press).

Kennedy, John F.: *Why England Slept* (Hutchinson).

Kennedy, Major-General Sir John: *The Business of War* (Hutchinson).

Kennedy, Major Robert M.: *The German Campaign in Poland, 1939* (Department of the U.S. Army).

Kiernan, R. H.: *President Roosevelt* (Harrap).

King-Hall, Stephen: *History of the War*, Vol. 2 (Hodder & Stoughton).

Kirkpatrick, Ivone: *The Inner Circle* (Macmillan).

Langer, Rulka: *The Mermaid and the Messerschmitt* (Roy Slavonic Publications, N.Y.).

Macleod, Iain: *Neville Chamberlain* (Frederick Muller Limited).

Martienssen, Anthony: *Hitler and His Admirals* (Secker & Warburg).

Mendelssohn, Peter de: *The Nuremberg Documents* (Allen & Unwin).

Ministry of Information: *The Outbreak of War* (H.M.S.O.).

Namier, L. B.: *Diplomatic Prelude 1938–39* (Macmillan).

Noel, Léon: *Une Ambassade a Varsovie* (Flammarion, Paris).

Norwich, Lord: *Old Men Forget* (Hart-Davis).

Odhams Press: *Ourselves in Wartime* (Odhams).

Paloczi-Horvath, George: *Khrushchev—The Road to Power* (Secker & Warburg).

Papen, Franz von: *The Memoirs of Franz von Papen* (Andre Deutsch).

Polonius, Alexander: *I Saw the Siege of Warsaw* (William Hodge).

Pope-Hennessy, James: *Queen Mary* (Allen & Unwin).

Prange, Gordon: *Hitler's Words* (American Council on Foreign Affairs).

Raeder, Grand Admiral Erich: *Struggle for The Sea* (William Kimber).

Rauch, Georg von: *A History of Soviet Russia* (Praeger, N.Y.).

Reynaud, Paul: *In the Thick of the Fight* (Cassell).

Richards, Denis, and Saunders, Hilary St. George: *Royal Air Force, 1939–45*, Vol. 1.

Riess, Curt: *They Were There* (Putnam, N.Y.); *Joseph Goebbels* (Hollis & Carter).

Robertson, Terence: *The Golden Horseshoe* (Evans).

Roosevelt, Elliott: *The Roosevelt Letters* (Harrap).

Roskill, Captain S. W.: *The War At Sea, 1939–45*, Vol. 1 (H.M.S.O.).

Ruge, Vice Admiral Friedrich: *Der Seekrieg—The German Navy's Story, 1939–45* (United States Naval Institute, Annapolis).

Sales, Count de: *My New Order—Hitler's Speeches, 1922–41* (Reynal & Hitchcock, N.Y.).

Salter, Cedric: *Flight From Poland* (Faber).

Schacht, Hjalmar: *My First Seventy-Six Years* (Allan Wingate).

Schellenberg, Walter: *The Schellenberg Memoirs* (Andre Deutsch).

Semmler, Rudolph: *Goebbels, the Man Next to Hitler* (Westhouse).

Shirer, William L.: *Berlin Diary* (Hamish Hamilton); *The Rise and Fall of the Third Reich* (Secker & Warburg).

Simon, Viscount: *Retrospect* (Hutchinson).

Simpson, J. S. M.: *South Africa Fights* (Hodder & Stoughton).

Spears, Major-General Sir Edward: *Prelude to Dunkirk, July, 1939 to May 1940* (Heinemann).

Taylor, Telford: *Sword and Swastika* (Gollancz).

Templewood, Viscount (Sir Samuel Hoare): *Nine Troubled Years* (Collins).

Thompson, W. H.: *I Was Churchill's Shadow* (Christopher Johnson).

Toynbee, Arnold and Veronica: *Survey of International Affairs, 1939–40—The Eve of War 1939* (O.U.P.).

Tuleja, Thaddeus V.: *Eclipse of the German Navy* (Dent).

United States Department: *Foreign Relations of the U.S.*, Vol. 1; *Nazi-Soviet Relations, 1939–41* (U.S. State Dept.).

Wegierski, Dominik: *September, 1939* (Minerva).

Weizsacker, Ernst von: *The Memoirs of Ernst von Weizsacker* (Gollancz).

Wheeler-Bennett, John W.: *King George VI—His Life and Reign* (Macmillan).

Windsor, Duchess of: *The Heart Has Its Reasons* (Michael Joseph).

Wing Commander, A.: *Bombers Battle* (Duckworth).

Wucher, Albert: *Seit Funf Uhr Wird Zuruckgeschossen—A Documentary Report on the Start of World War II* (Suddeutsche Verlag, Munich).

INDEX